Neither Dead nor Red

CIVILIAN DEFENSE AND AMERICAN POLITICAL
DEVELOPMENT DURING THE EARLY COLD WAR

ANDREW D. GROSSMAN

ROUTLEDGE
New York   London

Published in 2001 by
Routledge
29 West 35th Street
New York, NY 10001

Published in Great Britain by
Routledge
11 New Fetter Lane
London EC4P 4EE

Routledge is an imprint of the Taylor and Francis Group.

Printed in the United States of America on acid-free paper.

Library of Congress Cataloging-in-Publication Data

Grossman, Andrew D.
   Neither dead nor red : civil defense and American political development
during the early Cold War / Andrew D. Grossman.
      p.cm.
   Includes bibliographical references and index.
   ISBN 0-415-92989-X— ISBN 0-415-92990-3 (pbk.)
   1. Civil defense—United States. 2. National security—United States.
3. United States—Politics and government—1945–1953. 4. Cold War. I. Title

UA927 .G76 2001
363.3'5'0973—dc21   00-065329

For Kim, with love and deep respect

CONTENTS

PREFACE

Laws are silent in time of war.
—*Cicero, Pro Milone, 52 B.C.*

On a summer day in New York City in 1955, Times Square emptied to the wail of an air-raid siren warning citizens of a simulated nuclear attack, while the cameras of the government's Federal Civil Defense Administration (FCDA) recorded the almost surreal scene. Not a person or moving vehicle was on the streets as Manhattanites dutifully crowded into subway tunnels and buildings that had been identified as fallout shelters. Police immediately arrested the few who ignored the air-raid warning. The drill, one of many "Operation Alerts," was a success: The citizens of the most densely populated city in the United States, known even then for their cynicism, did what they had been trained to do—they found shelter and waited for the "all-clear signal."

What were the institutional conditions necessary for the acceptance of a program such as Operation Alert? Today, it is virtually impossible to imagine anything that would motivate New Yorkers to serenely clear the streets of their city in five to ten minutes, to say nothing of whether they would descend into the subways and wait patiently in summer heat for an all-clear signal from bureaucrats practicing for World War III. Yet these Operation Alerts were repeated many times between 1954 and 1960 in cities and towns across the United States.[1] A comprehensive Cold War mobilization of the home front induced the required response from citizens across the nation. The mobilization program was the kind of effective social control that specialists within the Truman administration deemed necessary for the success of American postwar national security policy. In retrospect, we can see that the American state engaged in a civic garrisoning process that shaped and ultimately solidified the domestic political consensus necessary for Cold War mobilization. The social and political mechanisms that made this process possible—not an attempt to prove that the United States became a police garrison state—is the subject of this book.

It has been more than a decade since the Berlin Wall came down and the Cold War ended. We now have some historical perspective from which to reexamine the consequences for the United States of waging and "winning" the half-century-long shadow war. Much of the new scholarship on the Cold War has been animated by newly declassified primary sources in both the United States and the former Soviet and Eastern bloc archives. As far I know, most scholars, political elites in most countries, public intellectuals of all stripes, and almost everyone else for that matter (including this author) were wrong about how the Cold War would end. The new scholarship on the Cold War is important because it reveals what the experts misunderstood about this dangerous period in postwar history. Much of the new knowledge that has been developed in the last decade about the early Cold War has focused on the *interpenetration* of external and internal policy planning.[2] This book continues that trend. By examining what seems, in retrospect, to have been an intrinsic connection between domestic policy planning and international politics, we can better understand not only the trajectory of the Cold War but also how postwar domestic political development was shaped. In the United States, newly declassified documents have enlivened an important debate (albeit at times too tendentious for my taste) about the effects of the anticommunist ideology of the early 1950s, spying in the United States during the 1950s, and whether Cold War mobilization and its consequences were worth the social, economic, and political price that was paid. Early Cold War mobilization had long-term institutional effects on American political development in three important domains: executive power, jurisprudence, and private day-to-day life. The indeterminate nature of the Cold War—was it a "real" war or not?—systematically and logically led to an increase in presidential power. Likewise, lawmaking in an atmosphere of emergency planning (1947–1954) institutionalized the centralization of power within the executive branch of government. Laws on "national security" conflated internal and external policy: The early Cold War threat was not only about the Soviet Union but also about ideas.[3] The "containment" of ideas (a much more difficult task than military-strategic containment) focused the attention of the federal government on internal threats as if there were little or no difference between external and domestic security policy. As a result, legislation was crafted with discretionary powers that helped advance the growth of a national security bureaucracy. Additionally, much of the national security legislation of this era reflected the narrow, constrained liberalism of the public institutions, discourse, and political culture of the time.

Two important interpretations at odds with the arguments of this study have developed out of the new Cold War literature. One, best represented by Aaron Friedberg's provocative book on the period, argues that America's historical anti-statism limited central-state expansion and facilitated an efficient Cold War mobilization process.[4] The argument that postwar American political development is an example of anti-statist political development is a revamped version of the traditional American exceptionalism thesis, which holds that because of its geographic, political, cultural, and ideological uniqueness, the eighteenth-century American state developed differently from European states. This thesis is based on three main premises: (1) unlike the long course of European history, there was no feudal period in the United States; (2) the United States did not have external strategic military threats in its first century of political development; and (3) the United States developed within an overarching liberal political regime that protected individuals from central-state expansion and the capriciousness of bureaucratic discretionary power. As a result, the founding period set in place a political and social order that fundamentally protected political participation and *purposely* decentralized central-state power, thus inhibiting centralized bureaucratic development. As Chapter One makes clear, I reject the American exceptionalism thesis because it is too narrow as theory and devalues comparative historical analyses in favor of more limited and often overdetermined studies of American political development. Additionally, I argue that postwar American political development depended on a robust, not a weak, state, thus rejecting the interpretation that Cold War political development is a crucial case study of how a benign, liberal-democratic, weak state implemented its Cold War grand strategy.

A second important position in recent Cold War literature argues that there was a causal link between the Cold War and the postwar civil rights movement.[5] This argument holds that without the pressure of Cold War mobilization, the civil rights movement would not have taken hold or, at the very least, the federal government would have moved much more slowly in making fundamental changes to the Jim Crow system and other matters of race and politics. Because the Cold War laid bare the contradictions between the stated international political goals of the United States for liberal democracy and its treatment of African American citizens at home, the Truman administration had to confront what it identified as the "colored problem," first in the armed forces and then, more slowly, within society as a whole. The key implication of this interpretation of postwar civil rights history is that the Truman administration acted "progressively" (in the context of the times) with respect to issues of race in American society.

As the reader will quickly see, I am dubious about the "no Cold War–no civil rights movement" thesis. The following chapters defend a different and much less sanguine interpretation of the social consequences of Cold War mobilization. The Cold War and the dominant concern about national security essentially limited what was possible with respect to civil rights and, more broadly, American liberalism. Under both the Truman and Eisenhower administrations, the federal government had to balance pressure to support civil rights for African Americans (and others) against what both administrations viewed as the primary grand strategic aim of the United States: the swift rationalization of national security policy. Protest of any sort was generally viewed by most of the public and politicians as an internal security problem that could threaten the United States. The Truman administration's approach to the early Cold War crisis provided the basis for the militarization of Cold War political culture through civilian defense planning and the demonization by the Federal Bureau of Investigation (FBI) of the postwar civil rights movement as a communist-inspired "fifth column." The Truman administration's effort to secure both domestic and international security thus hindered an expansive liberalism in favor of a constricted liberalism that refracted domestic politics through the lens of national security policy.

If this book is successful, the reader will learn two things about early Cold War mobilization that differentiates it from the two interpretations just outlined: first, that the Truman administration had at its disposal a more robust institutional capacity and political consensus for the implementation of its Cold War public policy than the newly resurrected American exceptionalism argument posits, and second, that long-term mobilization for the Cold War produced a narrow and at times illiberal, even repressive, domestic political environment that configured, for good or ill, postwar political culture, citizenship rights, and law. In a comparative historical sense, then, U.S. early Cold War mobilization, coming as it did on the heels of global economic crisis and then global war, was more European in its process and consequences than it was the product of American exceptionalism.

CAVEAT

A book cannot be all things to all people. *Neither Dead nor Red* is no exception, and thus an important caveat is in order about what this book is not. This project is not concerned with who caused the Cold War or who won it. These important questions of historical interpretation have and will be debated endlessly. They are independent of my analysis. This book is an analysis (not a story) of a discrete time period, 1946–1954; it does not stretch into the period of the civil defense protest movements of the late 1950s. Nor do I advocate a "power-elite" conspiracy theory of generals and "Wall Street bankers" colluding to sell to the American people a military-industrial complex that served their narrow interests.[6] On the contrary, Cold War mobilization, especially the mobilization of the home front, was driven by unintended and unexpected contingencies that were much too complex to fit the simplistic scheme of a conspiracy theory centered on "bankers and bullets."

Finally, this work is not an attempt to mock the civil defense program of the late 1940s and the early 1950s, after the fashion of the movie *Atomic Cafe* and Elaine Tyler May's chapter on civil defense in her book *Homeward Bound: American Families in the Cold War Era.*[7] This tack—for want of a better term, we can call it the "the silliness approach" to civil defense—misses the point of why such a program was launched, how it functioned, and what consequences it produced. The FCDA and its civic-education programs and operations offer us an interesting case of a line agency of the federal government that proposed the *quasi-militarization* of civilian life as the best way to manage and shape *how* the polity viewed nuclear war. The Cold War was serious business. The institutions for shaping public opinion and public culture were tied directly to the wartime state created between 1939 and 1945. They are still with us today.

ACKNOWLEDGMENTS

Writing a book is very hard work. When I first started this project I wondered why acknowledgments often run on for so many pages. I now have the answer: For most of us, our books would never see the light of day were it not for the kindness, mentoring, and time that so many people offer in the arduous process of turning an idea into a book. This book owes much to many. Everything that is good about this work is the result of the support, suggestions, and at times very tough criticism that I have received from colleagues and students over the last five years.

For financial support in the writing of this book I would like to thank Albion College and its Faculty Development Committee. In the last five years, I have received generous funding for this project from the Hewlett-Mellon Fund for Faculty Development at Albion College. I also want to acknowledge and thank the Harry S. Truman Library Institute, the MacArthur Foundation for a grant to the Department of Political Science at the New School, and the New School's Center for Studies of Social Change.

I owe special thanks to all my colleagues at Albion College, but I specifically would like to acknowledge Glenn Perusek, who taught me much (and from whom I continue to learn), especially about some of the deeper implications of central-state expansion in a liberal democracy. Joe Stroud offered an important critical analysis of Chapter Four, and he has been a great friend and supporter of the project. Thanks to Myron Levine, Nancy Levine, Geoff Cocks, Charles Schutz, Molly Mullin, Bindu Madhok, Gene Cline, Erik McKee, Jim Diedrick, Marcy Sacks, and Kim Tunnicliff, who have all supported me at different stages of writing and teaching at Albion. I owe a special debt to Jeffrey Carrier, who supported me when it might have been easier to let a visiting assistant professor who was filling in for a sabbatical leave move on.

This book would have been impossible without the help and training of some very special people in my life. Thanks to Charles Tilly and Louise Tilly, directors (1987–1996) of the New School's Center for Studies of Social Change, which provided an office and a remarkable intellectual environment for writing and research. To Ira Katznelson, Elizabeth Sanders, Richard Bensel, Aristide Zolberg, Herman Schwartz, and Alan Wolfe I owe a debt that can be repaid only by attempting to teach my students as well as they have taught me. My life would be very different and not nearly as rewarding were it not for these truly exceptional teachers who have also become good friends. To Daniel Kryder, who took the time, even as he was completing his own book, to offer detailed comments on almost every chapter, thank you, very much.

I also want to acknowledge my deep gratitude to Andrew Polsky, David Plotke, Victoria Hattam, Michael Barnett, Eric Hobsbawm, Roy Licklider, Vicky Grant, Marlene Kondelik, Michael VanHouten, John Kondelik, Peter Benda, and the librarians at Albion College; Denis Bilger at the Harry S. Truman Library; John Taylor at the National Archives; the librarians at the University of Florida, Gainsville; Princeton University's Firestone and Seeley-Mudd Libraries; and the librarians at the Schomburg Center for Research in Black Culture, New York Public Library. Additionally, many thanks to Eric Nelson and Nicole Ellis at Routledge and the two anonymous reviewers for Routledge—their suggestions and criticisms have been taken to heart and have made this a better book. The help of John J. Huckle, who copyedited the manuscript, was invaluable.

To my students at Albion College I owe a deep debt of gratitude. Beginning in fall 1996, many of the students in my "proseminars" in American political development, public policy analysis, and international relations read and commented on the chapters of the book. They did a great job in teaching the professor new things and making sure he remained humble. I specifically want to thank Thomas J. Raven, Kelli Zappas, Nathan Piwowarski, Corinne Johnson, Christopher Moore, Elizabeth Hutula, and Robert Harbaugh for doing research for me and for carefully and critically reading portions of the book as it was in progress.

I would like to acknowledge a group of colleagues from the New School for Social Research. Between 1986 and 1996 the Graduate Faculty of Political and Social Science was an exciting place to be a graduate student, and my friends who helped me, through thick and thin, have contributed so much to making me a better scholar and teacher: Jens Borchert, Catherine Holland, Robert Latham, Orin Kirshner, Lizabeth Zack, Joseph Luders, Andrew Schlewitz, Jytte Klausen, Brad Usher, Kate Peterson, Kathy O'Leary, Anne Raffin, Joseph Loundes, Michelle Stoddard, and, especially, Nancy Shealy.

Very special thanks are due to Kim Geiger, who has not only supported me in this project but has also made the book so much better by her insightful criticisms, suggestions, and copyediting. To mentor and friend Guy Oakes I offer a deep thanks: Long conversations and detailed suggestions about this book and related subjects have taught me much and have made me a better scholar and teacher. Marian and Stephen Grossman, thanks very much for your love and support and also consider this: All that fighting about politics around the dinner table actually got put to good use. To Patricia and Charles Geiger, thanks for your love and support also. To Susan Grossman, thank you for helping me through some very tough times, for your love, and for a place to stay whenever I was in New York City. Many thanks to my friends at the Shore: Steven Nelson, Mitchell Weiner, and Robert Campi. To Layla, Frodo, Mieze, and the inestimable Rollo, thanks for accepting full blame for any and all errors that may be in this book. To Himmelhund and the ABB, thanks.

ACRONYMS

Ad Council	Advertising Council
BBD&O	Batten, Barton, Durstine, & Osborn, Inc.
BBP	Bernard M. Baruch Papers
CDC	Centers for Disease Control
CIA	Central Intelligence Agency
DOD	Department of Defense
DOJ	Department of Justice
EOP	Executive Office of the President
FCDA	Federal Civil Defense Administration
FDRL	Franklin D. Roosevelt Library
FEMA	Federal Emergency Management Agency
FEP	Ferdinand Eberstadt Papers
FRUS	Foreign Relations of the United States
GOC	Ground Observer Corps
JVFP	James Vincent Forrestal Papers
NA	National Archives
NAACP	The National Association for the Advancement of Colored People
NSC	National Security Council
NSRB	National Security Resources Board
OCD	Office of Civil Defense
OCDM	Office of Civil Defense Mobilization
OCDP	Office of Civil Defense Planning

OF	Official File
OFF	Office of Facts and Figures
OWI	Office of War Information
PHST	Papers of Harry S. Truman
PNP	Philleo Nash Papers
PSB	Psychological Strategy Board
PSF	President's Secretary's Files
PTA	Parent-Teacher Association
RG	Records Group
RNSP	Ralph N. Stohl Papers
SQP	Spencer Quick Papers
WHCF	White House Central Files
WMD	weapons of mass destruction

ARCHIVAL SOURCES

President Harry S. Truman Library Institute, Independence, Missouri
Franklin D. Roosevelt Library, Hyde Park, New York
The Seeley G. Mudd Library, Princeton University
The Philip Wylie Papers, Firestone Library, Princeton University
The National Archives, Washington, DC
Millard F. Caldwell, Jr., Papers, University of Florida, Gainesville
New York Public Library
Schomburg Center for Research in Black Culture, New York Public Library
Papers of the NAACP, Part 18, Subject Files 1940–1955
Governor Alfred E. Driscoll Papers, New Jersey State Library

Chapter 1

FRAMING THE PROBLEM

War is the health of the State.
—*Randolph S. Bourne, 1919*

[The Cold War] was the defining issue in our political discourse and public policy from 1947 until last year. It made "national security" the justification for everything—the interstate highway system, the National Defense Education Act, the Vietnam War, the foreign aid program. J. William Fulbright used it to sell his scholarships and J. Edgar Hoover used it to sell wiretaps.
—*Richard Holbrooke, quoted in the* New York Times, *February 6, 1992*

INTRODUCTION

How was the Truman administration able to implement a long-term war mobilization process and garner the necessary domestic political consensus to support a process that, ultimately, hinged on the concept of nuclear deterrence, a concept that was alien to most Americans in the late 1940s? What were the institutional and political consequences of Cold War mobilization on postwar American political development?

Among the policy challenges confronting Truman administration national security planners in the early Cold War period was the problematic nature of life in the "atomic age," which explicitly connected public with national security policy. The "next war," policy planners such as Secretary of Defense James Forrestal claimed, would include the use of atomic, biological, and chemical weapons against the continental United States. For U.S. planners and the general public, Hiroshima and Nagasaki were the touchstones for the future of war in the modern age. By 1950, a picture of World War III was indelibly etched in the minds and imaginations of policy makers:

millions dead in the pulverized and radiating ruins of major cities in the United States. If the Cold War became a "hot" war, U.S. citizens had to come to grips with the possibility—even probability—that the Cold War would result in the ultimate challenge to the American social order: nuclear war.

The National Security Resources Board (NSRB) was one of the important administrative agencies developed to handle the problem of domestic Cold War public policy. Although short-lived, the NSRB not only dealt with the strategic-military-economic facets (much of which focused on industrial planning for and during a nuclear war) of Cold War mobilization but also promoted a home-front mobilization arm, the Office of Civil Defense Planning (OCDP). In December 1950, the OCDP became a stand-alone line agency of the federal government by virtue of the Civil Defense Act of 1950 and was renamed the Federal Civil Defense Administration (FCDA). I use the FCDA as a case for examining how long-term disaster planning shaped Cold War culture generally, as well as how civil defense planning reflected the rationalization of a set of important administrative and institutional links between public policy, propaganda, and public ethics. In the late 1940s and early 1950s, the Truman administration linked home-front preparedness and civil defense education about nuclear weapons to its Cold War grand strategy. The FCDA predicated its national policy planning on a general theory of emotion management or "crisis mastery." There were domestic prerequisites for home-front mobilization (the American public had to be prepared to fight and win a war and this had to be signaled in a credible fashion) and there were "moral foundations" to containment policy by means of nuclear deterrence. As sociologist Guy Oakes notes: "If the attempt to preserve peace by threatening nuclear war produced the very consequences it was intended to avert, the American people would be required to pay the price ultimately exacted by this strategy. If the price of freedom proved to be nuclear war, would Americans be willing to pay?"[1] It was the FCDA's mission under the Truman administration to make sure the answer to this question was yes.

From a political development perspective, the FCDA functioned as a mediating institution: It not only helped link the federal government with major research universities and newly developing think tanks and foundations throughout the country but also affiliated the Executive branch of the state with the major media outlets (print, broadcast, and film) in the same way a wartime information agency would have managed these affiliations.[2] The FCDA was part of a new postwar institutional and administrative architecture for long-term Cold War mobilization that was based on a public policy of national civic education regarding all facets of the Cold War. The

Truman administration's framework for rationalizing national security policy was capacious in both the scope and the depth required of the federal government. That is why I reject "weak state" interpretations of postwar American political development. The case study I present offers a detailed appraisal of how a federal agency of the state, the FCDA, intervened to change the way the American people saw with their own eyes the destructive capability of nuclear weapons when they looked at pictures of the post-attack devastation of Hiroshima and Nagasaki. As we will see, this was no easy feat. It required highly rationalized interagency governmental, private sector, and quasi–private sector relations (the research-university system) at the federal, state, and local levels. Additionally, the Truman administration's policy-of Cold War national security civic education is an example of *how* a liberal democratic state can expand its power into all spheres of both public and private life and use that power to garner the necessary domestic support for its larger grand strategy.

STRATEGIC MAKE-BELIEVE, POLITICAL REALITY, AND THE HOME FRONT

> Mr. President, I'm not saying we wouldn't get our hair mussed, but I do say not more than ten to twenty million killed, tops, depending on the breaks.
> —*George C. Scott as "General Turgidson" to Peter Sellars as "President Muffley" in Stanley Kubrick's* Dr. Strangelove or: How I Learned to Stop Worrying and Love the Bomb

In the United States, the development of postwar strategic thought was shaped by two concerns: the popularly held feeling that a war with the Soviet Union was more than a remote possibility and a more technical consideration about the effects of nuclear weapons themselves. The more specialized concern was especially evident within the Department of Defense (DOD) and among civilian national security planners who advised in the development of grand strategy for the United States in the nuclear age. From the perspective of policy planning, two basic problems loomed as obstacles to the development of a military grand strategy. First, nuclear deterrence, in its earliest conceptual incarnation, depended on projecting the perception of a broad-based agreement on how American interests would be defended: deterrence hinged upon credibility or, more broadly conceived, on "national will." The second problem was more complicated. If deterrence depended upon national will and nuclear weapons were part of American war plans, how was public information about nuclear weaponry to be handled? How was the public at large to be informed about the fact that the "front lines" in the next war might not be "over there," but right here? How could the U.S. public commitment to collective security arrangements be deemed credible if "nuclear fear" caused the American public to reconsider their acceptance of the risks involved in these strategic policies?[3]

Contemporary strategic studies were very influential and had a direct effect on policy planning in the immediate postwar period. Since, in theory, nuclear weapons transformed the military-strategic environment, defense policy makers and political elites in Washington depended on a select group of individuals who had written about the consequences of the nuclear revolution for American postwar planning.[4] Within this literature, both classified and public, the concepts of nuclear deterrence theory, nuclear war-fighting, and policies related to collective security for the postwar era were developed and elaborated. Since these concepts had to be explained to the domestic population, who stood to suffer the consequences of a policy failure, the home front took on an instrumental, strategic role.

Information pertaining to nuclear war depended on complicated, abstract, *theoretical* modeling drawn largely from economic science. These formal models were used by civilian and military planners in their development of war-fighting scenarios. However, since there was no baseline for nuclear war, formal nuclear war-fighting models were, more often than not, an amalgam of two ontologies: an abstract hypothetical "reality" and the tangible reality of conventional warfare—specifically World War II.[5] In one sense, the construction of a hypothetical strategic environment is understandable, for strategic planning had to be undertaken in some way. However, much of the strategic analyses developed in the early part of the Cold War assumed that the crucial cognitive jump from strategic abstraction to military and political reality could be achieved effortlessly.[6] Nuclear war-fighting scenarios abstracted from the make-believe world were proposed as workable options for American policy makers, as if the hypothetical scenarios were themselves real. The phenomenon of treating hypothetical scenarios as if they were real creates what one scholar of the development of U.S. nuclear strategy, Scott Sagan, calls "the usability paradox." The paradox was that deterrence fundamentally depended on the willingness of the United States to treat nuclear weapons as ordinary weapons and consequently threaten their use; at the same time, nobody was sure that nuclear weapons should be used in large numbers and, if they were used as planned, what the overall effects would actually be.[7] Nonetheless, nuclear war-fighting scenarios became fashionable not only within national security planning circles but also within the popular media and general public during the early to mid-1950s. By the beginning of the Eisenhower administration, the theory of massive retaliation was incorporated into U.S. strategic war plans and the public was being taught, by way of civil defense training, to "understand" what this strategy meant.[8]

The basic idea that nuclear weapons could be used as tools for either deterrence (weapons of punishment) or war-fighting (weapons of defense) can be traced to an earlier period in American postwar strategic thought: the years 1946–1949.[9] In this formative period of postwar strategic planning, national security planners viewed the domestic population as a vital part of overall deterrence theory. Additionally, any strategic calculation of the consequences of using nuclear weapons on the battlefield had to include a reconceptualized notion of the battlefield itself.[10] Given that nuclear weapons were so destructive, the traditional concepts of a "field of battle" became problematic at best.

Opposite the abstract world of strategic make-believe, political elites and policy makers had to fashion state policy within the contentious context of American domestic politics.[11] For example, the foundation of U.S. Cold War policy was the containment of the Soviet Union. Containment was effected not only through U.S. nuclear diplomacy but also through the deployment of collective security arrangements with the European allies.[12] U.S. commitment to collective security in Europe was viewed by the Truman administration as the cornerstone of the construction of an American-led postwar international order under the nuclear umbrella of the United States.[13]

The Truman administration had to sell the advantages of its two-pronged Cold War strategy of global containment and collective security to the American public.[14] The administration also had an ancillary objective: to educate the general public about the operational link between both strategies and the development of an immense nuclear weapons arsenal. In both the Truman and Eisenhower administrations, national security issues were discussed publicly by policy makers in order to facilitate this process of "domestic education." We might call this process the popularization or nationalization of the concept of national security. From the perspective of state aims and goals, this process served to affect congressional negotiations and to "deparochialize" the very concept of national security within the minds of the general public. Concerns about the effects of nuclear fear became acute when media reportage focused on four key issues within a five-year period: the human effects of the atomic bombing on Japan; the American nuclear weapons testing that took place in the South Pacific during the 1940s; the successful Soviet atomic bomb test of 1949 and the consequences for the United States of a Soviet nuclear arsenal; and the Korean War and its meaning as interpreted by planning and political elites. It was within this context of impending emergency that civilian defense and the mobilization of the home front became serious issues to policy makers.

TWO HYPOTHESES CONCERNING AMERICAN POLITICAL DEVELOPMENT AND EARLY COLD WAR MOBILIZATION

With few exceptions, contemporary state theory on the U.S. role in the international system since World War II does not view the postwar American state as potentially coercive and expansive.[15] The principal question posed by postwar American foreign policy—how the United States, a supposedly weak state with little capacity for long-term strategic planning of any sort, domestic or international, successfully implemented a grand political, military, and economic strategy such as its Cold War containment policy—can be answered in either of two ways: The United States was a functional weak state or it was a more expansive, democratically structured, civic-garrison state. This question about the postwar American state is especially important given that U.S. national security policy was enormously expensive in both financial and human terms. Both the Marshall Plan and the Korean War were explained to the general public as necessary and vital facets of U.S. foreign policy. Not only did the Marshall Plan and the Korean War impose costs that were immediately apparent to the general public, but central to both events was also the fact that U.S. postwar national security policy rested on the concept of nuclear deterrence. Early Cold War national security policy entailed real costs as well as potentially catastrophic risks for the domestic population. Yet if it were not for the broad domestic political consensus that legitimized U.S. Cold War strategy, American foreign policy would have been effectively undermined.[16] How the Cold War consensus was constructed and maintained in the face of terrifying risks is fundamental to a more comprehensive understanding of state behavior during the formative years of the Cold War. This book focuses on the home front and purposely shifts attention away from the domain of strategic-economic mobilization, which has been analyzed in the huge literature that deals with postwar American national security policy. For Truman administration national security planners and members of Congress, the postwar grand strategy of containment and deterrence could be achieved only by way of active international engagement, for the United States a historically unique commitment that was not yet convincingly sold to all sectors of a war-weary American society.[17]

Historic Anti-Statism: The Weak Democratic State

As World War II ended, the United States emerged as the most powerful nation-state in history. One of the key arguments in contemporary state theory is that central-state power and expansion are by-products of war mobilization and war-making. As a result, post-crisis states tend to develop highly centralized institutions and administrative capacities for implementing and managing public policy. The relationship between crisis mastery on the one hand and central-state development on the other is broadly understood as the "ratchet effect."[18] In historical perspective, the United States was (and is) a war-prone nation, yet some of the new literature on the Cold War argues that, against the ratchet effect model of state theory, the United States achieved its superpower status *without* creating a highly centralized state. More precisely, the weak state argument holds that the United States historically avoided the development of a strong central state because it has an "anti-statist ethic" built into its polity.[19]

This raises the following question: If the theoretical connection between political development, central-state power, and war-making is correct, then why does some scholarship on the Cold War hold that postwar American political development is unique with respect to the crisis/state-expansion model? In large part, the answer is that American political development, as a consequence of American exceptionalism, is historically and politically *sui generis*. In this view of American political development, the United States seemed to lack what one scholar of comparative state development points out are "the state capacities to pursue specific kinds of polices."[20] The ostensible absence of central-state planning capacity in the United States had little effect on the successful deployment of its Cold War economic, political, and military strategy between 1946 and 1990; as Aaron Friedberg cogently argues, this is exactly the point: "Out of weakness, strength." In other words, because the United States is structurally constrained by the polity's anti-statist ethic, early Cold War mobilization took place within a limited or highly constrained state-building model. Equally important, what state expansion did occur in the early postwar period did so because of the political tensions that developed out of a demobilization process or "rollback" effect, not any "ratchet" effect. As a result, postwar political development is characterized by a functional weak state that facilitated an efficient Cold War mobilization process because structural decentralization is compatible with American capitalism.[21]

This is an incorrect way to conceptualize American political development, at least with respect to the twentieth century. American exceptionalism is theoretically too narrow and, ultimately, is an unsatisfactory premise on which to base an interpretation of the development of early Cold War mobilization. It is essential that any thesis of American exceptionalism be grounded historically and comparatively.[22] In historical perspective, American political development became less and less exceptional as the United States engaged in more and more wars. Additionally, in comparative perspective, American political development followed a pattern of war mobilization, war-making, and state formation that is not all that distinct from European state formation and political development. As Aristide Zolberg has convincingly argued, there are many types of "exceptionalisms"; taken as a fundamental theoretical premise, the notion of American exceptionalism quickly collapses under the weight of comparative analysis and scrutiny, for *every* nation's political and military development is, as Zolberg argues, exceptional.[23] Following this admonition concerning the traditional reliance by scholars on American exceptionalism and its supposed consequences for American political development, I offer a different hypothesis to understand Cold War mobilization.

The Civic Garrison: The Robust Postwar Democratic State

Postwar American political development has been characterized by a robust and expansive central state, not a weak, decentralized central state. The various processes and types of twentieth-century state-building are fundamental themes in the American political development literature, and for good reason: There was, in fact, an enormous amount of state-building going on in the United States.[24] The crises of the twentieth century did not create anemic institutional and administrative capacity with which to carry out public policy. Quite to the contrary, institutions created to handle crisis and economic modernization were well-developed and *did not* disappear after the end of World War II. Broad-based institutional capacity for federal planning developed in the interwar years, with national security agencies being forged primarily between 1938 and 1945 and social welfare agencies being forged between 1933 and 1939. As a result, the Truman administration had enormous administrative and institutional capacity and *continuity with wartime institutions* to draw upon for implementation of its Cold War public policy. It is true that the implementation of a European-type grand strategy was a new experience for Truman administration planners, but they nonetheless had the institutional architecture in place to carry out a coherent grand strategy.[25] Institutions and line agencies tied to postwar national security had two characteristics. First, organizations for systematic planning for postwar policy were still relatively young. Because these agencies and their bureaucratic apparatuses were relatively new—some worked efficiently and some did not—postwar planning was *not* frictionless and needed to undergo a process of rationalization that entailed substantial bureaucratic and political infighting. Lynn Eden, for example, illustrates this nicely in her study of how early postwar national security planning played out in Congress and how the universal military training debate in particular became a focal point for internationalists and business nationalists to contest the U.S. Cold War grand strategy.[26] Still, these congressional debates, while extremely important for viewing how political contention worked itself out in the immediate postwar period, were ultimately about what kind of postwar dominion the United States was going to manage.[27] The debate *was not* about whether the United States should be a superpower that would protect its national interests. In short, the United States was going to protect its vital national security interests, defined either unilaterally (the business nationalist position) or collectively (the internationalist position) in the international political arena.

The absolute certainty that the United States would not withdraw from the international arena as it did after World War I leads us to the second characteristic of postwar institutional capacity—namely, that institutional and organizational capacity *was* politically insulated, ultimately allowing for a systematic approach to postwar planning. Organizations associated with national security policy were politically insulated in the sense that theoretical approaches to postwar national security and the attendant strategic schemes to carry out these policies were developed within the Executive Office of the President (EOP). Because *initial* postwar national security planning unfolded in politicized fits and starts, scholars committed to the weak state thesis use this early, erratic rationalization process as evidence of minimal state-building and state expansion in postwar America.[28] This is a mistaken reading of American political development. To argue that the Cold War state was configured by an anti-statist impulse within the American polity is inconsistent with how the Truman administration implemented its domestic public policy for civilian preparedness, a policy that was dependent on a powerful domestic political consensus and durable central-state institutions and administrative capacities. To use postwar political development and the political contention surrounding national security policy in the Truman administration as a crucial case of how a liberal-democratic state turned weakness into strength is an overdetermined claim about how the United States mobilized for the Cold War. The causal logic for such a claim works in the following way: (1) American democracy creates the conditions for (2) party politics, interest group politics, and deep political contestation regarding central-state planning, which in turn creates the conditions for (3) a decentralized and relatively weak central-state apparatus that is constrained in its ability to exercise programmatic planning. This logic is politically and historically facile. However, for all intents and purposes, this *is* the logical formula used by some scholars who hold that American exceptionalism is the necessary and sufficient condition for understanding how Cold War mobilization influenced American political development .

This study does not dispute two facts: The U.S. central-state apparatus was not (and is not) as politically insulated or "efficient" as that in European states, and the United States *did not* become a totalitarian, police-garrison state during the Cold War. The fact that postwar American politics was contested at many levels and early postwar bureaucratic development reflected this contestation or that American liberalism prevented the United States from becoming a police-garrison state fails to demonstrate that the Truman administration inherited a fragmented, weak government with which to successfully implement its Cold War policies. As the following chapters will establish, postwar planners adapted the decentralized American state structure to fit a particular kind of postwar expansion of central-state power.

In the case of the FCDA, the state literally entered the home with its preparedness training programs; this was a direct result of a comprehensive study on how to market civil defense training to people. The FCDA tapped community agents in its systematic recruitment, for example, of primary and secondary school teachers for community public education. It also used its connections to both large and small businesses to facilitate adult education within the workplace. Additionally, the FCDA recruited citizens from neighborhoods and communities for its warden program. The warden system, examined in Chapter Three, a program directly modeled on the community air-raid warden system of the war years, proposed, in part, to militarize everyday life, especially in the home. None of these events was being "freelanced" at the local level; the central state managed the rules of the game, if you will, of how the American polity would be trained and educated for the Cold War. In short, I do not offer the example of the postwar weak contract state; instead, I propose an interesting historical case where planners maintained the *illusion* of decentralization, as was done during World War II, as a means for state expansion. In this view, the United States *does not* avoid the centralization of federal powers that are consistent with a war mobilization–state expansion model. More important, the United States did not avoid, by a vaporous notion of an "anti-statist ethic," the social, political, and economic consequences of its Cold War mobilization project. The processes of garrisoning the civilian population were used by key agencies of the central state as a *technology* for successful long-term Cold War mobilization.

In addition, the early years of Cold War mobilization revealed something more ominous, even coercive, than the rosy, pluralistic, functional weak-state argument posits. Patriotism and loyal citizenship were continually redefined during the early Cold War era—especially by officials in Washington as they conflated internal and external security issues. Even the meaning of democracy was in a state of perpetual change. For instance, Cold War civic education, of which civilian defense training and exercises were a part, supported specific views on these fundamental questions concerning Cold War citizenship. FCDA civic education was an important part of a much larger national education project that affected all politics. In the popular magazines of the early 1950s, for example, many domestic programs (which by today's standards would be seen by most as exceedingly moderate) are systematically denigrated as "socialistic" or even "communistic." These terms resonated with the populace; they were terms that signified subversiveness. This kind of civic education and its consequences were the direct result of the construction of a civic garrison that had real effects on society during the period under study here. The *civic garrison*, then, is the result of the Truman administration program for a national civic (as in civilian) preparedness training and education policy to wage the Cold War with the Soviet Union.

MOBILIZING THE HOME FRONT FOR THE COLD WAR

Preparation for what has been called "the imaginary war" had very real social consequences for American society, and it configured fundamental institutional changes within the federal government.[29] The connection between war-making and war mobilization and the ability of the central government to manage information are of critical importance to this analysis and to the claim that a robust central state was developed to manage early Cold War mobilization. An internal logic to home-front mobilization—the actual political, administrative, institutional, and ideological logistics necessary to carry out such a program over time—profoundly affected society, especially as the political culture became militarized.[30] Cold War mobilization was an open-ended process that functioned most efficiently through politically insulated institutions that were relatively safe from constant political logrolling, budget cuts, and election-year grandstanding. Most important, however, these institutions of domestic mobilization were juridically endowed with enormous discretion to carry out their programs. Such highly insulated national security institutions and line agencies often, by their very nature, operate in opposition to liberal-democratic aims and objectives.[31] For Truman administration planners the antinomy between war mobilization and liberal-democratic norms was apparent, but the process of Cold War mobilization ultimately required that some aspects of traditional liberalism be eroded in the name of overall state survival.

When the National Security Act of 1947 was passed, President Truman and Congress established institutions that initiated systematic processes for continuous civilian, economic, and military mobilization.[32] The institutional capacity to mobilize the general public through institutions of the state and their agents by applying a sophisticated version of "communication science" developed during World War II was expanded, not demobilized, at the war's end.[33] Put otherwise, key facets of the war-making state of the 1940s were fixed in place so that the Cold War could be waged like a low-level "hot war." Additionally, the Truman administration's Atomic Energy Act of 1946 put the federal government in charge of determining what projects were, and were not, deemed secret in the mobilization of American science for the Cold War. The state enforced what one scholar of postwar American science has called "Draconian secrecy provisions."[34] In turn, continuous Cold War mobilization increasingly militarized civilian life and narrowed conceptions of American liberalism and citizenship. The fact that the nation was engaged in the Cold War as if it were a "hot war" fundamentally affected what constituted the "loyal" citizen, patriotism, and the acceptable margins of liberalism.[35] The early Cold War period was a historical moment in which the Truman administration—with bipartisan support in Congress and within the body politic—moved to collapse distinctions between external and internal threats because the emerging Cold War was conceptualized as a type of real war and because American national security policy reflected a strategic culture that saw the postwar world in Manichaean terms.[36] When planners within the Truman administration reflected on the key role of the domestic population and its essential support for postwar U.S. grand strategy, they made almost no distinction between planning for a real war and planning for a Cold War. The central state's apparatuses for external and internal security worked together to investigate potential and real saboteurs and "fifth columnists" who might be preparing the country for a surprise attack. The internalization of national security policy drove the process of garrisoning and in turn created the conditions that allowed "Cold War liberalism" and attendant illiberal moments to blossom in the early 1950s.

Three Components of Early Cold War Mobilization

The mechanics of successfully mobilizing the home front in the early 1950s were linked to the consolidation of three interrelated components. First is the functional component to war mobilization: How does a liberal democracy mobilize for war without undermining the bases (both norms and structures) of a democratic social order? Second is the state-expansion component: How did the state penetrate society so as to garner the necessary consensus to support a policy that was, at least theoretically, fraught with risks? Last is the consequential component: How are the consequences of the mobilization and penetration of society politically negotiated within a liberal-democratic state? The concept of a civic garrison evolves out of this third problem: the institutional consequences of long-term war mobilization within a liberal democracy.[37]

The functional component of Cold War mobilization has been appraised, albeit incompletely, in some detail within the postwar strategic literature. As a body of scholarship, this literature tends to be ahistorical and abstract. Within this narrowly focused scholarship, war mobilization and, specifically, early Cold War mobilization are viewed by strategic analysts as a simple, clear-cut dilemma of strategic capability versus strategic commitment. Put another way, consider the question that was posed in the late 1940s and early 1950s by strategic analysts who advised the government and produced treatises on grand strategy: How, if war comes, does the United States, essentially, "execute" the Soviet Union? Truman administration planners answered the question by developing a strategy that ultimately (by the first year of the Eisenhower administration) targeted seventy Soviet cities for annihilation, encouraging, so these planners hoped, a "morale collapse" that would effect the unconditional surrender of the Soviet Union.[38] Thus from a strategic analyst's point of view in the late 1940s, the capability-commitment problem became a simple dilemma of how the United States would develop the resources (strategic capability)—aircraft, nuclear weapons, trained personnel, and the organizational structure—to carry out the strategic commitment to obliterate the Soviet Union. In this view, nuclear war became a technical problem open to the scientific "fix," what Colin Gray critically views as the fundamental characteristic of American strategic culture: the "American engineering spirit." For U.S. war-planners, World War III is nothing other than a problem of more aircraft and more sophisticated nuclear weapons.[39]

The strategic literature on postwar American national security often reproduces the "engineering spirit" in its analyses, leaving unanswered numerous questions regarding how liberal-democratic states prepare for and fight wars. Does the general citizenry matter? Does voting matter? Does domestic structure matter? Do popular domestic politics matter? Does, specifically in the case of the United States, Congress matter, and, in general, do parliaments? The seemingly obvious relationship between social order and war is not, for the most part, addressed in the strategic war-fighting literature.[40] This is a fundamental defect of the literature, and it diminishes the scholarship. For example, the ahistorical, apolitical, and superrational approach to war preparedness that characterizes postwar literature on U.S. strategic policy produced the following mind-boggling analysis concerning human behavior in a post-attack environment:

> Now just imagine yourself in the postwar situation. Everybody will have been subjected to extremes of anxiety, unfamiliar environment, strange foods, minimum toilet facilities, inadequate shelters, and the like. Under these conditions some high percentage of the population is going to become nauseated, and nausea is very catching. If one man vomits, everybody vomits. It would not be surprising if almost everybody vomits. Almost everyone is likely to think he has

received too much radiation. Morale may be so affected that many survivors may refuse to participate in constructive activities, but would content themselves with sitting down and waiting to die—some may even become violent and destructive. However the situation would be quite different if radiation meters were distributed. Assume now that a man gets sick from a cause other than radiation. Not believing this, his morale begins to drop. You look at his meter and say, "You have received only ten roentgens, why are you vomiting? Pull yourself together and get to work."[41]

In sum, a critical survey of strategic war-fighting literature reveals at the very least that it elides the problem of domestic politics and its relationship to American society: It produces ahistorical analogies by focusing on past wars and war mobilizations (all of which in the twentieth century were mass-industrial conventional wars); it fixates on the imaginary; it becomes profoundly abstract in its analysis of the "art of warfare"; it transmutes the arcane theories of nuclear strategy and war-fighting into a "believable" reality.[42]

The second component to Cold War mobilization, the institutional consequences for society of central-state expansion, is considered in current war and state formation literature and American political development literature. This scholarship, to which this project is indebted, also owes a substantial theoretical debt to the richness of the German Historical School, which engaged many of the same questions in the early part of this century.[43] For example, both Otto Hintze and Max Weber wrote extensively on the relationship between state formation and war.[44] Hintze's essays on the state made two significant observations: first, that there is an integral relationship between the type of internal structure of a given nation-state and its external "strategic interactions," and second, that the internal structure and the geographic status of a major power (in his case, Germany) can shape the external international political structure. Hintze, then, systematically tied the domestic structure of a state with the kinds of external relations it might have, even going so far as to argue that the international system itself is shaped by the internal politics of major powers. It was, however, Max Weber who precisely saw the sociological link between social order and war-making. Hintze's somewhat more narrow and mechanical analysis lies in relief to the nuance and capacious scope of Weber's scholarship. In Weber we find a brilliant analysis of the intrinsic relationship between the dependence of modern armies on conscription in exchange for citizenship rights on the one hand and the rationalization of state bureaucracy and war-making potential on the other.[45] Furthermore, Weber's detailed analysis of how the state rationalizes coercive power, thus advancing the legitimacy of the state in the eyes of the "political community" and the legitimacy of the state's penetration of society, endures as a bedrock concept for this book, as well as other current state theory scholarship.[46]

Of particular interest to students of American political development is how institutions of war-making and war mobilization become politically insulated and part of what Charles Tilly has emblematically labeled the state-centered "protection racket."[47] This fundamentally Weberian notion of the relationship between war and discretionary state power is applied in this study to the American Cold War state and is used to illustrate how political and institutional insulation within national security organizations and agencies within the EOP centralized immense power within the Executive branch.[48] Because national security planners viewed internal security and external security as two sides of the same coin, Cold War mobilization required that emergency planning be normalized.[49]

Finally, the third component of democratic war mobilization has been a province of postwar political psychologists such as Harold Lasswell, who wrote at length on how the liberal-democratic state might garrison itself in order to confront the first two problems, while not undermining its raison d'être.[50] In his discussion of the antinomies between liberal-democratic norms and procedures and the potentially deleterious effects of continuous war mobilization, Lasswell was prescient. Furthermore, one can tease from his work of the late 1940s and early 1950s a suggestion of the current vogue in American political science (and among today's elite policy planners in Washington) for "democratic peace theory" when he alluded to the connections among the democratic civic garrison state, the protection of civil rights, and Cold War mobilization. My final chapter engages and extends Lasswell's idea of the civic garrison and examines some of the implications for postwar American political development of the early Cold War mobilization. Lasswell's scholarship is worthy of a careful reexamination, especially in light of the fact that new scholarship on the Cold War employs an oversimplified version of his writings in order to explain how the United States skirted the garrison state problem, while simultaneously achieving a frictionless "total victory" in its Cold War with the Soviet Union.[51] Additionally, Lasswell's scholarship was interdisciplinary in approach, crossing the boundaries of political sociology, political psychology, and postwar Anglo-American behavioralism; most important, it was infused with an enduring historical sensibility that keeps the scholarship fresh and worthy of reexamination.

Institutional and Administrative Continuity

The case for institutional continuity of the Cold War state with the war-making state of the early to mid-1940s is uncomplicated but worth restating: The strategy of long-term, low-level, economic, military, and political mobilization for Cold War hinged on the support of the home front. This support was forged in large part by a select but energetic postwar expansion of the central state combined with an enormous expansion of bureaucratic discretionary power—in the name of national security—that fundamentally shaped postwar American political development.[52] However, this study also analyzes the domestic consequences of a momentous technological and historical change in human history: the discovery, use, and integration into the U.S. armed forces of nuclear weapons. When one thinks about how the atomic age was integrated—in political, economic, ideological, cultural, and strategic terms—into postwar American political development, it becomes very tempting to frame the analysis within a thesis of historical discontinuity.[53] Clearly, there were political, scientific, and ideological facets to postwar America that were very different from the prewar period. Nevertheless, while it is tempting to take an uncomplicated route and focus only on historical discontinuity, an insufficient understanding of how the American state mobilized the domestic polity behind its early Cold War policy would result. More important, on a theoretical level, an analysis of historical discontinuity would produce a study that would add to a long list of research that uses historical breaks in American history not only to periodize political change but also to accentuate American exceptionalism.

The following chapters highlight the importance of political and institutional continuity with wartime state-building projects of the twentieth century. Thus my argument operates against an interpretation that views U.S. political development as periodized by a clear-cut historical and political break somewhere between the years 1940 and 1945. Yet one cannot ignore the fact that the dawn of the atomic age on a rainy, wind-swept night in Alamogordo, New Mexico, in July 1945 fundamentally changed how humankind viewed itself and its place within the postwar world.[54] However, from a political development perspective the dawn of the atomic age did not propel the development of a contract state as a way to handle the new postwar policy planning processes. To the contrary, the Truman administration turned to the tried-and-true methods used during World War II to implement its domestic preparedness policies.

Assertive international engagement was a bedrock principle of Truman administration postwar grand strategy, and this policy meant that the United States, if necessary, would use nuclear weapons to protect its national interests around the globe.[55] As Chapter Two details, the elite consensus in support of this presupposition of the use of power in the postwar international arena was almost complete before the war had even ended. Whether one was a so-called Taft Republican or a Truman administration "liberal internationalist," the far-reaching idea that the United States would act to protect and nurture its postwar national interests in the fashion of the last great maritime trading power—Great Britain—was, for all intents and purposes, a given. In short, there was firm consensus around what has come to be called "security internationalism," and this elite consensus limited alternative trajectories for U.S. Cold War policy planning.[56]

However, postwar planners, politicians in Washington, and national security specialists within the Truman administration were *not* convinced that the American people had accepted the elite interpretation of the postwar world or its concept of the place of the United States in the postwar international political arena.[57] In an established wartime manner, Cold War civic education was premised on the idea that the public had to be taught that accepting the risk of a nuclear war and understanding the threat of Soviet communism were essential for the nation's political, economic, and social security.

Agency

The following chapters mirror *exactly* how Truman administration planners envisioned the public policy of educating the home front about the effects of nuclear weapons, the meaning of the Cold War, and the purpose of national preparedness—namely, as traditional marketing challenges where coordination between producers, marketers, and consumers is the key to success.[58]

In this framework, *producers* are seen as the policy-planning elites who actually assess postwar national security needs and plan strategy. These producers of policy are referred to throughout the book as "policy elites," "national security elites," or "Truman administration planners."[59] The institutions in which many of the individual actors and their staffs worked are regarded here as *institutional producers*, for example, the NSRB, the FCDA, the DOD, the National Security Council (NSC), the Atomic Energy Commission, the State Department, and the various agencies within these larger institutions.

There are two principal loci—civilian and military—in which the strategic planners and actors were situated. The main civilian locus was the Executive branch, specifically the EOP, where, after 1947, the NSC and its staff were located. The chief military-strategic axis was not only the upper echelons of the Pentagon (i.e., the Joint Chiefs of Staff and the various high-level interservice coordinating committees) but also academic national security specialists who were affiliated with the DOD.[60] These defense intellectuals were located within top research universities, forming the core epistemic community that dealt with the theoretical aspects of nuclear war and its impact on postwar grand strategy. Furthermore, technical counsel concerning nuclear weapons and their effects was drawn from the universities that had participated in the Manhattan Project and other associated projects that dealt with advanced weapons development, especially at MIT and Stanford University.[61] Universities incorporated (in the business/legal sense of the term) research subsidiaries that contracted with the federal government on national security issues. These proto–think tanks worked on advanced weapons research projects and created an entity in which faculty from various universities could collaborate at different times and on different projects throughout a given period, without giving up their positions in their own schools.[62] In other words, many physical and social scientists spent time in Washington in the equivalent of "academic holding companies," advising military and civilian planners about grand strategy, war mobilization, and the art of modern war-fighting.

Marketing the principles of postwar grand strategy depended on maintaining institutional arrangements originally forged during World War II between the central state and the aforementioned major research universities and, most especially, a relationship between the federal government and quasi-private business organizations and trade associations. The Advertising Council (Ad Council) was an important institutional locus where the home-front mobilization campaign designed by the NSRB and instituted by the FCDA was publicized and marketed. The Ad Council continued and refined its "war advertising" techniques to sell the Cold War civil defense preparedness programs.[63] The Ad Council was enormously important because it had substantial, practical business arrangements with the Hollywood movie studios that were, in turn, used by the FCDA. The Ad Council also had ties with numerous small businesses that it accessed through the client lists of the major advertising agencies that comprised the Ad Council itself. These arrangements between the state, the Ad Council, small and large businesses, and Hollywood were crucial when the NSRB's Office of Civil Defense Planning (OCDP) and the FCDA moved to "mass market" their Cold War civic education programs about war preparedness, communism and its threat to the American social order, patriotism, and civilian defense.

There were two *internal* (within the Truman administration) loci where specific key actors can be associated with the alliance between the federal government, quasi-private organizations such as the Ad Council, and media-oriented businesses. First, within the EOP, John R. Steelman (assistant to the president and, for a time, chairman of the NSRB) and Spencer Quick handled much of the liaison between the administration and the Ad Council. Second, within the Ad Council proper, relations between the government, council members, and other businesses used by the council for government-related work was handled by Allan M. Wilson, who was the vice president of the Ad Council during the early Cold War period. Additionally, the prestigious Madison Avenue advertising agency employed by both the OCDP and FCDA was Batten, Barton, Durstine, & Osborn, Inc. (BBD&O), whose top-level staff interacted—on personal, political, and official business—with top Truman administration personnel as well as with personnel at the OCDP and then the FCDA. The institutional continuity here is important. During World War II the Office of War Information (OWI), under the direction of the Ad Council, employed BBD&O to carry out many of its home-front mobilization campaigns. Promoting and marketing Cold War civic education relied on a corporatelike relationship between the Truman administration and the Ad Council.

Finally, the general public appears in this study as the object or target of both producers and marketers; thus the general public is the *consumer* of the home-front mobilization process. What kind of consumers, how much they "bought into" the war preparedness programs of the FCDA, and the manner in which the state fine-tuned its civic education program at the local and national level are examined in detail in the remainder of this book.

Chapter 2

THE NEVER-ENDING THREAT: POLICY PLANNING AND THE COLD WAR

We are not at war. Neither are we really at peace."
—*Ferdinand Eberstadt, 1947*

Before World War II had ended, planning for the "next war" had begun. As one historian has shown, as early as November 1941, a month before the attack on Pearl Harbor, Army General George C. Marshall and his aide, Brigadier General John McAuley Palmer, were already preparing for the postwar peace and the next war to follow it.[1] As the war drew to a close, key civilian planners and military advisors to presidents Roosevelt and Truman became increasingly concerned about postwar relations with the Soviet Union and its potential to threaten American economic, political, and military interests. These concerns were premised on a realist interpretation of Soviet power and a newly evolving bipolar international system. By the end of World War II, Britain's role in the international system was supplanted by the United States, completing the decline of British power that began in the late nineteenth century.[2] In the United States it was clear to both Roosevelt and Truman administration planners that the United States would be the driving force behind the reconstruction and maintenance of a new liberal economic order that they hoped would prevent another global confrontation.[3]

Overlaying the fact that World War II rearranged the international system and its power structure was the certainty that the "other power" was the Soviet Union. To political elites and key planners in the United States, the Soviet Union under the leadership of Josef Stalin was essentially indistinguishable from Germany under the rule of Adolf Hitler.[4] Soviet *ideology*, derived from the Soviet variant of communism, was envisioned by advisors in the United States as the main threat to immediate postwar plans. It is important to note that this ideological threat was different from strictly strategic military threats. Military threats represent problems on which planners can get concrete analytical "traction," whereas the containment of *ideas* represents a much more difficult planning problem. Truman administration advisors made the problem of ideological containment more difficult for themselves, for they were skeptical about liberalism in general and thus the capability of liberal democracies to defend themselves against Soviet expansionism.[5] In other words, the postwar vision of a liberal economic and political world order was premised on the assumption that democratization would be one beneficial by-product of such a reconstructed postwar world order.

Yet democratization, especially that modeled on the American experience, was perceived, ironically, by Truman administration advisors such as George Kennan, John Foster Dulles, Clark Clifford, and Averell Harriman as producing weak-willed, self-interested, consumerist polities that did not have the intellectual facilities to see the "real threat" to Western principles of democracy. According to this cynical analysis, democratization and its consequences made especially easy targets for Soviet communist penetration via the various "left-of-center" political parties in Western European states. By 1950, when interpretations of Soviet omnipotence were commonplace, national security elites referred to democratic or semidemocratic countries whose political systems were thought to be susceptible to Soviet-directed communist penetration as "soft spots."[6] From the perspective of the Truman administration, the early postwar period represented a danger for the citizens of both Western Europe and the United States, who, for different reasons, were perceived as potentially easy "prey" for Soviet propaganda.[7]

In the case of Europe, advisors to both presidents Roosevelt and Truman were convinced that the Soviets would exploit the immediate postwar economic and political flux. For national security planners in the Truman administration, on the one hand, it was clear that postwar Europe was devastated, its social, economic, and physical infrastructure left in ruins, resulting in an extraordinary economic dislocation and a massive refugee problem. On the other hand, an immense worry grew, and for good reason, within official Washington circles that the United States would be forced for domestic political reasons to return to its historic isolationism, leaving a devastated Europe to fend for itself. In this sense, Truman administration planners remained skeptical about whether the U.S. polity understood, in any real sense, the connection between postwar recovery in Europe and in the Pacific and U.S. domestic security.

Now, there is little evidence that citizens in the United States *misunderstood* this fairly easy-to-understand thesis, but the "guardians" of postwar

American policy planning believed the American public would choose to turn inward as an alternative to the United States becoming a postwar "global policeman." The framing of Soviet communism as an ideological disease, where *ideas* can be understood as pathogens that use vectors to infect their hosts, was one way to educate the public at large about the postwar threat at hand. As we know, this is exactly how many understood Soviet communism; nor, it should be noted, for many of the planners associated with both President Roosevelt and then President Truman was this a cynical interpretation of how ideology could be used as a weapon. Thus, from the point of view of the U.S. foreign policy establishment, Soviet communism was a contagion that would exploit postwar political and economic conditions in Europe at the expense of American interests. The logic of the pathogenic theory of Soviet communism is sketched in a 1943 memo from William Bullitt to President Roosevelt pertaining to postwar planning. Presaging George Kennan's "long telegram" of 1946, the Bullitt memo clearly articulates an early version of the postwar strategic policy to circumscribe Soviet influence and power:

> In what countries in Europe may we reasonably hope to set up de facto administrations, followed by de jure governments, that will work for a world of liberty, democracy and peace? The answer to this question lies largely in Stalin's hands. He may set up Soviet governments in many of the countries in which we now expect to set up democratic governments.... We have to demonstrate to Stalin—and mean it—that while we genuinely want to cooperate with the Soviet Union, we will not permit our war to prevent Nazi domination of Europe to be turned into a war to establish Soviet domination of Europe.... *When Germany collapses, we must (1) be in a position to prevent...the flow of the Red amoeba into Europe;* (2) set up in the liberated countries in Europe democratic administrations which, working together, will be strong enough to provide the requisite defense against invasion by the Soviet Union.[8]

CONSENSUS FORMATION AND THE HOME FRONT

As World War II entered its last year and a half, postwar planning became the focus of presidential advisors such as James V. Forrestal, Averell Harriman, Secretary of War Henry L. Stimson, John J. McCloy, John Foster Dulles, and George Kennan. These advisors, as well as many influential politicians in Congress, viewed the Soviet Union as anything but a partner in the postwar period.

However, with the exception of some important individuals like General George Marshall, between 1941 and 1944 many of the military chiefs were not overly concerned with Soviet postwar political aims. They had actual strategic concerns related to war-fighting, but civilian planners concerned about postwar planning thought it absolutely crucial to get the officer corps "on board" with respect to a consensus about containing, even actively engaging, the Soviet Union after the war had ended. It was not until second-front operations began in June 1944 and a working strategic relationship had to be hammered out with the Soviet military that the ambivalence on the part of the chiefs of the armed services began to change. The initial ambivalence stemmed from the fact that, from the point of view of the American officer corps, the Soviet Union was an ally that pinned down and bled the German war machine (a fact not lost on Stalin) while mobilization programs in the United States had time to go into full gear.[9] However, once integrated strategic planning with the Soviets was begun, high-ranking officers involved in the operations of these plans became unnerved. They interpreted Soviet grand strategic interests and goals, and the ruthlessness with which the Soviet military sought to protect and achieve them, as being at odds with the overall allied grand strategy to win the war in Europe.[10] More important, it also indicated to the U.S. military that divergent strategic interests in wartime might translate into an antagonistic clash of national security interests in a postwar environment.[11] As Michael Sherry has noted, "measuring the Russian threat" was an ad hoc and contested process within the military until the later stages of the war. By late 1944, however, the military perception that the Soviet Union represented the *primary* threat to postwar U.S. interests was generally acknowledged and accepted in principle by both military and civilian advisors to President Truman.[12]

In late 1944, a civilian/military consensus coalesced around the proposition that postwar national security interests in Europe depended on controlling what was called the "sovietization" of Eastern Europe and the Baltics. While debate among and between different bureaucratic organizations, political factions in and out of the Congress, influential academics, and individual advisors to the president over the *means* by which the United States would manage postwar relations with the Soviet Union was fierce and continued well into the 1950s, the fundamental question about whether the Soviet Union represented an obstacle to postwar planning for the United States was, for the most part, uniformly answered in the positive before World War II had even ended.[13] Containment, defined broadly, of the Soviet Union's postwar plans and its political and ideological influence became the basic organizing doctrine on which U.S. postwar national security planning and postwar grand strategy were based.[14] Navy Secretary James Forrestal, clearly a "hawk" on any issue concerning the Soviet Union, nevertheless concisely outlined this general viewpoint in a September 1944 memorandum:

I find that whenever any American suggests that we act in accordance with the needs of our own security he is apt to be called a god-damned fascist or imperialist, while if Uncle Joe suggests that he needs the Baltic Provinces, half of Poland, all of Bessarabia and access to the Mediterranean, all hands agree that he is a fine, frank, candid and generally delightful fellow who is very easy to deal with because he is so explicit in what he wants.[15]

Seven months later, in April 1945, the U.S. Ambassador to the Soviet Union, Averell Harriman, cabled Washington with a very dismal "official" analysis of the postwar aims of the Soviet Union:

We must clearly recognize that the Soviet program is the establishment of totalitarianism, ending personal liberty and democracy as we know and respect it. In addition the Soviet government is attempting to penetrate through the communist parties supported by it the countries of western Europe with the hope of expanding Soviet influence in the internal and external affairs of these countries.[16]

Harriman's cable makes obvious the new "gospel of national security"—namely, that U.S. long-term national interests were systematically tied to Western Europe.[17] With this interpretation of postwar national security policy, a globally engaged United States that eschewed any kind of neo-isolationist sentiment within the domestic polity was an absolute requirement for success.[18] Truman administration planners were concerned about a resurgence of isolationism, especially because of the very vocal public calls to swiftly demobilize the United States after the war ended and the "high-friction" domestic politics surrounding the continuation of wartime commitments. The tension between domestic promises about demobilization and postwar planning turned on the fact that rapid postwar demobilization was the polar antithesis of what the United States required to carry out an active, internationalist foreign policy. There was, in short, a fundamental rift with respect to policy planning between demobilization planning and the elite-centered consensus on postwar containment policy. Writing in his diary, James Forrestal viewed this policy disjunction with dismay when he noted that the citizens of the United States were "going back to bed at a frightening rate, which is the best way I know to be sure of the coming World War III."[19]

It would not be easy to sell a new view of American national security that mirrored "Old World" European grand strategic planning, which regarded domestic and international issues as interpenetrated and not just a logistical problem of "guns and bombs" and continental defense. Planning for postwar national security required a mobilized and *schooled* home front that was not, as Forrestal had worried, "going back to bed." Even though the United States held a monopoly on the atomic bomb and had a huge military advantage over any nation, President Truman's advisors were still anxious about the "contagion" of Soviet communism, or in the lexicon of the day, the threat of "Red Fascism." Cold War preparedness meant not only the capability and willingness to wage political, ideological, and economic warfare as well as military warfare, but also the ability of a liberal democracy to innoculate itself by "civic education" from the threat of Soviet "contagion."[20]

An early planning document for the National Security Resources Board, *The Eberstadt Report* (1948), discusses the connection between a properly schooled domestic population and successful Cold War mobilization: "Something to this end [successful public relations] can no doubt be done by more carefully considered public relations policies on the part of the board—ranging all the way from regularly published official reports, through the 'seminars' or 'indoctrination courses' such as the military services are employing to keep their policies and needs in the minds of prominent civilian leaders, down to the more direct methods of public education."[21] The comprehensive planning outlined in NSRB documents entailed integrated plans for mobilizing an array of resources—human, political, military, ideological, and industrial-economic—so that the United States could manage multiple strategic interactions and crises. To achieve this end, the Truman administration had to find a way to permanently institutionalize a structured relationship between the state and society that mirrored the kinds of relations that obtained during war *without:* (1) undermining the U.S. economy; (2) undermining the critical political coalition between northern and southern Democrats within the Democratic Party; and, most important, (3) undermining liberal-democratic structures in the name of national security. It seems that only one of these issues survived the Cold War mobilization process—the U.S. economy did not collapse, for the rise of a military-industrial complex in support of postwar national security had both short- and long-term beneficial economic consequences.

In summary, by the end of World War II key advisors and officials in Washington concluded that Soviet power had to be severely circumscribed. In order to carry out the containment of Soviet power, officials produced a new grand strategy, premised on a complex interpretation of U.S. national security, which embraced two fundamental and interrelated concepts: U.S. security was fundamentally tied to the domestic politics of Western Europe and the allied nations in the Pacific and the United States was vulnerable to external threats in a way that had not existed before in its history. The perception of vulnerability, especially in the age of atomic weapons, thus affected how national security elites thought about the home front. Given the decentralized and parochial nature of American politics, the home front could either facilitate or severely hinder the implementation of an internationally engaged postwar grand strategy. Thus a domestic political consensus was a vital component of postwar national security planning.

THE PERCEPTION OF VULNERABILITY, THE ATOMIC BOMB, AND PLANNING FOR CIVILIAN DEFENSE MOBILIZATION IN THE POSTWAR PERIOD

Few events and discoveries have evoked the kind of introspective and passionate reportage that developed around issues concerning atomic weapons and their proliferation. In late summer 1945, the atomic age and its potential consequences for warfare and humankind were made clear. The Japanese cities of Hiroshima and Nagasaki were destroyed by atomic bombs dropped from an American B-29. By the end of the war, the "military-economic synthesis" for war-making had delivered to humankind major advances in weapons of war: jet aircraft, radar, missiles, long-range strategic bombers, and the atomic bomb, which Bernard Baruch called "the winning weapon."[22]

In the United States, the institutional arrangements between the federal government and society produced a highly efficient war-making state, one that could extract enormous quantities of war materiel and maintain a democratic social order at the same time. This was no mean feat. The capacity of the central state to organize mobilization for global war and to simultaneously manage the home front and maintain democratic procedures and institutions represented a model for planners concerned about the postwar era.[23]

A profound *perception* of vulnerability on the part of both political elites and the general population was one consequence of World War II.[24] Most apparent was the sense that the United States was no longer a continent protected by geographic isolation, a feeling intensified by the advent of the atomic bomb.[25] In November 1946, Secretary of the Navy James Forrestal and Secretary of War Robert P. Patterson sent a top secret memorandum to President Truman in which they expressed their concerns about American vulnerability and postwar national security planning in an era of "unconventional weapons":

> The Joint Chiefs of Staff have been considering plans for the defense of the continental United States and its outlying bases and possessions in case of emergency. It is apparent that a significant portion of the plans and preparations required apply to matters other than military defense against conventional

attacks and weapons now in existence. The impact of initial surprise assaults which will involve new weapons such as the atomic bomb and which will be accompanied by widespread sabotage may cripple the mobilization of the nation for war and at the same time result in a large demand for defensive resources.[26]

In June 1947, President Truman and his civilian advisors were given a detailed top secret evaluation of the Operation Crossroads atomic weapons tests that were carried out in the South Pacific in 1946.[27] Offering an analysis of the military-strategic significance of atomic weapons, the report illustrates in graphic detail the organic and physical effects of nuclear weapons, as well as how national security planners and advisors perceived American vulnerability in a world with such weapons:

> (1) If used in numbers, atomic bombs not only can nullify any nation's military effort, but can demolish its social and economic structures and prevent their reestablishment for long periods of time. With such weapons, especially if employed in conjunction with other weapons of mass destruction as, for example, pathogenic bacteria, it is quite possible to depopulate vast areas of the earth's surface, leaving only vestigial remnants of man's material works. . . .

> (4) The value of surprise attack has increased with the increase in the potency of weapons. With the advent of the atomic bomb, surprise has achieved supreme value so that an aggressor, striking suddenly and unexpectedly with a number of atomic bombs might, in the first assault upon his vital targets, achieve such an order of advantage as would insure the ultimate defeat of an initially stronger adversary.

> (5) There must be national recognition of the probability of surprise attack and a consequential revision of our traditional attitudes towards what constitute acts of aggression so that our armed forces may plan and operate in accordance with the realities of atomic warfare. Our policy of national defense must provide for the employment of every practical means to prevent surprise attack. . . .

> (10) Any target study must include a critical consideration of the vulnerability of this country to atomic attack and should lead to the study of ways and means of reducing this vulnerability, not only by physical dispositions and military measures, but by suitable training and indoctrination of the military personnel and the civilian population.[28]

In 1946 and 1947 the Truman administration began to redefine what constituted postwar national security. The process of arriving at a national security policy was intensely debated and politically dynamic.[29] Policy formulation and implementation were often contingent on the vagaries of domestic political coalitions, sectionalism, and inexactitude in assessing the Soviet threat. At the highest levels of government, the political friction turned on how much military planning and military decision-making would be fused with foreign policy development. In other words, the debate broke along lines of how much influence military planners should have in civilian decision-making. Also important was the fact that Congress was not totally convinced (in 1946–1947) that ad hoc approaches to containment or pronouncements about containment policy absent the resources to carry out such a policy—such as the Truman Doctrine—were in the national interest. As Melvyn Leffler has argued, "Congress seemed no more eager to take positive action (with respect to containment and, in particular, the case of Greece in 1946) than did the American people."[30] It was not until the National Security Act of 1947 was passed by Congress that the first step in a long process of rationalizing postwar national security policy was achieved.[31] With its enactment, the National Security Act set up the institutional, administrative, and legal capacity to carry out Cold War mobilization, setting the foundation for the rise of the "national security state."

Thus, even though there was significant debate about the means for achieving a coherent postwar national security policy, there was little debate in Washington about the primary foreign policy interest: containing the Soviet Union and Soviet communism (a threat that, contrary to some recent scholarship, was clearly defined).[32] The National Security Act laid the bureaucratic foundation for analyzing and then deploying swift war mobilization processes, which became the cornerstone of early Cold War national security planning. Truman administration planners, as evidenced by the Eberstadt Report, believed that an institutionalized relationship between some agencies of the central state and the civilian sector, like those that existed during World War II, had to be reestablished.[33] The central premise on which the National Security Act and the subsequent Cold War mobilization programs rested was that the Cold War was to be understood as a continuation of a "hot" war. The very notion of Cold War as a type of low-level "hot" war was the logical result of postwar elite anxiety about U.S. vulnerability.

In light of the prevailing view of American vulnerability, planners linked home-front readiness to the idea that civilian preparedness was a means to communicate the credibility and commitment of U.S. policy.[34] Home-front readiness became an important part of rapid mobilization; conversely, the lack of preparedness on the part of the civilian population was a weak link in the "critical consideration of the vulnerability of this country to atomic attack."[35] In an era where the concept of a "front line" had been completely shattered, planners wanted to institutionalize a program that could immediately produce an efficient military-economic synthesis in an emergency.[36] In the atomic age, national preparedness would require a sophisticated and *con-*

tinuous low-level, civilian, industrial-economic, political, and military war readiness. The totalistic quality of modern war thus placed a premium on a strong popular consensus in support of continuous war mobilization, even though the country was at peace.

The A-Bomb and the Pedagogical Role of Civilian Defense Plans

The atomic bomb, especially the reportage concerning its effects—even its "magical powers"—presented national security specialists with a potential problem.[37] As the press reported it, an "atomic" Pearl Harbor would leave whole cities pulverized in a matter of hours.[38] Adding to the concern of national security elites was the fact that the U.S. monopoly on nuclear technology was tenuous at best. Although the United States was the sole nuclear power in the immediate postwar period, the diffusion of this technology and the science on which it was based was believed to be only a matter of time. At some point in the near future, the Soviet Union and perhaps other countries would also be nuclear powers.[39]

Thus planners had to concern themselves with how the general public would react to the Soviet development of atomic weapons. If the public became overly fearful of atomic weapons, this fear might cause a return to isolationism, undercutting the credibility of "nuclear diplomacy."[40] This was not an unreasonable concern for planners, for the media had detailed, often in gruesome fashion, the frightening physical and human effects of these weapons. The popular media correctly depicted Hiroshima and Nagasaki as omens for New York and Chicago in a future nuclear war. This reportage was read by officials in Washington as alarmist and counterproductive to the formation of postwar national security policy.

How Americans would react to a Soviet atomic bomb was envisioned in two ways. In one, the general public would overreact and become excessively fearful, undercutting American political and military credibility. Labeled "nuclear fear" by historian Spencer Weart and referred to by planners at the time as "the problem of panic," this public reaction had to be avoided.[41] A second answer suggested that public reaction could be managed by means of a massive public relations and preparedness program to educate and train the public so that it would not fear atomic weapons and withdraw into isolationism. This was the result that the U.S. government wanted to achieve. Policy planners consequently posed the question of managing public information about atomic weapons in the following way: How do we simultaneously mobilize, train, educate, and garner the support of the home front, given that the United States, in a worst-case scenario sometime in the near future, could come under attack? To answer this question both the mass-education and strategic dictates of postwar policy had to be made understandable and integrated into a coherent mobilization program that would place the citizenry in a position to be schooled under the direction of the central state.

As part of the overall Cold War mobilization effort, an organized civilian defense program would be well suited to deal with public education about atomic weapons and their effects. Likewise, civilian defense as home-front mobilization also gave the illusion that the government could *do* something if atomic war came and that individuals could protect themselves and their loved ones if the worst happened.[42] From a strategic perspective, civilian defense would serve as part of a deterrent strategy in an uncertain and risky future in which other nations had atomic weapons. Most important, a civilian defense program would put the central state in a position to redefine atomic weapons, their uses, and their effects for the general public. This could preempt the "problem of panic" and thus one of the potential consequences of the new era of American vulnerability—a retreat into atomic-age isolationism.

In sum, an assessment of American vulnerability led to a systematic analysis of postwar mobilization needs. Out of this reevaluation, the link was made between domestic support and preparedness and the steadfastness and credibility of U.S. postwar national security commitments. To policy planners in the Truman administration, continuous war mobilization planning and preparedness training were seen as the best way to achieve a U.S. postwar deterrence strategy within a context of engaged global activism.[43]

Planners worried that a postwar domestic political consensus did not exist for an internationalist agenda, especially in light of public concerns about atomic weapons. The belief that the general public would support an activist postwar national security policy *was not* taken for granted in the immediate postwar period. Well before World War II had ended, planners, committed to the belief that the United States would have to remain fully engaged in the international system, were concerned that the general public would not support such an agenda. Advisors to both presidents Roosevelt and Truman knew that there was a tremendous gap between their postwar grand strategic plans and what the general public was being told about postwar politics. The Office of War Information (OWI), which produced domestic propaganda in support of the U.S. war effort, spent much of its time exhorting the home front to support the war so that the nation could once again return to "normalcy," that is, to focus on domestic issues in a peaceful world without economic hardship—and with the Soviet Union as a close and important friend and ally! Thus postwar plans that entailed universal military training, limited demobilization, potential economic sacrifice, and aggressive international engagement aimed specifically at the Soviet Union were at odds with the "sales pitch" about U.S. postwar plans. Advisors and planners were so concerned about this gap in public understanding and knowledge concerning the postwar role of the United States that in 1943 they instructed the OWI to prepare a study on how to "resell" the public on an activist postwar foreign policy.[44] Within the framework of continuous mobilization planning, there was a need to school and train the polity in the requirements of a new kind of politics of sacrifice.

As was the case during World War II, mobilization of the home front was understood as an exercise in government-managed mass education and propaganda. The ultimate goal of such an exhortation and education program is the methodical management by the central state of public relations during wartime. During World War II the OWI and the Office of Civil Defense (OCD) were the agencies charged with the management of the home front and the production of domestic propaganda.[45] Thus the institutional memory and capacity for continuing a state-centered education and preparedness program were available for use during the early Cold War period.

THE COLD WAR AS A CONTINUOUS EMERGENCY

At war's end, the United States found itself at a historical crossroads framed by two new realities of the postwar world: the new geopolitical situation and the scientific/technological revolution in warfare. These fundamental changes complicated American postwar planning and policy formulation. The bipolar geopolitical reality was interpreted in Washington (and not without basis in fact) as a continuation of the clash between democracy and totalitarianism. Some members of Congress, the media, and most advisors to President Truman presented the Soviet Union as a "Red Fascist" power. Likewise, the new scientific/technological revolution was viewed by both civilian and military policy planners inside and outside of "official" Washington as portending an extremely dangerous new era for the United States; the historical evidence with respect to weapons development suggests they were correct in this assessment.

Institutional Capacity for Home-Front Mobilization
During World War II, a systematic home-front mobilization program was instituted. Under the direction of the Office of Emergency Management, numerous highly insulated wartime presidential agencies were created that massively expanded the power of the central state.[46] Wartime linkages between state and society forged under the administration of these presiden-

tial agencies facilitated this home-front mobilization. These important connections between the state and society were produced in three domains. First, in the name of "emergency management," very tight institutional ties between the central state and the industrial private sector were constructed. This established what economic historian Harold Vatter has called an "economic controls bureaucracy of a magnitude never known before or since in the history of the country."[47] The key aim and the result of these links was the maximization of the industrial and economic war production capability of the state. Second, connections between the central state and disparate epistemic communities in academia and business were developed. These linkages created an avenue for recruitment into government of various specialists, bringing together "hard" and social scientists, as well as organizational experts from the business sector. This produced, by the end of the war, a streamlined relationship between the state and quasi-governmental organizations that facilitated scientific/technological breakthroughs in weapons designs and logistical planning.[48] Finally, a government-managed, home-front mobilization campaign was developed that brought together public and private "information professionals" under the jurisdiction of government-run agencies such as OCD and OWI. This yielded a sophisticated and coherent mass civic education and domestic propaganda program that focused the attention of the civilian population on the war effort so that vital domestic support for that effort did not wane.[49]

As the Cold War began, advisors to the Truman administration viewed the general public in the same instrumental fashion as they had during World War II. Without a doubt, all of Truman's advisors, both civilian and military, understood that there was a significant difference between the prewar and postwar eras. Conceptually and intellectually there was an acute awareness of the "new" world order, but policy planning and implementation—especially concerning propagandistic home-front mobilization—were based on pragmatic institutional continuity with agencies created during the war years, for no other reason than because the basic theories—bureaucratic, administrative, and propagandistic—on which the OWI had coordinated its domestic programs during World War II had worked so well.[50] Key advisors took this lesson to heart when mobilization of the American public for the shadow conflict of the Cold War became part of overall national security planning.

Presidential advisors and civilian planners Ferdinand Eberstadt, James Forrestal, John Ohly, and John Steelman learned from the war effort the necessity of having institutions and legislation in place for war mobilization in time of emergency or crisis. These high-level planners and advisors actively sought to influence and manage how the postwar United States institutionally organized itself for what historian Martin Van Creveld terms "mobilization warfare."[51] Therefore, while planners were fully cognizant of the differences between the prewar and postwar years, they interpreted the new geopolitical and scientific realities in a way that resulted in two general postulates that would shape early Cold War mobilization programs. First, the geopolitical reality portended a continued crisis for democratic nations and their allies. In this view, the emergency of World War II was not entirely alleviated by the unconditional surrender of Germany and Japan. A period of crisis would continue in the form of East-West rivalry and conflict. The second postulate, derived from the first, had to do with developing a workable model for crisis management within a democracy. Since the Cold War meant continued uncertainty and risk for the United States, early Cold War mobilization efforts, especially civilian defense mobilization, would look to the experience of World War II as a baseline standard for home-front mobilization and planning.

Given the perception of uncertainty in the postwar environment, planners and advisors considered a speedy and ad hoc dismantling of the civilian wartime state-society arrangements as shortsighted. From the point of view of anyone committed to some form of postwar internationalism, a headlong rush to demobilize wartime agencies would re-create the conditions that had characterized the highly disorganized and politicized planning of the interwar years. At the very least, it was argued by Truman administration national security specialists and influential members of Congress that ad hoc and disorganized demobilization was illogical, at best, as it produced organizational inefficiencies; at worst, it was downright dangerous.[52] Instead, advisors such as Eberstadt, Ohly, and Forrestal envisioned a totally reorganized national security apparatus with a separate civilian-controlled agency charged with rationalizing domestic mobilization and readiness policy for the early Cold War. The National Security Act piloted the reorganization of the national security apparatus and created a new mobilization agency that was specifically dedicated to centralizing home-front mobilization planning—the relatively short-lived but extremely important NSRB.

The NSRB and the Ethos of Emergency Planning

In 1947, with relations between the United States and the Soviet Union rapidly deteriorating, the perception that the postwar era would be buffeted by international crises became commonplace in the Executive branch, the State Department, and Congress. Deputy Director of the State Department's Office of European Affairs John Hickerson expressed this perception in a top secret memorandum in February 1947, appraising the deterioration of postwar U.S./Soviet relations:

Actions of the Soviet Government in the field of Foreign Affairs leave us no alternative other than to assume that the USSR has aggressive intentions.... If the right of free men to live out their lives under the institutions of their free choice is to be preserved, there must be a vigilant determination on the part of peoples and governments of the U.S.A. and the U.K. to resist Soviet aggression, by force of arms if necessary. It seems clear that there can be no question of "deals or arrangements" with the USSR. That method was tried with Hitler and the lessons of that effort are fresh in our minds. One cannot appease a powerful country intent on aggression. If the lessons learned from the efforts to deal with Hitler mean anything, concessions to the Soviet Union would simply whet their appetite for more.[53]

As noted, the National Security Act reenergized state and society relations so that they mirrored those that had existed during World War II. Following a "defense-in-depth" organizational and institutional scheme, Cold War mobilization placed a premium on the domestic political support derived from a home-front preparedness program.[54] Straightforwardly enunciating the organizational continuity between Cold War mobilization and preparedness and the lessons of World War II, Ferdinand Eberstadt commented on the relevance of the ties that bound the NSRB and the new national security apparatus as a whole to the recent war experience:

At the end of World War II, exhaustive studies and analyses were undertaken. Out of these emerged a body of sound organizational forms, principles and procedures. This knowledge and experience was embodied by Congress in the National Security Act of 1947—an organizational pattern and operating establishment superior to anything which previously existed in this Country.[55]

The NSRB based its programs for Cold War mobilization and home-front preparedness on the premise that low-level, continuous mobilization was the most efficient way to adapt to changing strategic requirements without overburdening the domestic U.S. economy:

In the performance of our duty to advise the president concerning the coordination of military, industrial, and civilian mobilization, we have adopted the concept of continuous mobilization planning—to assure continual adjustment to changes in strategy, tactics, and the weapons of warfare; to changes in technology; to changes in the international position; and generally to changes characteristic of a dynamic economy.[56]

The concern about the potential consequences of continuous preparedness planning on the national economy and on fundamental democratic structures highlights the peculiarity of Cold War tensions. Since, organizationally at least, the state and its agencies planned as if to fight an actual war, the NSRB organized its programs as if war were inevitable.[57] Thus two working assumptions framed NSRB planning: One, the United States could no longer depend on its geographic isolation to allow for a slow war mobilization process; and two, when and if war came, it would be in the form of a massive, probably surprise nuclear attack on the United States: "In the future, war may come suddenly and may be launched through mass assaults on our strategic, industrial, and population centers with weapons of mass destruction. We can look forward to no respite; and there may be no one else to hold the line while we prepare. In consequence, the national security requires continuous mobilization planning and, to maximum feasible degree, a continuous state of readiness."[58]

Given these organizational premises, mobilizing the home front to support U.S. Cold War policy and preparing for war fell to an internal agency of the NSRB, the Office of Civil Defense Planning (OCDP). The OCDP was originally located in the Office of the Secretary of Defense until March 1949, when it was relocated within the NSRB, moving it out of the military sphere and into a civilian planning domain. Following the pattern of World War II, Cold War home-front mobilization was organized in a decentralized fashion through local and state governments, civic organizations, and trade associations. This produced the appearance of minimal central-state expansion and intrusion into state and local affairs.[59] Civil defense planning epitomized this organizational strategy for the home front. Drawing on a series of analyses that dealt with the efficacy and feasibility of a national civil defense policy, the OCDP produced a basic architecture for a coherent training process that routinized procedures before, during, and after nuclear attack and, most important, a comprehensive, national civic education policy in support of the training process.[60] This two-faceted, simultaneous program of mass national education and militarylike regimentation would, in theory, train the populace to act "properly" in a crisis. Managing fear through systematic training and public education was a fundamental part of early plans for a national civilian defense program: "Related to training is the means for informing the public. How to allay fears and control the panic that could come with attacks by modern weapons, and yet to keep the public informed on the dangers and the means of protecting against them—these are the basic functions requiring attention in Civil Defense organizations not only in the national office but in the state and local organizations."[61]

Mass civic education was a domestic propaganda enterprise; its fundamental purpose was to govern how the general public thought about atomic weapons and their effects. The education program would seek to reconceptualize atomic weapons so the public would comprehend these weapons as nothing more than powerful conventional weapons. This reconceptualization became the cornerstone on which all civilian defense education programs rested.[62] An example of this premise is the NSRB-produced booklet *Survival Under Atomic Attack*. By June 1951, 16.5 million had been sold or given away. Through its message that atomic weapons were really no different from very powerful conventional weapons, *Survival Under Atomic Attack* sought to assuage any fears about the catastrophic consequences of an atomic attack: "To begin with, you must realize that atom-splitting is just another way of causing an explosion. While an atom bomb holds more death and destruction than man has ever before wrapped in a single package, its total power is definitely limited. Not even hydrogen bombs could blow the earth apart or kill us all by mysterious radiation."[63]

The second facet to civil defense planning was a community mobilization effort at regimentation, crisis training, and crisis management. This training effort put into operation the key features of the mass-education program, especially its panic-prevention components, which were theoretically tied to the "nuclear-as-conventional" weapons thesis. These community-based civil defense programs operated on the theory that the effects of atomic weapons could be controlled; just as conventional weapons were handled during World War II they functioned as important reinforcements to the overall program of morale supervision, offering the illusion of normal life in both an attack and post-attack environment.[64]

Civil Defense Pedagogy and the Creation of the FCDA

Given theoretical presuppositions on which civilian defense plans were based, the NSRB's overall plan for comprehensive, national civil defense should be understood as a blueprint for social control. According to this interpretation of civil defense, the ultimate goal was the mass "conditioning" of the home front so that it would gain a "healthy respect" and understanding of the effects of atomic weapons, thereby preempting nuclear terror. In May 1948, Russell J. Hopley, Director of Civil Defense Planning for the Secretary of Defense, made plain the pedagogical and the social control facets of civil defense:

> There is one great potential problem and that is mainly a psychological one. Because it is an atomic bomb that has been used, there is liable to be an increase in hysteria and panic, if our people have not been "conditioned" by educational programs and complete familiarization with the defense plans.... A program of "healthy respect" and familiarity with the effects of atomic bombs rather than

"fear and lack of familiarity" paid dividends in safety during those tests [the Crossroads weapons tests].[65]

Following on the heels of the Berlin crises of 1948, the successful explosion of a Soviet atomic device in August 1949 produced apoplectic reactions in Washington and within the general public at large, creating an atmosphere of dread that peaked in June 1950, with the start of the Korean War.[66] From the perspective of Truman administration planners, the Soviet Union was behind the North Korean invasion of South Korea. There was palpable fear in the United States that World War III might be under way. Gallup polls suggested, in fact, that a substantial percentage of the general population strongly believed that World War III had begun.[67] In a letter to President Truman in August 1950, Clarence Cannon, Chairman of the powerful House Appropriations Committee, articulated the fear that gripped Washington and the nation in the summer and fall of 1950:

> Unfortunately many people on the home front are still somewhat confused and critical of the minor inconveniences and various governmental actions. They do not realize that this is the final show-down between slavery and freedom. The great seriousness of the situation must be demonstrated to them so that they will carry forward and do their part willingly and voluntarily in the difficult times ahead when our citizens must fact [sic] higher taxes, shortages, many sacrifices and even hardships.[68]

Within the NSRB and especially within the OCDP, these events helped to shape an organizational culture of emergency planning that was reflected within civil defense education programs. As a result, the conviction that global war might come at any moment was reinforced not only within the Truman administration proper but also within the general public.[69] Within this setting of "war fear," the federal government moved to activate a vigorous civil defense program that would implement massive public education and training to preempt effects of panic and nuclear terror.[70] One of the central documents of the Cold War, National Security Counsel Directive 68, is perhaps the most well-known artifact of this atmosphere of emergency policy planning. In the closing paragraph of NSC-68, the mood of impending crisis reinforced the official reinterpretation of the Cold War as a real war: "The whole success of the proposed program hangs ultimately on the recognition by this Government, the American people, and all free peoples, that the cold war is in fact a real war in which the survival of the free world is at stake."[71]

It was under these circumstances in 1950 and 1951 that elites posed, analyzed, and attempted to actively solve "the problem of panic." The concern about nuclear terror would now have to be handled much earlier than had been expected, for the United States was at war in Korea and national security planners believed that the United States might be at war with the Soviet Union in the near future.[72] Overlaying this concern about the possibility of war with the Soviet Union was concern that the Soviets had a viable atomic weapons capability and that the Korean War was a tactical diversion in preparation for a general attack on Western Europe. Thus, especially within the NSRB, the sociological relationship—a theoretical connection that was presupposed by planners—between national will and nuclear terror took on expanded importance in the Truman administration.

In 1950, in response to the deepening Cold War crisis, Congress passed the Civil Defense Act of 1950. This act created the FCDA, which began official operations in January 1951. A civilian line agency separate from the NSRB, the FCDA would assume and expand the responsibilities of the NSRB's OCDP.[73] The top priority of the FCDA was to deploy the civil defense information, training, and education program that already existed in the NSRB/OCDP operational plans.[74] Mass public education was the foundation of home-front mobilization, and it was dependent on the active participation of private-sector organizations such as the Ad Council, the major media networks and organs of the mass media, and the Hollywood film studios and their contract actors and actresses.[75] Following the sequence developed during World War II within the OWI, private-sector organizations engaged in public education campaigns that were contracted out by the central state; however, these organizations engaged in active self-censorship and submitted to official censorship as well (see Chapter Three). As a result, public education programs were marketed through the private sector under the fiction that they were *independent* of the federal government, when in actuality the programs were developed and carefully managed by the FCDA.

FCDA operations established a kind of state expansion that was subtle and well adapted to a decentralized political structure. The agency reestablished a dual-track approach to home-front mobilization: a national civic education program that was overtly administered by the federal government and a seemingly less centralized, more autonomous community-based training program that was administered at the grass roots through local government.[76] By refining government relations among public information specialists, various epistemic communities, and principal private-sector organizations like the Ad Council, the FCDA education project created and marketed the myth that the atomic bomb was basically a large conventional weapon.[77]

At the community level, the central state would depend on the active participation of state and local governments to carry out the lion's share of civil defense drills as well as the "nuts-and-bolts" local organizational planning that would routinize life under atomic attack. The local mobilization program exemplifies how state expansion was maximized by adapting to a decentralized political system. For example, local civil defense training drew on syllabi that were compiled from an array of scientific studies undertaken by the federal government. Once these studies were converted into training programs and accepted by the FCDA, they were integrated into the national mass-education apparatus, which in turn delivered the programs to the various grassroots locales. Thus, when students in school communities were taught to "duck and cover" by their fourth-grade teacher, they were ritualizing a carefully planned training program developed by the central state, but delivered at the community level by way of the local school system.[78]

Ultimately, early civilian defense plans were successful enough at mobilizing communites that the program could clear the streets of New York City in less than fifteen minutes with an air-raid siren, have children—wearing FCDA-approved dog tags—fall beneath their desks with militarylike discipline, and send families rushing to their "well-stocked" cellars or bomb shelters in the belief that a nuclear attack could be managed in the same way the British handled the bombing of London during the Blitz.

CONCLUSION

The development of a home-front mobilization and education program through civil defense operations depended on reestablishing, refining, and ultimately institutionalizing the wartime home-front state-society relations forged during World War II. Planners within the NSRB saw the benefits of using a "tried-and-true" scheme for public education and morale building as the most efficient way to deploy a domestic social control program. The program was set up to use a decentralized political system to produce the illusion of minimal central-state interference in local and state affairs when, in fact, under the rubric of national security, these FCDA plans presupposed an extensive expansion of the central state. This approach to state expansion was achieved by adopting the dual-track approach, developed and refined by the OWI and the OCD during World War II, which established a federally administered national education program on the one hand and community-based training on the other. The next chapter will focus on specifically *how* and through what agents and agencies the national civic education program was set in motion.

Chapter 3
FROM CIVIC EDUCATION TO SOCIAL CONTROL

Every person and every community has a part to play in the civil defense program. Remoteness from places considered probable targets does not exempt any community from playing its part in the over-all program, since evacuee reception and care must be planned, and a support program organized. The civil defense program for this country must be in constant readiness because for the first time in 136 years an enemy has the power to attack our cities in strong force, and ... that attack may come suddenly, with little or no warning. ... More important, civil defense could spell the difference between defeat with slavery for our people and victory in a war thrust upon us.[1]

The opening quotation for this chapter is from an NSRB civil defense publication known as the *Blue Book*. Published in 1950, it detailed civil defense plans that were produced under the direction of the NSRB, which was later folded into the FCDA in 1951. The quotation illustrates three key policy objectives of civil defense training: (1) There is a specific, *shared* community responsibility for war preparedness; (2) there is a clear and present danger to the civilian populace and good reason to fear the capabilities, aims, and overall military objectives of the Soviet Union; and (3) winning and losing a war in the nuclear age should be understood by the public in a traditional sense—there actually could be "winners" and "losers" in a nuclear war. Both the NSRB and then the FCDA used the language of war preparedness and war mobilization as a tool for their civic education programs.

The first theme of self-help and community preparedness was directed toward individual responsibility: It was ultimately up to individuals to protect their families and community, which they could achieve through the practice of civilian defense drills. However, the second and third themes were also extremely important for the success of the government's policy of emergency mobilization. Preparedness training depended on hammering home the idea that an impending attack was imminent, that at any moment the security of middle-class life and its social order could be destroyed. In its civil defense planning, the federal government always depicted the United States as an exposed and vulnerable nation at probable risk of a surprise nuclear attack by the Soviet Union. In this fashion, the FCDA intended to produce a manageable level of fear that could then be channeled into civil defense operations and training, thus preempting panic.[2] Finally, the themes of self-help and vulnerability were linked to the core myth of early Cold War emergency planning: Not only was strategic nuclear war manageable from a civil defense perspective, but it was also no different from a conventional war that the United States could and would "win." All three narrative themes were used by the FCDA public affairs division to offer the American public a "normalized" explanation of the ultimate social consequences of nuclear war and the use of nuclear weapons.[3] In other words, the policy of the FCDA was to try to establish a benevolent model of post-attack nuclear reality within which emergency planning and training programs could be situated so that preparedness training would make sense not only to policy planners but also to the citizenry. This ambitious program of national schooling entailed both a national- and community-level program of civic education.

This chapter analyzes the FCDA's national-level program in three parts. The first is a brief overview of how the concepts of national will and national morale affected elite thinking about the home front. This overview situates the rest of the chapter's analysis by advancing an explanation as to exactly *why* civil defense plans and education shifted in emphasis from a problematic strategic role to a less problematic domestic propaganda role. Second, I explore the relationship between the central state, public information outlets in Hollywood and within the national media, their mobilization for civil defense education, and the use of wartime propaganda techniques as a means for information management. Third, I introduce the 1952 "Alert America" campaign. A detailed examination of this program is taken up in Chapter Four; here I consider how, at the national level, the tight relationship between the FCDA and the university system led to the idea for the Alert America campaign and how it would work as an agent of mobilization at the grass roots. This high-level brainstorming about a civil defense "campaign" offers us a window through which to see how the FCDA rationalized its private-sector connections, especially within the research-university system, and how it incorporated modern marketing and propaganda techniques into public education, home-front preparedness, and mobilization.

THE HOME FRONT AS FRONT LINE: DEFENSE INTELLECTUALS
AND CIVIL DEFENSE

With the development of nuclear weapons, existing military strategies became obsolete. The idea of a traditional battlefield was transformed forever as the integration of nuclear weapons into war-planning ushered in a new era of strategic thought in the United States.[4] During the late 1940s and early 1950s, war-planning in the United States focused on the integration of nuclear weapons into overall military plans. As early as late 1946, there also was serious consideration of using these new weapons in a "preventive war" against the Soviet Union: "Our policy of national defense must provide for the employment of every practical means to prevent surprise attack. Offensive measures will be the only generally effective means of defense, and the United States must be prepared to employ them before a potential enemy can inflict significant damage upon us."[5] Bernard Brodie, one of the founders of modern nuclear strategy, remarked to his wife in 1945 after reading accounts of the atomic bombing of Hiroshima, "Everything I have written is obsolete."[6] Brodie and other members of Yale's elite Institute of International Studies (the key members of which were later to become the core of the Rand Corporation) believed that nuclear weapons would forever change the way grand military and political strategy could be formulated and carried out by the United States.[7] Whether this view of modern war was correct is open to debate, but the fact that national security planners at the very beginning of the Cold War believed it to be true forced them to consider the *strategic* role of the home front.[8]

Postwar political-military national security policy relied, in part, on nuclear diplomacy. Nuclear diplomacy, even in the very early years of the Cold War, was premised on the theory of rational deterrence, the logic of which entailed a strategic role for home-front preparedness.[9] In theory, as the United States became vulnerable to atomic attack, the general population not only had to be made aware of such a possibility but also had to be prepared for such an attack in order to deter it.[10] It was also important for the home front to be prepared for the consequences of nuclear war should deterrence fail. Thus, especially during the early Cold War years, civilian defense preparedness was considered a component of a larger comprehensive plan for national security.[11] However, from the perspective of early postwar strategists, civil defense programs were conceived as a form of "passive deterrence," as opposed to the more "active" deterrent that regular armed forces represented. It was as a so-called passive deterrent that civil defense came to represent an important *signal* of national resolve and credibility.[12] But how does a nation-state communicate "resolve"? How does a democratic nation signal its resolve in the face of popular belief that a future war would obliterate most of the nation's urban industrial centers, its basic social order, and many of its citizens? At its most basic level, this question can be answered only if the theoretical relationship between psychology and rational deterrence is understood.[13]

The ability to exercise power on a global scale and contain Soviet expansion ultimately depended upon the capacity of the United States to project a credible threat to fight and win a nuclear war. From a policy-planning perspective, the degree to which this threat was made credible depended on the *character* of the American people. Truman administration national security planners conceived this as the problem of national will and morale, which provided the occasion for numerous declarations of apprehension and anxiety, private and public, on their part.[14] These doubts about the moral strength and character of the American public were discussed explicitly in late 1946 in a secret report to President Truman:

> Even a cursory examination of the characteristics of the American people and of the cultural and material fabric of their national life invites the conclusion that this nation is much more vulnerable to the psychological effects of the bomb than certain other nations. A study of the factors involved should not only assist us in determining the vulnerabilities of other nations, but, also, should lead to the development of measures to lessen the effects of these phenomena should we be attacked.[15]

From the standpoint of Truman administration planners, nuclear terror could subvert the strategy of nuclear diplomacy and deterrence by producing an apathetic American public, an isolationist American public, or widespread support for the "one-world-or-none" policy, the view that nuclear weapons should be withdrawn from sovereign American control and placed under the authority of an international organization. Any of these contingencies would destroy the domestic basis of early postwar national security policy. Thus if nuclear terror jeopardized the domestic consensus required by deterrence, the postwar grand strategy of active international engagement, ultimately defended by the American nuclear umbrella, could not be sustained. As the secret 1947 report noted, "of primary military concern will be the bomb's potentiality to break the will of nations and of peoples by the stimulation of man's primordial fears, those of the unknown, the invisible, the mysterious."[16] National security elites were convinced that the "primordial" fears of the average American could be evoked at a very low threshold, much lower than that of the average Soviet citizen.

Planners seemed to have little faith in the citizenry they were working to protect. For example, James Forrestal, George Kennan, and John Foster Dulles thought of themselves as enlightened guardians fighting against Stalinist communisim, yet they also distrusted the very social order they were defending. These "wise men" of American foreign policy believed that postwar consumerism, combined with the kind of democracy that was practiced in the United States, would not generate the kind of citizen necessary to combat what was known as "Red Fascism."[17] Drawing on their experiences of both world wars, policy planners believed that the psychological abstraction of national will and national morale could be attributed to the whole of society and identified in a scientific fashion.[18] Consider how sociologist Hans Speier—an important academic advisor to the Truman administration—crisply defined the theoretical link between the home front, mass psychology, and strategic planning:

> No Modern army can wage a war without the persistent support of the whole country. Political conflicts at home, sabotage in the factories and offices or mere malaise among the citizens may incapacitate the best armies. With more truth than ever the ancient metaphor of the fighters as the arm of the state can be applied to modern war. When the body, the economic and social system, is sick, the arm cannot strike. Thus under the conditions created by these three factors— the development of technology, mass participation in war, and nationalism—the morale of the nation itself becomes of decisive *military* importance.[19]

Emergency-management planners conceived the home front as a malleable object with a mass psychology that could be conditioned. Early civilian defense planning and operations shifted quickly to a domestic propaganda function as against a passive strategic-military function. By 1952 (the first full year of FCDA operations), civilian defense programming, training, and civic education would attempt simultaneously to mobilize the home front, manage the problem of national will/morale, and preempt nuclear terror by seeking to change how people viewed nuclear weapons and their effects.[20]

Comprehensive, national civil defense education thus hinged on a two-pronged strategy: the establishment through public civic education of an imaginary nuclear reality in which nuclear weapons and their effects are transformed into conventional weapons, and then the systematic marketing of this contrivance to the public. The reconstitution of nuclear reality was fundamentally dependent on the help of defense intellectuals and other knowledge communities within academia.[21] Individuals and academic institutions offered the theoretical underpinnings that linked mass psychology, fear, and civilian morale to propaganda and emotion management. The FCDA used these data pertaining to the hypothetical management of crises before, during, and after a nuclear war and produced numerous training syllabi intended for the general public.[22] Once the pedagogical architecture for a national civic education program was established, the FCDA moved swiftly in its campaign, using well-established governmental connections (forged mainly during World War II) to private organizations, particularly to national media outlets whose mobilization made the goal of redesigning how citizens thought about nuclear weapons and modern war possible.

Perfecting the Aesthetic of the Home Front at War

When it came to mobilizing the domestic population around issues of national security, Truman administration planners used the World War II model as a template for formalizing more than just simple business affiliations with key facets of the national media.[23] During World War II, under the emergency war powers granted the Executive branch, the OWI systematically fed information to the mass media as part of its wartime domestic mobilization and propaganda effort. The key to the OWI's success lay in the fact that both patriotic and commercial goals could be achieved through private-sector organizations—for example, the Hollywood film studios—by working in partnership with government information agencies to disseminate wartime propaganda. During the early Cold War, the FCDA (staffed with OWI veterans) capitalized on and streamlined the OWI model of information and communication science.

The best example (of numerous instances) of FCDA relations with national media was the seamlessness with which both official and self-censorship was incorporated into the day-to-day routines of national magazines, newspapers, radio, and the nascent television industry. An illustrative case is how the Mutual Broadcasting System (MBS)—at the time the world's largest radio network—moved on its own to request that the FCDA review a recorded lecture by Dr. Richard H. Gerstall on "How to Survive an Atomic Bomb" in February 1951. However, the MBS did not simply want a fact check (which would be understandable); on the contrary, the FCDA was offered the opportunity to delete and reshape whatever it deemed necessary from the lecture before it was broadcast:

> We are desirous of scheduling this [the pre-recorded lecture] as soon as possible and I would therefore appreciate your having the appropriate authorities there review the transcript. As I have told you, we are anxious that this important subject matter be reviewed by the Federal Civil Defense office prior to broadcast.... Will you therefore kindly return the attached to me at your earliest convenience, indicating thereon any deletions which the Federal Civil Defense office would like to make.[24]

On its face, this instance of media-state relations and "cooperation" seems fairly harmless, but the matter of self-censorship and official "editing" became more problematic as the FCDA standardized its media relations between 1952 and 1954. As the Cold War deepened and the conflict in Korea ground on, the national news organizations would essentially *fake* ostensibly "hard" news interviews in order to deliver the mobilization message to the general public in the way national security agencies such as the FCDA wanted it delivered.

Consider the example of the National Broadcasting Corporation's (NBC) highly rated television news program *Meet the Press*. In February 1951, Millard Caldwell appeared on televison to be questioned by Lawrence Spivak and the other members of the *Meet the Press* panel about the FCDA, its plans, and its reason for being. The audience was led to believe that Spivak, NBC, and the other "interrogators" (this was how they identified themselves) would ask Caldwell hard questions that were spontaneous and tough so that Caldwell's responses could be measured by the public at large. However, NBC and the FCDA not only rehearsed—with all the participants—the "news program" but also prearranged with the FCDA exactly what questions Administrator Caldwell would be asked and how he should answer them.[25] This same model of information management was used when the Columbia Broadcasting Network (CBS) asked Caldwell to appear on its television and radio show *The Facts We Face*.

My purpose here is not to criticize but to elaborate how Cold War home-front mobilization commanded a wartime model of domestic relations between the national media and the government. Without being overly abstract, one must consider what happens to truth claims when the central state nourishes the kind of relationship with the national media—an essential institution for both the education and socialization of the public—that the Truman administration began in 1947. As a result of a consensus between the state and private-sector organizations regarding Cold War mobilization, the popular media, for the most part, became a *willing* client of the state; this limited both ideological and political discourse within the general public.

Using the OWI communications model, FCDA bureaucrats methodically and specifically targeted the major radio networks and the new medium of television, important national magazines such as *Collier's* and *Life*, and Hollywood talent agencies in order to rationalize the civic education side of the preparedness effort.[26] In this ongoing task, nothing was more important than the connection between the agencies of government and the film industry. Hollywood studios voluntarily commissioned smaller film companies to produce informational civil defense "movie shorts," just as they had contracted out government public service films during World War II. The institutional and organizational connection between the OWI and the FCDA is extremely important for understanding how the media, especially the film studios, moved to help the FCDA create the institutional architecture for its civic education program. In an internal memo written in October 1950, just before the FCDA was created by Congress, public policy planners were forthright about the need for continuing and deepening the relationship forged during World War II between media and government.[27] The memo argued the importance of a strong private-sector–oriented approach to marketing civil defense education:

1. During World War II the Government produced or sponsored the production of more than 10,000 film subjects that were related to the general defense problem. Many of these were directly related to civil defense....
2. If such films served a useful purpose in the last war, it may be assumed that similar films can serve a useful purpose in the event of another war.
3. I am not suggesting the Civil Defense Office should undertake an actual film production [ultimately the FCDA did just this]; such a program would offer many budget, staff, space, and equipment problems. But I feel strongly the need for utilizing motion pictures in every way possible to implement the program we have already launched. This emphasizes the need for sponsorship of one kind or another, encouragement to private industry and others, and a limited program of assistance and guidance as the most logical participation we might undertake.[28]

Not only were such links to the private sector politically acceptable (and a standard approach for state expansion in twentieth-century American political development), but, most important to the FCDA, these large media organizations were also part of a lucrative and powerful business sector that had particularly deep roots reaching into communities throughout the country. Using crucial aspects of the private sector built economic efficiencies into the overall cost of the preparing for Cold War and permitted high levels of operational discretion to be shifted to agencies, such as the FCDA.[29] Additionally, Congress tended to favor "privatizing" low-level war mobilization because it provided for constituency service opportunities. For example, both Carl Vinson (Chairman of the Armed Services Committee) and Richard Nixon (at the time a member of the Committee on Labor and Public Welfare) lobbied hard for FCDA training facilities to be located in their districts; both continued their avid support of FCDA operations.[30]

Marketing War Preparedness: The Ad Council and the FCDA
The quasi-private Ad Council played a pivotal role in the government's civic education enterprise. The Ad Council served the FCDA (as it did other government agencies) as the primary conduit to key national media distribution outlets.[31] The council designated the agency BBD&O to be sole representative to the FCDA. BBD&O, acting in its advisory role, engineered the marketing of ideas and images related to civilian defense through various types of media.[32] In offering its services pro bono to the federal government and proposing that Cold War mobilization be presented to the American public in exactly the same fashion as World War II had been, the Ad Council represented another important organizational and institutional tie to the wartime state of the mid-1940s.[33]

The Ad Council, and in particular BBD&O, advised the FCDA to market its national education campaign by reproducing the aesthetic of "war advertising" initially developed during World War II. This aesthetic incorporated the use of glossy images combined with short explanatory narratives that reinforced the notion of the country's immediate danger and the importance of home-front readiness to deterring that danger.[34] As the admen of BBD&O suggested, the FCDA drove this message home by the heroic portrayal of the civil defense volunteer who acted as an "equal partner with the military in defense of the nation."[35] Consequently, FCDA posters and literature often depicted graphic and frightening pictures of devastated cities aflame in the aftermath of atomic attack, where (tempering the impact of these pictures) brave volunteer citizen-soldiers trained by the FCDA did their jobs during and after the attack. War advertising as a method of information delivery was refined between 1942 and 1945 when the largest advertising agencies uncharacteristically worked together to help the wartime state.

War advertising was premised on three interrelated concepts, which, when taken together, created an elaborate structure for producing mass-marketed information and propaganda.[36] First, "public service" advertising aimed at a popular domestic constituency should develop an ethos to which average citizens could adhere and contribute. Thus the citizenry could conceive of themselves as part of the reality that was being portrayed in a wartime civil defense poster, for example. Second, the advertisement would attempt to provide a pathos to involve the individual in its manufactured reality, thus achieving the goal of a concise and coherent message. Finally, and perhaps most important, war advertising attempted to produce didactic images from which the citizenry could draw "correct" conclusions about their role in the war effort.[37] The FCDA adopted this approach in its marketing and mobilization campaign under the rubric of civil defense for national security. As a result, FCDA posters, advertising strategies, patriotic extravaganzas, and all forms of civil defense paraphernalia reflected the wartime propaganda approach to mobilization of the general citizenry (see Figure One).

Producing an almost palpable sense of impending emergency through the use of wartime propaganda techniques was one of the desired goals of the FCDA's public information program. In theory, the production of a manageable quotient of fear within the public had at least two immediate purposes: It focused attention and it established a context in which the home front could be mobilized and schooled by the FCDA, putting the state in a position to preempt nuclear terror and produce the legitimating ideological framework for its Cold War policy. As Ad Council members advised, the management of popular emotions depended on citizens concluding on their own that national preparedness and vigilance were fundamental to a successful U.S. policy of containing the "communist threat."[38]

Even with the coordination of the Ad Council, policy planners in the FCDA understood that more than just slick advertising posters would be needed to fully mobilize the general public behind its overall project.[39] Successful implementation of Cold War preparedness as *public policy* required that the FCDA engage in delicately balancing two impulses: fear and panic. FCDA planners had to foster within the general public the belief that the Cold War was potentially as dangerous as a "hot war" while simultaneously *not* producing a sense of panic. From a policy perspective, war advertising as a model of communication and a civic education tool was highly dramatic in order to draw attention to civil defense and its role in national security. However, dramatic images of nuclear war—destroyed cities and a devastated social order—sent a message that undermined the FCDA's reason for being by inducing nuclear terror. In short, simple war advertising in the atomic age might spawn the very thing—nuclear terror—that the FCDA was established to prevent. Thus FCDA planners knew they had to expand the marketing model and its overall architecture to allow for both a visual and a narrative transmutation of post-attack nuclear reality into a conventional context. Thus war advertising techniques as public policy would have to be combined with images that portrayed nuclear war like conventional war. This reconstituted nuclear reality would become a tool for civic education by way of a thoroughly mobilized national media network.

Making the Best of the Worst: The Reconstitution of Nuclear Reality

The FCDA's raison d'être required that the effects of nuclear weapons be regarded by the public as banal and manageable.[40] Given that neither claim

Figure One
Common FCDA Posters, 1952.

Source: PHST, Papers of Spencer R. Quick, Box 5, Civil Defense Campaign Folder.

was true, this was a daunting task for the FCDA and the Truman administration. Early media reports (1945–1947) correctly portrayed nuclear weapons as singular and horrifically powerful weapons that revolutionized modern warfare. From the point of view of policy planning, the FCDA's goal of conventionalizing nuclear weapons was made even more difficult because most of the scientists involved in the Manhattan Project also went public, in 1946 and 1947, about the effects of nuclear weapons. They argued to Congress and the American people that modern war with atomic weapons was so unique that the United States could be completely annihilated.[41] For example, physicist James Franck, a senior member of the Manhattan Project and one of the earliest critics of the American atomic weapons program, envisioned a "Pearl Harbor disaster repeated in thousand-fold magnification in every one of our major cities," introducing into public discourse the horrifying concept of a "nuclear Pearl Harbor."[42] David Lilienthal, having visited Los Alamos in February 1946, was concerned enough about the new reality of atomic bombs to write in his journal:

> I can't write these things down, safely at least until I return home so I won't be carrying the notes around with me without the precautions that top secret limitations require. But I shall certainly never, never forget them. There on that mesa, with high mountains forming a majestic backdrop, we went into casual little buildings, saw things only few men have seen, talked with soft-spoken, gentle, intelligent men about the things they had done—all most disinterested. Now I have a sense that this thing of atomic bombs is *real*, and to do something about it is a matter of immediacy, of urgency.[43]

Testifying before the Special Committee on Atomic Energy of the U.S. Senate, the distinguished physical chemist Irving Langmuir claimed that forty atomic bombs exploding over forty American cities would kill forty million people, destroy the entire political structure of the nation, and constitute the "complete annihilation of the...country as such."[44] Perhaps even more disturbing, he suggested that atomic bombs "a thousand times as powerful as those that now exist" could almost certainly be produced. With cheaper means of bomb manufacture, it would be possible to reduce every square mile of the United States to Hiroshima-like devastation. Such an attack would not only nullify the retaliatory force of the American military but would also kill virtually the entire population. In Langmuir's gloomy estimate, "there might be 2 percent of the people left."[45]

Perhaps the most widely publicized contribution of a concerned scientist was that of Harold Urey, the discoverer of the heavy isotope of hydrogen and an activist in the Federation of Atomic Scientists. On January 5, 1946, *Collier's* published Urey's open letter addressed to the American public. "I write to frighten you," Urey declared. "I'm a frightened man myself. All the scientists I know are frightened—frightened for their lives—and frightened for *your* life."[46] It was, of course, the prospect of an atomic attack that frightened Urey and his colleagues. Quickly disabusing readers who might be naive enough to believe in the possibility of a defense against such an attack, Urey stressed the unique destructive force of atomic weapons: "In an [atomic] explosion, thousands die within a fraction of a second. In the immediate area, there is nothing left standing. There are no walls. They are vanished into dust and smoke. There are no wounded. There are not even bodies. At the center, a fire many times hotter than any fire we have known has pulverized buildings and human beings into nothingness."[47]

Given this kind of early coverage of the atomic bomb, civil defense planners had to construct a new view of what nuclear weapons and nuclear war would be like. The FCDA had to peddle the illusion of commonplace life during and after nuclear attack as if it were selling the idea of "victory gardens."[48] By the early 1950s, mobilization of the home front in the atomic age was not simply an attempt at mass education; it became an enterprise of domestic propaganda and dissimulation. Since the Cold War was construed by political leaders and planners in Washington as a form of real war, a state-centered program that systematically obfuscated and censored key facts about the effects of nuclear weapons was justified in the name of emergency planning and continuous war mobilization.[49] Just as in World War II, the government managed what the public should know.

Accordingly, the first step in the FCDA's civil defense education program was to persuade the general public that their initial perceptions of post-attack Hiroshima and Nagasaki—the only concrete reference point anyone had regarding atomic weapons and their effects—were in fact incorrect. Home-front mobilization for civil defense was *always* premised on the theory that the public could be trained to conclude that the atomic bomb was a powerful but basically conventional weapon. As we saw in Chapter Two, this was exactly the assurance offered to the readers of one of the first mass-produced civil defense booklets, *Survival Under Atomic Attack*:

> Because the power of all bombs is limited, your chances of living through an atomic attack are much better than you may have thought. In the city of Hiroshima, slightly over half the people who were a mile from the atomic explosion are still alive. At Nagasaki, almost 70 percent of the people a mile from the bomb lived to tell their experiences. Today, thousands of survivors of these atomic attacks live in new houses built right where their old ones once stood. The war may have changed their way of life, but they are not riddled with cancer. Their children are normal. Those who were temporarily unable to have children because of the radiation now are having children again.[50]

FCDA literature such as *Survival Under Atomic Attack* illustrates the agency's commitment to the modern advertising principle that properly marketed information can change one's view of reality.[51] It is also an example of how civil defense literature, through the use of carefully structured narrative stories, strove to transform the frightful impressions and emotions held by the general public about the atomized remains of Hiroshima and Nagasaki. Ultimately, by 1961, the FCDA and its successor agency, the Office of Civil Defense Mobilization (OCDM), had published and circulated more than 503 million pieces of literature dealing with civil defense. Of this figure, more than 400 million pieces of civil defense literature were aimed specifically at the general public in the form of booklets and training manuals, almost all of which treated nuclear weapons as large conventional weapons (see Table One).

For civil defense planners, the reconstitution of nuclear reality began with the manufacture of a curious universe where the properly prepared and mobilized American people ride out global nuclear war as if such a war would parallel the sequences, strategies, and effects of World War II. This aspect of home-front mobilization was extremely important to the process of managing how people conceptualized what a modern war might be like. The management of panic and terror depended on assuring the public that life would be ordinary after a nuclear attack. The major urban centers of the United States may lay in pulverized and radiating ruins, but the basic fabric of the American social and economic order would still remain intact. In this gloss on nuclear reality, the trained, educated, and mobilized community would be back at work within days after the start of a nuclear war. The most efficient means for disseminating this view was through mass-market national magazines that worked closely with FCDA as well as other government agencies.

A remarkable example of this process can be observed in the October 1951 issue of *Collier's*. This popular magazine, which had close ties to the FCDA, published an entire issue under the title "Preview of the War We Do Not Want." Every article was written by famous World War II correspondents, pundits, and essayists, who were invited by the editors to reprise their World War II roles and contribute essays in the guise of war correspondents covering a fictional eight-year global nuclear war with the Soviet Union.[52] According to the editors, this "spectacular" issue of the magazine had a national security message for both domestic and international constituencies. They wrote:

> Alarmed at the time [January 1950] over the creeping pessimism of the free world as it faced the threat of an unending series of Korea's [sic], Collier's planned this unprecedented project. Its purpose was no less than this: (1) to warn the evil master of the Russian people that *their* vast conspiracy to enslave

Table One FCDA Public Relations Materials per Year Production in Thousands

Fiscal Year	1952/1953	1954	1955	1956	1957	1958	Total
Administrative guides	128,782	67,780	117,186	104,853	118,375	23,924	1,560,900
Flyers	0	0	0	33,970	444,669	41,611	520,250
Handbooks	60,510	168,183	424,266	733,767	2,243,385	1,431,102	5,061,413
Instructor guides	0	0	53,250	143,586	74,504	37,776	309,116
Kits	0	0	0	0	0	32,874	32,874
Leaflets	0	0	0	0	9,391,889	21,819,414	31,211,303
Manuals	23,230	7,804	1,947	8,454	18,237	3,801	63,473
Pocket manuals	0	0	0	0	31,628	30,471	62,099
Posters	318,251	42,378	23,049	543,154	2,368,599	420,299	3,715,730
Program guides	0	0	51,866	53,669	87,887	66,453	259,875
Public booklets	13,994,395	2,921,088	1,424,607	6,024,330	5,018,125	2,094,728	31,477,273
Technical bulletins	109,363	188,755	287,609	954,006	908,746	2,407,892	4,856,371
Technical manuals	477,355	405,271	104,982	313,190	210,943	153,771	1,665,512
Technical reports	0	0	33,975	85,774	43,471	145,130	308,350
Training bulletins (Officer Series)	163,014	77,376	24,106	29,012	1,081	1,100	295,689
Training bulletins (School Series)	57,585	23,969	6,511	0	460	0	88,525
Training and education bulletins	128,913	1,269	1,568	10,054	0	0	141,804
Volunteer manpower	259,014	30,815	93,783	12,707	0	0	396,319
Miscellaneous	47,505,908	4,594,986	19,953,084	40,778,238	37,051,192	24,387,787	174,271,195
Total	64,226,320	8,529,874	22,601,789	49,828,764	58,013,191	53,098,133	256,298,071

Source: Compiled from *FCDA Statistical Annual* (Washington, DC: GPO, 1960).

humanity is the dark downhill road to World War III; (2) to sound a powerful call for reason and understanding between the peoples of the West and East—before it's too late; (3) to demonstrate that if The War We Do Not Want is forced on us, we will win.[53]

In this issue of *Collier's*, nuclear war becomes a romanticized version of World War II: American factories working overtime; the home front mobilized within an intact social, political, and economic order; B-36 bombers flying long-range atomic bombing raids on the Soviet Union as if it were Berlin in 1944; American special forces parachuting into the Ural Mountains to capture a nuclear weapons stockpile; and finally, the Soviet Union occupied and "liberated from communist slavery" in 1962. According to the magazine's editors, nuclear weapons were simply weapons, and nothing more. In the imaginary war, whole cities in both the United States and the Soviet Union are annihilated, subjected over and over to atomic bombing. For the most part, there are no real consequences. Cities and urban-industrial regions disappear in clouds of radioactivity and fire, but normal life goes on. Not surprisingly, one outcome discussed is that the citizens of the United States begin to take civil defense training very seriously.

For example, in an essay written by Pulitzer Prize winner Robert E. Sherwood, "The Third World War," Chicago has been subjected—for the second time, no less—to an atomic attack by a Soviet bomber. The city is obliterated. What happens? According to Sherwood, the president arrives the next day to stand in the ruins of the second largest city in the United States to give a pep talk to the survivors and to the nation. In Sherwood's account, not only is the social order basically unaffected, but so is the technological capacity for the president to address the whole nation through mass communications networks. Sherwood writes:

> The day after the first attack on Chicago, the President flew to that stricken city and broadcast a speech which had a reassuring effect on the entire nation. He explained the enormous problems involved in making entirely secure "the new frontiers of freedom, which cover thousands of miles of arctic wilderness all the way from the Bering Strait to the island of Spitsbergen."... In general, the President's speech expressed a sober optimism which was justified by subsequent developments.[54]

Pulp science fiction author Philip Wylie also contributed to *Collier's* "Preview of the War We Do Not Want." The readership was not told that Wylie was a paid consultant to the FCDA and that he had worked for the OWI during World War II. A fervent proponent of national civil defense training and a passionate supporter of the FCDA's mission throughout the early 1950s, Wylie worked very closely with the agency during the writing of his best-selling novel *Tomorrow!* The book, one of a spate in the early 1950s about nuclear war, was dedicated to the FCDA and told the story of one city's commitment to civil defense training and its subsequent survival of a surprise Soviet nuclear attack on the United States.[55]

These narratives illustrate what historian Paul Boyer has called the "domestication" of nuclear war,[56] which made a romanticized interpretation of World War II combat the referent for the general population. This fanciful view of combat, specifically air combat, was employed by magazines like *Collier's* under the direction of the FCDA to obviate the abstract, unknown, and terrifying aspects of modern war for the average citizen. In this sense, the Truman administration used the "last war" to domesticate the "next war." What is remarkable here, however, is not the absurdity of the stories in "The War We Do Not Want," but the fact that much of the popular national media *did not* publish independently of the scrutiny of government agencies. Whether it was issues tied to the domestic politics of demobilization after war, the domestic political economy, issues of race relations, or more internationally oriented national security issues, the media worked with the government to distribute information in a way that the state wanted it disseminated. The mass popular media thus became an important instrument for Truman administration planners in disseminating a policy that bolstered home-front mobilization and provided an instrument for shielding the domestic Cold War consensus from political and ideological criticism.[57]

SOCIAL SCIENCE AND SELLING COURAGE

The FCDA's adoption of the war-advertising paradigm for its civil defense education program converted a more or less benignly tendentious enterprise into an internal disinformation campaign about the effects of nuclear weapons. Systematic dissimulation, in which the FCDA engaged, had more in common with psychological warfare methods employed against external enemies than with mainstream, government-run civic education programs for its own polity. In the case of civil defense operations, the connection drawn by civil defense strategists and national security elites between morale and nuclear terror on the one hand, and the debilitating effects that such fear might have on U.S. national security policy on the other, put the FCDA in the position to forge links with a rather strange and highly insulated national security organization, the Psychological Strategy Board (PSB). The sole purpose and legislative charge of this organization was *external* propaganda and political warfare. Eight months after the FCDA began operations, an informal meeting between FCDA officials and PSB officials took place to address "problems of mutual concern." During this meeting, Jack DeChant, Director of Information for the FCDA, and Donald Sheehan, an FCDA consultant, argued for a close working relationship between the two agencies on the grounds that propaganda and information programs, whether externally or domestically oriented, had problems that were interrelated:

> The burden of their argument was that there is an inescapable inter-relationship between our overseas and domestic information activities. [DeChant and Sheehan] have been constantly aware of the reaction on their state and local volunteer organization of speeches and other informational activities of the government which have been directed at overseas audiences.... In addition they stated a need for a place to which they could come for expert advice concerning matters relating to the technical defense of the U.S. civil population against psychological warfare offensives.[58]

Even more fascinating than the attempt to tap a propaganda agency for domestic purposes was the suggestion by DeChant that the PSB could function as a "mental CIA," developing and distributing national security estimates concerning the mass psychology of the general population:

> However, the meeting brought out a suggestion from Mr. DeChant that some kind of an authoritative "psychological estimate" would be very useful to them in adapting [the FCDA's] information program to the requirements of overall national psychological strategy. They suggested that the PSB could very well function as a "mental CIA" in developing such estimates for the authoritative and restricted use of the top government officials somewhat in the same manner as CIA functions with respect to intelligence matters.[59]

The informal ties between the FCDA and the PSB were fateful not only because they indicated that political and psychological warfare techniques were considered for use domestically but also because they opened up a second avenue for the FCDA to access experts in psychological warfare and propaganda within academia.[60] It was the research universities that supplied the FCDA (among the many national security agencies of the early Cold War period) with an operational model for the "protection" and surveillance of the emotional well-being of the American public. In the early 1950s, the FCDA policy planning staff drew heavily on the research-university system for its theory of panic prevention and for a general *working* theory on the sociology of emotions, that is, a theory that could be used as public policy. One of a series of Truman administration national security studies carried out by the major research universities was called Project East River, which dealt specifically with civilian mobilization, civil defense, and the development of a working theory of fear management.

Project East River: Fear Management and Panic Prevention

"The prevention and control of panics in time of attack are important tasks of civil defense. For the possibility always exists that where people panic under attack, more death and injury may occur from that cause than from the direct effects of military weapons."[61] So begins an analysis of fear management and panic prevention in the most influential and comprehensive government-sponsored academic civil defense study, Project East River. The study was begun under the auspices of the NSRB and completed under the control of the FCDA by a consortium of research universities known as the Associated Universities, Inc.[62] The exhaustive examination of civil defense was initially part of the larger collection of national security studies known as the "Cape Cod series," begun in 1948 at MIT. These secret national security research projects, which are striking evidence of the institutionalization of the wartime relationship between the government and the major research universities, dealt with various aspects of national mobilization for waging the Cold War: the development of high-technology weapons, various nuclear war-fighting scenarios, propaganda programs, psychological warfare measures, and a civilian defense program.[63]

The multivolume Project East River research study is a fascinating artifact, not only as a source for understanding the genesis of a particular kind of home-front mobilization but also because it precisely represents how national security organizations and the top bureaucrats within them conceptualized the importance of postwar social science. National security and civil defense planners, as well as political elites, conferred immense prestige on social-scientific analyses of society, placing such analyses on the same plane as, for example, a "hard" scientific endeavor to develop a new weapons system. The Project East River analysis of civilian defense and its theoretical connection to fear management and panic prevention reflected the "cutting edge" of the behavioralism that dominated the social sciences in the late 1940s and early 1950s. Part nine of the study and its appendix, "Panic Prevention and Control," offered a meticulous analysis of fear and panic prevention and the role of civil defense in the management of these emotions. According to the Project East River study, mass panic could be prevented by managing fear through ritualized training behavior, self-surveillance, and emotion management that civil defense instruction strove to produce in individuals and communities around the country. In theory, a successful civil defense program would achieve the goal of individual and group emotional control by *channeling* fear so that it would not become panic. The main concern of the authors of Project East River was that once nuclear terror and mass panic had taken hold, they would be very difficult, if not impossible, to quell: "The return of the individual to rationality is not easy. Further, the group panic which he may incite around him strongly sustains his emotionality.... The devices [to manage panic] which should be tried center, in any event, in the effort to channel crowd behavior in an organized direction."[64] The "device" of channeling individual and crowd behavior was premised first on the view that fear was an understandable and pragmatic response to danger and second on the idea that fear could be used to both mobilize and motivate individuals to take seriously the importance of controlling themselves under conditions of extreme stress.

The concept that a natural emotion such as fear could be used as an *instrument* for broad social control was one of the principal presuppositions on which Project East River based its analysis of panic and panic prevention. The use of fear as an explicit tool for controlling emotions is discussed in the following way:

> Fear is a normal response to any danger. Some of the physiological responses of fear—increased rate of heartbeat and breathing, increased muscle tone, and release of blood sugar—are useful in sustaining the physical effort which may be required to cope with a danger. What is crucial, however, is whether the activity which is thus initiated and sustained in the individual will be channeled into behavior actually useful in combatting the danger (organized behavior) or into behavior which is not useful (disorganized behavior: panic, paralysis, senseless aggression).[65]

According to this analysis of mass fear, the "useful channeling" of mass behavior can be achieved through training regimens patterned on military combat training. Conforming to the logic of the Project East River findings, average American citizens could be trained to control their fears in the midst of a nuclear conflagration—to witness the agonizing deaths of their loved ones and the disintegration of their social order—and still carry out their patriotic duty of staying calm as a "learned response," just as soldiers in combat control their fear in order to carry out their assigned roles:

> To the extent that training is feasible, it stands as the surest single preventive measure against panic. It is the device used effectively in combat training—implanting of habitual estimates of danger situations and habitual responses in consequence of such estimates.... For civil defense, the goal is intensive training of the public to recognize the main sources of danger in foreseeable emergencies and practice effective actions to combat these dangers. As in

combat training, every approach toward realism in the training situations will be a gain inasmuch as it guarantees greater transfer of the learned responses to the situation of real danger.[66]

Policy implementation of civilian defense programs that conformed with the recommendations and analysis of Project East River rested on two important prerequisites: a marketing scheme that emphasized "personalized selling" and the reconstruction of nuclear war as a survivable conventional war. The first requirement was a dominant theme for Project East River. Project East River's analysis of direct marketing illustrates why, as policy, the FCDA moved so quickly to develop and adopt an enhanced community-level campaign such as the Alert America extravaganza (analyzed in the next section of this chapter) as a way to mobilize the general public. Consider the following observation about marketing strategy and note how the authors of the study use World War II as a touchstone: "There is some evidence that face-to-face solicitation succeeds in enlisting public support where other methods fail. Studies of the sale of United States Savings Bonds during the last war showed that despite the intensive advertising in radio, magazines, and newspapers, the single most effective selling device was a personal visitation."[67] The study's prescriptions about how to preempt mass panic and channel fear were also contingent on the illusion of the "conventional" nuclear weapon. In particular, Project East River stressed the importance of minimizing the effects of radiation, noting that "dangers from radiation are, of all effects of atomic attack, least perceptible to the public at large. As such, these dangers become stimuli to panic at time of attack."[68] The report continues in the following vein:

> Research on the public's ideas on effects of atomic attack indicates a tendency for a majority of the people to regard radiation effects as a major hazard. The public needs to be advised of the general error in this belief and acquainted with the circumstances under which the belief might be true.... As other weapons, such as radiological warfare, become more imminent, their realities and potentialities should be presented to the public in such a manner that their panic potential is reduced and the public learns how to minimize their effects.[69]

Finally, Project East River concludes its theoretical considerations about the debilitating and dangerous effects of general fear and panic with a section ominously titled "THE SPECIAL PROBLEMS OF MOB AGGRESSION: RIOTING, SCAPE-GOATING, LOOTING, ETC."[70] In this section, which makes reference to race relations and the treatment of Japanese Americans, the American public is portrayed as a xenophobic, irrational, violence-prone mass:

The fact of lynching, race riots, and other well-known attacks on scapegoats in our society is not reassuring. Neither is the public opinion which readily supported indiscriminate seizure of Japanese-Americans in World War II, nor is the present atmosphere, to the extent that it condones aggression toward merely unorthodox persons as symbols of Communism. The very real possibility exists that in event of sudden attack, mob action could readily break out.[71]

However bleak their outlook, the authors offered a prescription for controlling the "mob": Since mob violence stemming from mass panic presents the worst of all possible outcomes of uncontrollable fear, it must be handled aggressively. In a classic statement of social control, researchers first suggested the standard behavior modification processes outlined throughout the report to control mob violence; if this failed, they argued for direct action aimed at removing the leadership structure of panic-stricken groups. Thus,

> As with panic, the effort must be to substitute appropriate goals of behavior for the destructive ones upon which the mob has become intent; and for this, the same techniques of calm suggestion and exemplary action should be tried. Mobs are usually characterized by the emergence of leaders. If leaders can be identified and isolated from their followers, substitute control may become possible.[72]

Project East River was the most comprehensive analysis of national civilian defense of its time. Its theory of fear management was fully incorporated into the FCDA's public policy. By late 1952, FCDA policy implementation was backed by a sophisticated theory of fear management drawn from academia, the institutional capacity to mobilize the mass media and private-sector business organizations, advice on war-advertising methods from the Ad Council, and links to even more insulated national security organizations that were engaged in external political warfare. The FCDA's Alert America campaign offers us a prime example of how these increasingly tight working relationships between various sectors of both state and society were used in the implementation of public policy.

The Alert America Campaign

In early 1952, the first administrator of the FCDA, Millard Caldwell, Jr., described what the agency hoped to accomplish with its Alert America campaign:

> The exhibits offer highly dramatic visualizations of the entire civil defense problem. Through photographs, movies, three-dimensional mock-ups, and scientific action-dioramas they depict the possible uses of atomic energy in both peace and war. Visitors to the exhibits see the damage that could be done to American com-

munities by atomic bombs, nerve gas, and germ warfare. Visitors experience a vivid dramatization of a mock A-bomb attack on their own cities. They learn what they can do through civil defense to protect themselves and the freedoms they cherish.[73]

Billed as the "show that may save your life," the FCDA's first national campaign to mobilize the general public behind its public education program centered on a mobile Alert America civil defense extravaganza that was modeled on the same concept as a "freedom train." In conjunction with the Valley Forge Foundation, a nonprofit organization like the Ad Council; the Ad Council itself; and the United States Army, an extensive nationwide mobile tour was deployed to sell the importance of civil defense to the home front. The idea of a nationwide caravan to promote the importance of civilian vigilance was developed by the FCDA in late 1951 and put into actual operation in 1952. In marketing terms, the Alert America campaign was an example of face-to-face, personalized sales marketing. This approach to delivering the civil defense message was carefully planned by civil defense strategists (some of whom were members of Project East River). Using simplified visual techniques, it fused three important messages of the civil defense public relations campaign: Cold War patriotism, national responsibility for civil defense, and the important message that the effects of nuclear weapons were manageable.

As testimony to its scope as a public relations project, the FCDA's year-end *Annual Report* for 1952 noted the reach and form of the civil defense caravans: "More than one million Americans in 82 cities had the civil defense story brought forcefully to them during 1952 by three identical, motorized Alert America Convoys carrying comprehensive civil defense exhibits. Each convoy exhibit was transported in ten specially painted 32-foot trailer trucks manned by United States Army personnel from the Army motor pool at Fort Eustis, Va."[74] The principal aim of this public spectacle was to convince the general public not only that civil defense was part of broader national security strategy, for which a collective national responsibility had to be shouldered, but also that nuclear war—having been made to seem ordinary—would easily be winnable and survivable if basic civil defense measures were heeded (see Figure Two).

The FCDA operation to "alert America" exemplified how a marketing strategy to reconstitute nuclear reality and to promote the importance of civilian defense could be integrated with a "scientific" theory on how to train the general population to discipline their own emotions. Two related marketing axioms (drawn from Project East River) characterized Alert America: One, there was a national morale that could be engineered; and two, a basic

Figure Two
Alert America, 1952.

Source: PHST, Papers of Spencer R. Quick, Box 5, Civil Defense Campaign Folder.

theory of emotion management could be used to condition the general public in order to preempt panic in time of emergency. The Alert America campaign was explicit: "The *Alert America* Convoy helps you meet the threat of enemy aggression, shows you the steps you can take, right now, to safeguard yourself and your family."[75] Emergency planners within the FCDA held the belief that the *successful* supervision of national morale in the nuclear age ultimately depended on the view that nuclear terror and panic could be preempted through specific kinds of training programs. *All* FCDA programs were dependent on a theory of fear management that was the result of social science research in academia. FCDA planners, along with other national security agencies such as the PSB and the Central Intelligence Agency (CIA), tapped these important epistemic communities within the university system for national security planning advice. It was within the research universities that networks between national security agencies that were charged with *external operations* and *domestic*-oriented agencies were forged.[76]

One of the consequences of these informal relations was the creation of a set of interagency committees consisting of the FCDA, the CIA, the FBI, the State Department, the DOD, the NSRB, and the Office of Defense Mobilization. These interagency committees were legal and acted to promote close communication and coordination among agencies that were charged by Congress with national security policy in the international arena and domestic agencies. In other words, operations that were based on studies regarding propaganda and morale that, for example, the PSB used in its externally aimed "political warfare" against the Soviets, were generated within the same academic community that the FCDA had cultivated. Thus it was logical for the FCDA to establish informal ties with, for example, the PSB and, ultimately, employ various aspects of propaganda theory for use in its national civic education program for civil defense.[77] In Alert America, we have an example of a sophisticated form of propaganda as "performance art." As the following chapter details, local-level mobilization was a goal of Alert America, which worked very well, indeed, as a tool for recruiting people into local civil defense corps.

CONCLUSION

A national "civic education" program to prepare the American public for the uncertainty of nuclear war involved a robust central-state involvement in society-based organizations. In the case of the FCDA and its program of home-front mobilization and preparedness, three kinds of state-induced interactions took place. The first collaboration stemmed from the firm belief by national security elites, politicians in Congress, academics, and key members of the Executive branch that there was an integral connection between the abstract notion of national morale and the ability of the United States to carry out its postwar strategic policies. This understanding of strategic policy helped to shape an instrumental view of the home front on the part of policy planners in the Truman administration. The home front as an instrument of grand strategy was reflected in civil defense policy planning within the Truman administration, where the American public was conceived as either ambivalent about U.S. Cold War nuclear policy or, at worst, apathetic and thus "weak-willed" regarding early Cold War planning. The importance of national will and national morale, coupled with a dim view of the American public at large, led the Truman administration to implement a public policy to reeducate the public about nuclear weapons and their effects. This policy of Cold War civic education was set in motion on a national level by the passage of the Civil Defense Act of 1951 and the creation of the FCDA.

The second important interaction was the use by the state of quasi–private-sector organizations such the Ad Council and private-sector businesses, especially within the national media, to plan and market a reconstructed reality that portrayed nuclear weapons as conventional weapons. The state's relationship to media outlets was an effort to apply the new "science of communication" and propaganda, much of which was refined during the war years, to a peacetime program of civil defense preparedness. The alliances and networks that were formed and formalized between the government and information managers in the private sector allowed for a massive dissimulation campaign to be carried out in the name of national security.

Last, government agencies such as the FCDA incorporated academic theories on morale and emotion management as a new communication science in its national campaign for civil defense training and awareness. The interaction between research universities and line agencies such as the FCDA opened the door through which different national security agencies—some of which were legally prohibited from engaging in domestic operations—used the same knowledge communities, sharing information, operational procedures, and in some cases personnel. Further, under the cloak of the academy and the legitimacy it lent to postwar social science, the U.S. population was subjected to a massive campaign of state-sponsored dissimulation. Project East River is a prime example of a university-supervised study incorporated into public policy. The state used the research universities to cultivate social scientists who helped the FCDA with the production of civil defense syllabi, narratives about nuclear reality, and self-help pamphlets. The American public was subjected, with the full authorization of their government, to preposterous explanations of the effects of nuclear war and the ease with which such a war could be fought and won. The melding of "scientific" theories about fear management with extravaganzas like Alert America and civilian defense programs in general allowed the state to oversee *how* issues concerning national security policy and especially nuclear weapons policy would be framed for debate by the general public.

Chapter 4

COMMUNITY MOBILIZATION AND THE FCDA

Understand this—there can be no shirking of civil defense duties. Civil defense is not something that is done for you.... [I]t is something you do for yourself. It is self-protection. No one person can escape the individual and collective responsibilities of civil defense.[1]

This chapter argues that FCDA policy planning was essentially successful at mobilizing communities across the United States to prepare for World War III. Equally important, however, it also elucidates how community mobilization fostered the garrisoning process, which in turn animated the legitimating ideologies we recognize today as the distinguishing features of the early Cold War era.[2]

Nevertheless, implementation of FCDA policies was not without its fair share of political and organizational friction. As we know, there is a decidedly mixed history of success in public policy planning and implementation in the United States. The institutional character of the American state and the constitutional structure of federalism guarantee that crucial points of political, ideological, and fiscal friction will dilute and reconfigure *how* national policy is implemented, especially at the community and local level of government.[3] In the case of the FCDA, policy implementation did run into problems in the familiar arenas of political friction: between urban and suburban areas, between rural and more populated parts of the country, and along sectional lines of North and South. However, it is intriguing that implementation problems were (with the exception of a key issue having to do with race relations, discussed below) chiefly a product of successful *overselling* of civilian preparedness education by the state.

TWO ISSUES CONCERNING COMMUNITY MOBILIZATION

Whether the FCDA achieved its goals at the subnational level depends on what we mean by "success." Two questions come to mind. First, did the FCDA implement mobilization plans in an environment that provided for a politically frictionless process of community-level emergency planning and training? The second question twists the first a bit and asks: Did civilian defense training, education, and planning—although not without some administrative problems—ultimately realize most of the objectives of FCDA planners? To this, the answer is yes. This second issue is a primary part of this chapter's analysis.

However, with respect to the first question, if it is a given that smooth implementation of any public policy in the United States, whether at the national or subnational level, is rare, even in times of real war, as might be expected, the FCDA did not succeed in achieving complete success with *all* of its programs. There were obstacles—mostly fiscal, but also policy oriented—that were not surmounted by the FCDA; thus some policies failed when broad-based community programs were instituted by local civil defense officials and volunteers. There was, as mentioned earlier, a paradoxical quality to the local implementation, directly related to how civil defense was marketed. For the most part, operational problems for the FCDA did not reflect a fundamental rejection of the Truman administration's national plan for civilian defense mobilization but were a consequence of the "overselling" of civil defense preparedness.[4] FCDA archives contain numerous documents that paint a picture of (especially) core industrial states and their local communities eager to move faster with civil defense mobilization programs and training than the FCDA was capable of managing.[5] In other words, FCDA plans to meld a public policy program with the concept of national security were so successful that the local-level mobilization phase demanded more from the central state than it was capable of delivering.

This was one of the many important institutional developments of Cold War mobilization, for even though the institutional capacity to deliver a mass education and community mobilization campaign existed, the FCDA was not nearly large enough to deliver on the scale that the local communities demanded.[6] The willingness of local communities to mobilize in the late 1940s and early 1950s is a rare example, in American history at least, of the local community demanding more from a federal line agency than it could quickly deliver. In this sense, then, the marketing of ideas about preparedness, vigilance, individual and collective responsibility, and the meaning of Cold War citizenship made things easier for the central state. Thus, in the language of sales, "selling" the need for the communities to unite and engage in preparedness planning was unnecessary—especially after the beginning of the Korean War in June 1950.[7] On the contrary, for the FCDA it literally was a matter of restraining various local organizations from developing their own civil defense plans *without* the support of the government agency—which they believed was moving too slowly.

That the communities wanted to move more swiftly than the federal government on civil defense mobilization presented policy problems for the FCDA. Imagine local and state governments independently researching the consequences for civilians of atomic warfare and the best means to provide civil defense. Two obvious problems would have developed, both of which would have undermined the Truman administration's argument regarding the banality of nuclear weapons and thus the raison d'être of the FCDA. First, high-level Executive branch planners in the Truman administration would have been removed as the arbiters of what should and should not be disseminated about nuclear weapons; individual states and localities would have made these decisions. This possibility raised profound issues with respect to national security and secrecy. Second, and most important, given the first consequence, sustaining the Truman administration's conventional-ization thesis would have been impossible. In particular, the FCDA's fanciful world where global nuclear war is fought like World War II and where post-attack normalcy was guaranteed would have been revealed to the general public as a homespun anodyne without any scientific basis. Thus FCDA officials found themselves in the self-contradictory position of trying to slow down the speed with which communities throughout the country wanted to institute their own civil defense education and mobilization programs, while at the same time publicly advancing a position of minimal central-state inter-ference and local independence in matters of civil defense. In sum, then, problematic administration of local civil defense programs, where they arose, was often a problem of *successful* marketing and overeager consumers, *not* the disbelief and apathy that developed within the general population in the late 1950s and early 1960s.

This chapter is divided into two main parts: The first deals with the pol-icy logistics and techniques for community mobilization; the second, with the ramifications for political development of emergency planning scenarios. Part one concentrates on the specialization of grassroots community mobi-lization, especially the FCDA's integration of direct sales marketing strate-gies into civil defense schooling and its use of the Alert America campaign and the public schools, and analyzes, as well, the warden system and home-training programs.

The second part considers the intended and unintended political out-comes of the central state's attempt to inoculate the general population against nuclear fear. The policy of continuous emergency planning had consequences for political development, predicated, as it was, on a framework that, for different reasons, was exclusionary, geographically biased, and gendered.

GRASSROOTS MOBILIZATION AND CIVIL DEFENSE EDUCATION

The State, Direct Marketing, and Community Education

The FCDA marketed its civil defense program to metropolitan suburbia between 1951 and 1953 with a three-tiered approach. The FCDA (1) used its Alert America convoys to spur local organizations not only to adopt the "civic education" programs but also to develop local community civil defense organizations, (2) employed a far-reaching use of the public school system as a way to distribute its training syllabi to local governments and civic organizations, and (3) used its warden system as a recruitment mechanism to further establish a basis for mobilization of the community. All three levels of FCDA community education were premised on a set of assumptions regarding the sociology of the individual, the home, the neighborhood, the community, and what constituted the private and the public divide during the early Cold War.

As noted in Chapter Three, the Truman administration's FCDA had close relations with social scientists because its primary objective was the management of human behavior. Social science research that focused specifically on theoretical aspects of mass behavior, propaganda, and psychological warfare linked postwar theories of fear management to the ritualized administration of the home and the important narrative discourse within FCDA literature that connected individual patriotism, community engagement, and voluntarism.[8] As was the case throughout the early Cold War, the FCDA drew on the institutional groundwork laid during World War II as the organizational structure for mobilizing grassroots interest in civil defense. During World War II, the efficiency of marketing war preparedness to local communities was enhanced by the Office of Facts and Figures (OFF), which adopted sophisticated methodologies for identifying relationships between "target" markets on the one hand and the statistical analysis of those markets on the other.[9] For planners concerned about the potential consequences of modern war on U.S. Cold War planning, the principal markets for civil defense were strategic (military and economic) and civilian. Both areas of civil defense planning depended on social science research for the basic theories that framed all emergency planning. Consequently, after World War II funding continued *uninterrupted* for a host of social scientific research projects intended to aid the Cold War effort at home and abroad. By 1952, total government spending on such research (in current dollars) was $39,900,305.

Clearly, a substantial amount of money was spent by the Truman administration on developing social science research networks in and out of academia.[10] Major foundations, including Rockefeller, Ford, Carnegie, and Russell Sage, received grants for various projects related to external and internal national security goals, the results of which were then used by federal agencies in the Cold War mobilization project (see Table One).

> At least six of the most important U.S. centers of postwar communication studies grew up as de facto adjuncts of government psychological warfare programs. For years, government money—frequently with no public acknowledgement— made up more than 75 percent of the annual budgets of Paul Lazarsfeld's Bureau of Applied Social Research (BASR) at Columbia University, Hadley Cantril's Institute for International Social Research (IISR) at Princeton, Ithiel de Sola Pool's Center for International Studies program (CENSIS) at Massachusetts Institute of Technology, and similar institutions. The U.S. State Department secretly (and apparently illegally) financed studies by the National Opinion Research Center (NORC) of U.S. popular opinion as part of the department's cold war lobbying campaigns on Capital Hill, thus making NORC's ostensibly private, independent surveys financially viable for the first time.[11]

Additionally, science research funds, which were budgeted by Truman administration agencies for behavioral studies, were delivered to the major televison and radio outlets throughout 1952 as part of the popular mobilization effort (see Table Two).

The Ad Council, which played a vital role in the FCDA's Alert America campaign, was closely tied to academic centers that were doing "cutting-edge" survey research, such as the Survey Research Center of the University of Michigan. In a real sense, there was a historical moment, a nexus, if you will, during the late 1940s in which the central state was able to use a set of social science methods to establish both a communication science and a "science" of sales for purposes of mass public education regarding national security. The fusion of social science methods to domestic civic education nudged the Truman administration and especially the FCDA to adopt direct marketing techniques for selling continuous long-term Cold War mobilization to the American public. By 1952, the triangular relationship among the state, research universities, and private organizations that had been forged during World War II had become a permanent organizational structure of the developing postwar national security state (see Figure One).[12]

Although the Alert America campaign remains, even by today's standards of consumer marketing, a classic example of merchandising concepts as if they were consumer products, the FCDA was initially resistant to incorporating advanced marketing techniques into its local civic

Table One
Funds Dedicated to "Social Science Research"
in Fiscal 1952: Foundations

Foundation	Total (1952 Dollars)	Total (1999 Dollars)
Rockefeller	$3,000,000	$18,415,525.68
Carnegie	$2,000,000	$12,277,017.12
Ford	800,000	$4,910,806.85
Mellon	225,000	$1,381,164.43
Sloan	130,000	$798,006.11
20th Century	90,000	$552,465.77
Russell Sage	160,000	$982,161.37
Brookings	75,000	$460,388.14
Total	6,500,000	$39,900,305.64

Table Two
Funds Dedicated to "Social Science Research"
in Fiscal 1952: Media

Media Group	Total (1952 Dollars)	Total (1999 Dollars)
CBS	$900,000	$5,524,657.70
NBC	$750,000	$4,603,881.42
ABC	$450,000	$2,762,328.85
Mutual	$200,000	1,227,701.71
Dumont	$100,000	$613,850.86
Total	$2,400,000	$14,732,420.54

Source: Compiled from PHST, PSB, Box 2, Social Science Research, folder 2 of 2.

Figure One

State–social science–private sector linkages. Solid lines denote direct funding; dashed arrows denote intellectual property/policy outputs.

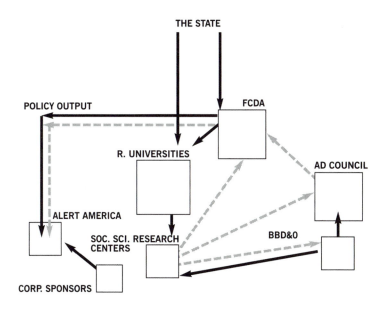

education programs. FCDA administrator Millard Caldwell and his executive staff at first brushed off advice to incorporate direct sales marketing techniques for getting the civil defense message out. They believed that a "Madison Avenue" approach to community mobilization trivialized the civil defense effort and distrusted admen because they used "gimmicks" to market ideas. After an initial planning meeting concerning a role for the Ad Council in the Alert America campaign, Alan M. Wilson, vice president of the Ad Council, had this to say in a letter to President Truman's assistant, Charles Jackson, about the views of the FCDA's director of public affairs, John A. DeChant, on the Ad Council and New York admen in particular: "DeChant's attitude was definitely antagonistic. He began by saying that the voluntary agency would have to take orders, no smart advertising agency is going to come down here and tell us what to do. He also said, I know those New York agency characters. They do public service campaigns because they are after a fast buck all the time, and it makes me sick."[13] Obviously these were not sentiments that anticipated a close working relationship between a government agency and the Ad Council. Nevertheless, neither DeChant nor Caldwell could ignore the fact that in order for the FCDA to efficiently deploy its community education program it had to depend on grassroots organizational and institutional structures. Furthermore, top FCDA officials could not deny that the wartime endeavors of the Ad Council had been successful. Ultimately, the FCDA moved swiftly in 1952 (about six months after the calamitous meeting between DeChant and Wilson) with the Alert America campaign, incorporating a "face-to-face" mass-marketing/sales approach in its community mobilization efforts.[14] This strategy for community mobilization was also a consequence of lobbying by public relations bureaucrats (not Caldwell's executive staff) in the FCDA, who knew from personal experience how successful this kind of marketing design had been for the OWI and OCD during World War II. From a public policy perspective, then, there was simply no need to "reinvent the wheel."[15] The public relations branch of the FCDA was staffed in large part by people with experience in the OWI, and they understood well the importance of selling ideas that would stimulate a precise public reaction—a reaction that could be measured, improved upon, or abandoned. Depicting life as "normal" after a global nuclear war was the central message of the grassroots civic education approach adopted by FCDA public relations officials. Since almost everyone had seen the graphic pictures of Hiroshima and Nagasaki, this was no easy sell.

The Suburban Ideal and the Illusion of Survival
FCDA public relations specialists understood that selling the illusion of post-attack survival in fast-developing metropolitan suburbia was primary

to the overall success of the national civil defense program. Ultimately, for domestic political reasons—mainly having to do with electoral considerations—civil defense was aimed at postwar suburbia. There were two main reasons for this belief on the part of the Truman administration and its FCDA. First, it was practical to protect suburban and rural areas because it was easier. If nuclear war broke out, industrial centers and large cities were viewed as prime targets. Although it was not publicly discussed, there was no way to protect the inhabitants of large cities in a nuclear war. Given the technology of the time, a nuclear war would have left large portions of rural and suburban America *initially* unaffected. Second, there was a fundamental political reason why suburban areas were objects of civil defense narratives and propaganda regarding post-attack normalcy. By the early 1950s, the out-migration to suburbia from cities such as New York was underway. Postwar "Levittowns" in Long Island and Pennsylvania and enormous housing developments of single-family homes on one- and two-acre lots in central and coastal New Jersey were being built and occupied as if there were no end to the new postwar middle classes streaming out of large cities. Literally millions of people were moving out of the cities to get a piece of the "good life" that has come to represent the mostly white, middle-class, suburban America of the early 1950s.[16] Thus for domestic political reasons, both the Truman and especially the Eisenhower administrations viewed this constituency as vital for sustaining the Cold War political consensus. These newly middle-class, first-generation suburbanites had to be unequivocally convinced that their government could do something to protect them if the worst happened and the Cold War became a "hot" war.

The FCDA's Alert America campaign in 1952 was an important first step in selling an illusion of protection for the suburban middle classes.[17] Alert America caravans announced their arrival in various towns across the country as the "show that could save your life." The surrealistic "doomsday carnival" assuaged the nuclear fear of visitors by promising to teach everyone "how Civil Defense protects you and your family from modern terror weapons." Visitors to the exhibition were shown FCDA-produced and Ad Council–packaged movies, three-dimensional exhibits, and dioramas of the American family surviving and winning World War III. The gist of the message to the attending public was the importance of individualism, patriotism, voluntarism, and the "happy life" in the bomb shelter where families played popular board games and rehearsed FCDA "Home Protection Exercises" while urban America was reduced to radiating ruins.[18] Most important to FCDA training, Alert America promoted the concept of the "responsible Cold War citizen": *Each individual* shoulders collective responsibility for civil defense and does so as a nuclear-age citizen-soldier. The public's internalization of this message was fundamental in the garrisoning process and in shaping the architecture for politically correct behavior in a democratic state that was engaged in continuous levels of mobilization for the possibility of war (see Chapter Five).

Unlike the national civic education campaign that focused on how *both* urban and suburban populations had a patriotic duty to take preparedness training seriously, the FCDA's grassroots campaign provided a more nuanced message to the suburban middle class about how they could rally their communities. As one advertising mat for Alert America noted: "You'll see how organized Civil Defense works to protect you and your family...how you can beat the bomb."[19] There is evidence that this approach worked well.[20] When an Alert America convoy arrived at a city or town, the following marketing design was followed:

> Each showing was arranged and planned by local civil defense officials, civic leaders, and media representatives. Special events such as parades, civil defense exercises, and military maneuvers were tied in with the Alert America show to attract public attention and promote greater interest in civil defense. The information media in each city gave unusually widespread publicity to the exhibits. Local merchants and industries advertised the shows in hundreds of public service announcements. City mayors frequently proclaimed "Civil Defense Week" during the Convoy visit."[21]

The language of the Alert America program as it related to mobilization demonstrates that the transference of responsibility for civil defense to the individual and the local community was part of a well-planned strategy to provide the locales with the pretext of local government control. The image that states had "local control" was enhanced by the fact that each state did have civil defense agencies located, for the most part, under the control of the governor. The fact is, however, that each state agency ultimately answered to the FCDA and was *entirely* dependent on the federal line agency for everything from money to civil defense literature. Very little was ad hoc about Alert America or the "autonomous" community mobilization effort it promoted.

Within the FCDA there was much discussion between its public relations branch and top BBD&O personnel in New York City about how to systematically employ a direct-selling approach to community mobilization for civil defense. Like the morale-boosting movies and government-sponsored pronouncements that the Great Depression would soon end or that the United States would rise to the threat of the Axis Powers and avenge Pearl Harbor and defeat Germany, BBD&O's work for the Ad Council and the FCDA continued the tried-and-true strategy of using local-level direct sales marketing designs. These strategies created both a national and a local structure for the federal government to manage the dissemination of information regarding civil defense, as well as other issues of the day.

By early 1952 and with a new-found vigor, FCDA public relations director John DeChant commented in a memo to President Truman's press secretary, Joseph H. Short, about the prospects for configuring Alert America as a government-run marketing campaign. DeChant observed, "Close observation at the Colorado state fair [where an early local civil defense education and recruitment program was instituted] revealed that people were willing to learn by seeing rather than reading. Audiences watched motion pictures and examined photographic displays, but in many instances failed to pick up literature." DeChant further observed that "'direct contact' is paying off."[22] The capacity of the FCDA to make adjustments in how it targeted local audiences was strengthened when the FCDA employed the Survey Research Center of the University of Michigan to carry out two (nine months apart) public opinion fact-finding surveys regarding civil defense mobilization at the local level. As noted in a progress report memorandum from the FCDA to the National Advisory Council, there were four clear objectives to commissioning the surveys: "Continuing measures of public opinion are needed to determine (a) the success of all civil defense public information programs alerting America, (b) the speed with which progress is being made, (c) the methods that have been most effective and economical and (d) the size of the job remaining to be done."[23] The preliminary results of the first survey clearly illustrated how FCDA civil defense pamphlets, publicly aimed and locally distributed, became the second largest source from which the general public learned about civil defense. The survey sought to identify how individuals acquired information about civil defense. In comparing the years 1950 (before the FCDA was up and running) and 1951 (the first year of FCDA operations), survey data demonstrate that in 1950 only 1 percent of those surveyed received civil defense information from locally distributed pamphlets. In contrast, by the end of 1951, a full 30 percent of those surveyed had received information on personal protection and civil defense from FCDA-published pamphlets. Only newspapers (most of them local and participating with local civil defense organizations) were a larger source of civil defense information, at 43 percent of those surveyed (see Figure Two).[24]

By uniting a sales/marketing approach with a message aimed specifically at suburban America about the "normal" post-attack social order, the FCDA mobilized large groups of people to volunteer in its local programs, such as the warden system (see below) and the Ground Observer Corps (GOC), which, by the end of 1954, had enrolled 375,000 active members.[25] One example of the success of the FCDA's grassroots approach to marketing was the impressive accomplishment of New Jersey's Division of Civil Defense. New

Figure Two
Civil defense information 1950–1951:
Comparison of information distribution.

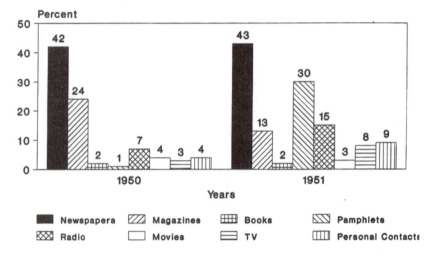

Source: Preliminary Report on Public Attitudes towards Civil Defense. Survey Research Center, University of Michigan, 1951: PHST.

Jersey civil defense officials divided the state into thirteen "civil defense areas" that were mostly suburban, consisting of one- and two-acre-zoned family homes. By the end of 1952 New Jersey's *total* civil defense mobilization effort was able to recruit 231,875 people into the program (see Table Three).

Public Schools and Administrative Expansion

During the Truman administration the FCDA institutionally "piggybacked" on an existing social welfare agency—Housing, Education, and Welfare (HEW, previously the Federal Security Agency)—to save money and to employ a deeply entrenched public welfare institution to disseminate its grassroots message concerning national preparedness. Within the FCDA, a subordinate organization, the Civil Defense Education Project, directed the public school program under the nationally advertised slogan "education for national survival." By the end of 1952, the FCDA instituted civil defense training in 87.4 percent of all elementary schools and 88.4 percent of all secondary public schools.[26] The Civil Defense Education Project also had extremely close ties to youth organizations like the Boy Scouts of America. The scouts, with its affectation of a martial "way of life," was the model for the Civil Defense Education Project's program for all public schools. In short, the FCDA hoped to organize the local communities in a quasi-militarized fashion, just as the Boy Scouts of America was already organized. The public schools would be the principal institution for such an organizational strategy.[27] FCDA officials and local civil defense organizations rallied public school teachers to the cause through dramatic appeals to patriotism:

> Once again the schools and the teachers of the Nation are called upon to undertake a new task. It is an urgent task, directly involving the daily personal safety and security of more than one-fifth of our total population; that fifth is the dependent fifth. Our future as a free people may well be determined by the skill and promptness with which our system of education is able to respond to the conditions that make necessary the development of civil defense education.[28]

The appeal to teachers to "do their duty" and prepare the students of the United States for an impending war characterizes the central marketing aspects of grassroots mobilization, but it also highlights the not-so-subtle formula for administering the local mobilization effort: the militarization of civilian life. Educators were draftees in a civilian strategy of preparing for the next war. In New Jersey, for example, education for civil defense was justified in part in the following way: "Unless our schools can strengthen and extend their services to include the new areas brought about by the present world crisis, our heritage of freedom may completely disappear."[29] Of pri-

Table Three Community Mobilization, State of New Jersey, 1952

Area	Transportation	Staff	Fire	Police	Rescue	Medical	Wardens	Welfare	Public Works	Communications	Clergy	Total
Palisades	1,836	1,089	4,233	6,953	1,652	3,522	7,287	1,929	2,246	702	246	31,695
Hudson	1,332	230	2,844	4,261	946	2,591	6,484	1,197	1,589	143	143	21,760
Essex	1,955	569	3,825	4,913	576	2,280	6,955	1,682	2,315	751	46	25,867
Union	888	909	1,897	3,531	1,452	2,976	6,505	1,969	1,494	418	68	22,107
Lake	1,035	435	2,344	3,757	521	1,057	3,616	1,399	1,641	408	90	16,303
Western	167	223	2,412	1,949	293	1,741	2,476	1,980	1,240	112	80	12,673
Raritan	1,391	669	2,603	4,339	459	2,647	2,053	1,343	1,442	219	88	17,253
Mercer	124	116	2,768	2,603	918	1,621	3,876	1,884	1,455	184	8	15,557
Coast	843	410	2,970	2,812	1,878	1,159	2,915	1,273	1,273	249	73	15,855
Pines	210	788	1,330	1,770	708	1,433	2,914	1,189	1,330	123	57	11,852
River	441	432	2,891	2,097	804	1,874	4,280	3,560	1,344	282	109	18,114
Cape	419	174	1,935	1,817	156	1,450	4,006	773	1,219	124	30	12,103
Bay	105	125	2,791	1,914	75	1,158	2,817	819	867	41	24	10,736
Total	10,746	6,169	34,843	42,716	10,438	25,509	56,184	20,997	19,455	3,756	1,062	231,875

Source: Compiled from the State of New Jersey Division of Civil Defense, *Annual Report, 1952*, p. 33.

mary interest here is that New Jersey's Division of Civil Defense adopted, almost exactly, the organizational link between local and state organizations and the FCDA that Project East River had set forth as crucial. Following the findings of Project East River on training and fear management, New Jersey's community civil defense operations sought first to mobilize the community through the use of fear as a tool of control. This goal was achieved through an ideological narrative that would frighten people—but just enough to get their attention:

> Public apathy is the first obstacle to overcome. Such apathy results from ignorance of the true nature of the struggle for survival which our country faces. Until Americans are aware of the fact that a great power, through its philosophy of aggressive expansion, is threatening free people everywhere, apathy will continue to retard progress in meeting the threat. It is imperative, therefore, that education inform citizens, young and old alike, of this threat to their very existence.[30]

Once mobilization was achieved, the importance of *channeling* fear (the influence of the FCDA's Project East River study is clear) was explained:

> Once [mobilization] is accomplished, apathy will disappear. In the process of overcoming apathy, it is important to take care that apathy shall not be supplanted by fear—a fear that might paralyze our people and make them ineffectual in time of emergency. This fear can be overcome by careful study of the potential enemy's intent, his capabilities of carrying out that intent, and how best to meet it.[31]

Thus from the perspective of propaganda and public relations, when combined with organized community activities, public school civil defense lessons gave federal, state, and local government extraordinary access to individual families across the nation.[32] The FCDA's Civil Defense Education Project had two fundamental aims. One was to communicate directly with the students. The FCDA supplied school administrators and teachers with syllabi, curricula, propaganda films concerning nuclear war, and safety "check lists" for shelter life. These materials reflected data developed by the FCDA and the major research universities that were dealing in disaster research. The second objective was to communicate indirectly with parents using children as interlocutors. Not only subtly delivered, this second goal was also very important for FCDA community mobilization, since it dealt with the problem of panic and fear on the part of parents: "Civil Defense includes everybody, not merely certain groups in our society. In development of curricula, administrators should not overlook opportunities to provide students with 'home work' which involves the parents in training. The leaders of other organized groups have developed successful techniques for training both the members and their parents in personal survival."[33]

The ubiquitous FCDA theme that not only was nuclear war survivable but also that, with a civil defense plan in place, the return to normalcy would be fairly swift, was ultimately aimed at adults. Consider, for example, the understandable fear of parents contemplating separation from their children, especially if they were in danger. It goes without saying that the specter of a "nuclear Pearl Harbor," the metaphor most often used in the early years of the Cold War, was a terrible event for parents to imagine. Civil defense training curricula and syllabi painted a picture of bomb shelter life as a kind of "Boy Scout" experience in which children, properly trained, were always safe in the public school. Thus the federal government through the FCDA sought to contain parental fear of nuclear war by portraying the public school system as a center of security for their children.

Evidence of this process can be found in FCDA-produced and distributed "home exercises," which were mailed directly to families as part of civil defense "home kits."[34] The Civil Defense Education Project's primary-school training took the form of skits in which children would practice both at home with their parents and at schools, routinizing civil defense training. These skits, which had titles such as "Let's Plan What to Do Now," "Operation Home Shelter," "Operation Family Car," and "Until the Doctor Comes," complemented and reinforced the training programs that "home exercises" reproduced for the children's parents.[35] Remarking on this mode of civil defense education in 1952, an FCDA staff member noted that "mental hygiene" worked because it promoted "underlying qualities of cheerfulness and optimism." Thus, in the language of the social scientists who developed the rationale of fear management for the FCDA, the "stay calm" message to children and parents exemplified the "mental hygiene" approach to information management.[36]

Urban public schools took part in all the civil defense programs of the FCDA, which worked hard with municipalities to implement civil defense education. For example, New York City's public schools went so far as to have children wear dog tags. "It is recommended that a metal tag attached to a necklace or bracelet be worn permanently around the neck, wrist, or ankle. Tests have been made to assure the FCDA that this method of identification will, in all probability, remain serviceable under any or all anticipated attack conditions and be universally applicable."[37] Nevertheless, it was the postwar suburban public schools that pounced on the FCDA programs. From a sociological perspective, suburban America (as opposed to urban centers) fit the FCDA message like a glove for various reasons. First, FCDA literature presupposed that one had a particular kind of house in which one could build a bomb shelter, either in the backyard or the cellar. The Truman administration tax code that offered a *tax credit* for the building of a home bomb shelter had the effect of favoring the new postwar suburban neighborhoods. Perhaps most obvious, one needed a backyard or a cellar—not something readily available for city dwellers in apartment complexes or row-housing—in order to build a home bomb shelter. Second, the warden system also, while set up for both urban and suburban communities, really functioned optimally in the postwar suburban community. Like a Parent Teacher Association (PTA), individuals could also join the local warden program, take federally funded training, and then partake in the kind of community solidarity that one would find at a PTA or local community meeting. Third, and perhaps most important, the very social order that the FCDA argued it could preserve if war came was the social order of suburban America. While FCDA literature clearly instructed all Americans how to protect themselves, the pictures, the movies, and especially the FCDA's descriptive training narratives almost always depicted suburban towns and communities. These communities survive World War III almost unscathed and without much hardship. As the Trenton State Bank declared in New Jersey's civil defense magazine *The Siren*, "It will be business as usual in the post-attack environment."[38]

Compared with this account of survival in suburbia, the fate of urban centers and large cities was almost always pictured rather less optimistically. A fantastic example of the difference between urban and suburban civil defense is corroborated by an Operation Alert poster that appeared in New York City's subways in 1952, showing a mailed fist smashing a city—and everyone in it—under the headline, "ENEMY TARGET NO.1—CIVILIANS."[39] Not only frightening in its depiction of modern war, the poster also offered little in terms of "hope" for those who lived in big cities (see Figure Three). The more one examines the massive array of civil defense education and training literature of the FCDA, it becomes clear that the agency was peddling the vision of the "normal" post-attack *suburban* social order, not that of urban America. Thus the suburban public school became the hub for community civil defense mobilization, just as the local school was the center for much community activity during the 1950s.

The Warden System and the Community

As public policy, the Truman administration established the warden system as a coherent and politically acceptable way to militarize the neighborhood. The institutional referent for the way that the system was coordinated was the community warden program that was implemented throughout the United States between 1941 and 1945 by the OCD:[40] "Historically, the war-

Figure Three
Operator Alert Poster, 1952.

Source: PHST, Files of Spencer R. Quick, Box 5, Civil
Defense Campaign Folder.

den is a public figure and a public servant. The average citizen who knows little of the intricacies of municipal government and civil defense will know his neighborhood warden and will cooperate with him. By their training and leadership wardens will be in a position to bring the principles of Civil Defense home to every householder in this country."[41] FCDA planners reconstituted the World War II warden system with updated training manuals and civil defense narratives to reflect the "realities" of global nuclear war. The key to the warden system was routinized training and regimentation as the basic means for managing mass panic.[42] The first warden's handbook (1951), *Before Disaster Strikes: What to Do Now*, precisely illustrates this point in a section called "Training Gets Results":

> Besides helping to save lives, the training you give your residents will be instrumental in preventing panic and confusion in an emergency. Knowing what to do under emergency conditions will bolster their confidence and morale and they are less apt to give way to panic and emotional reactions. When an emergency occurs they will realize that there is remedial action that can be taken and that they must take such action. If they are well trained their reactions will be automatic, and the greatest possible amount of order and effective civil defense action will result.[43]

Like New Jersey, the state of New York also stressed the importance of uninterrupted training as a key instrument against both public complacency and fear, as FCDA lecture notes for training sessions highlight: After a New York state civil defense instructor shows prospective wardens a short film entitled *A Tale of Two Cities*, which showed Hiroshima and Nagasaki after the atomic bombings, he poses a rhetorical question: "Picture to yourselves how Rochester, or Syracuse, or some other American city would look if it were hit by similar bombs."[44] The instructor is then directed to answer his own question: "Can we afford to be so complacent, so self-confident, that we are sure that it won't happen here? We may not be able to prevent an atomic attack, but we, in Civil Defense—*if we are trained*—can do an enormous amount to reduce the distress and danger resulting from such an attack."[45] Finally, the instructor sums up the ultimate rationale for civil defense planning and the importance of community mobilization efforts in these plans: "Civil Defense is the collective means through which a community, or group of communities, is able to take the enemy's Sunday punch, and get up from the floor to continue to support the nation's military effort to the utmost, while providing for restoration of the normal living routine as rapidly as possible."[46]

Clearly, the warden system operated as a form of social control, with the local warden as the commander of the neighborhood under conditions of emergency.[47] Civil defense wardens were people everybody knew and trusted, and they oversaw the many practice civil defense alerts. The FCDA especially viewed "block wardens" as the main liaisons between the local community and Washington, DC. Thus, like the civil defense plan during World War II, the organizational structure of the warden system was premised on the theory that your neighbor could control neighborhoods more efficiently than could, for example, a soldier.[48] By using local citizens, the FCDA was able to exert a substantial level of social control over those who did not take civil defense seriously.[49] The training of wardens within their communities and the practice alerts the wardens conducted reinforced the concept of civic and national duty in a wartime environment and advanced a process of garrisoning not only in the community but also in the home itself.[50]

There were other social benefits to a comprehensive warden system that did not escape the notice of FCDA officials: "It should be noted that while civilian defense in this country in World War II was not called upon for action against enemy attack, it served many useful purposes. It should not be forgotten that when air raid wardens patrolled the streets during blackouts, there were fewer crimes."[51] Certainly this type of community-based empowerment was an effective type of state expansion, for the state was not represented by a soldier but by the "citizen soldier," the neighborhood warden. It was the warden, your friend and acquaintance next door, who conveyed and reinforced the core ideas that the central state deemed vital for home-front preparedness during the early Cold War period.[52]

Organizational Structure and Effectiveness:
The Case of Suburban New Jersey

In actual practice, the warden system worked well in suburban communities. Again, New Jersey's civil defense program offers us an example. By the end of 1952, after only one year of recruiting for its warden service, the state of New Jersey's Division of Civil Defense was able to post impressive recruitment numbers: a total of 56,184 were enrolled in the warden system (see Table Three).[53] These numbers are even more impressive when we factor in the individual time and energy costs invested in warden certification. Recall, the FCDA was committed to producing a quasi-professional and quasi-militarized national organization of civil defense wardens. The best way to think of the warden services is to imagine an adult version of the Boys Scouts of America. Accordingly, official training to become a warden was mandatory. In the state of New Jersey, for example, all members of the warden service had to complete forty-two hours of instruction. Much of this training and education was first vetted in Washington at the FCDA and then passed on to state-level civil defense organizations. The syllabus covered a wide range of areas, from one hour of training in "Internal Security, Espionage, Sabotage, and Subversiveness," to six hours of training in "Methods of Survival Under Atomic Attack."[54]

The warden services not only were comprehensive in sheer size, but they also exhibited a high level of organizational rationalization. The program was differentiated and specialized at its core in Washington, DC, and at its grassroots locales. In New Jersey, the warden system subdivided the state into thirteen geographically distinct civil defense zones. Within each zone there was a further subdivision into "posts," "sectors," and "beats," all of which would be patrolled and handled by a chief warden and his staff. Each civil defense "beat" was a neighborhood that assigned twenty to thirty-five families to each warden. These wardens were known as beat wardens, or what commonly came to be called "block wardens." From this grassroots level, a chain of command within the warden service consisted of the following levels: Chief Warden, Deputy Warden, Zone Warden, Sector Warden, and Post Warden. All of these civil defense wardens had to work with a special set of "air-raid wardens" who, with the Ground Observer Corps, worked in filtering centers to deliver information to the Air Force and other national authorities. Finally, at the neighborhood level (the block or beat level), there was a further division of labor based on volunteers' individual skills. For example, organizational specialization would include Fire Wardens, Rescue Wardens, First Aid Wardens, Evacuation Wardens, and Communication Wardens. These subspecializations within the organizational structure of the warden services were staffed by professionals like doctors, nurses, dentists, first-aid and fire personnel, and police.[55]

The civil defense warden system was premised on a sociology of space that effectively ignored urban centers. Both warden-service literature and the operational plans for mobilizing neighborhoods had almost nothing to do with the characteristics and use of space in industrial cities such as New York, Detroit, Chicago, or Boston. There were, to be sure, wardens in New York and the other cities, and their training was just as comprehensive as that of the suburban civil defense wardens, but the home as conceived in FCDA preparedness training manuals and descriptive narratives did not even exist in the urban milieu. To clarify, there was a significant civil defense program in the urban centers even though FCDA literature and operational planning were primarily aimed at suburban areas of the country. Why the big cities ended up with fairly large civil defense apparatuses had little to do with whether large city populations could be protected; instead, it had everything to do with the FCDA funding formula. A matching-funds formula was used, and the delimiting factor was population density: The more population density the more money, so no mayor of a major city failed to take advantage of this formula to add more money to his fire and police departments. In the language of bureaucratic politics, the FCDA funding formula was, among other things, an excellent tool for big city mayors to engage in "shirt stuffing." In short, the paradox of large-city civil defense on the one hand, and the reality that FCDA planners regarded core industrial cities as a logistical nightmare in terms of protection from nuclear attack on the other, was the consequence of how the Civil Defense Act of 1950 had been written, not an indication of what planners actually believed was possible concerning civil defense in the nuclear age.

Between 1951 and 1954, the FCDA extensively tested communities in civil defense preparedness and the warden services functioned as planned. Local evidence from small communities in New Jersey suggests that citizens took their responsibilities as wardens quite seriously. For example, on a fall Sunday in 1952, the New Jersey community of Glen Ridge sounded a civil defense alert as part of a surprise test. As strange and as dangerous as it might seem today, an "aerial bomb" was exploded over the town to achieve a high level of realism. The New Jersey Division of Civil Defense went so far as to have "official umpires" in place in order to assess the defense drill and the speed with which the warden system could be activated. We do not know how frightened the unsuspecting citizens of Glen Ridge were, or if they questioned the intelligence of their political leaders in allowing a bomb to go off over their town, but we do know that this early civil defense drill was successful. Especially effective was the warden services, which, according to *The Siren*, reported to their assembly areas, with block wardens immediately beginning to patrol assigned areas.[56] By the end of that Sunday in Glen Ridge, people were in their bomb shelters, wardens were patrolling and carrying out their duties, and the FCDA, through its liaison in New Jersey, was producing the kind of community response it had hoped for when it began its operations.

The FCDA's warden system successfully mobilized citizens within communities to actively participate in civil defense programs. The ability to achieve this kind of mobilization at the grassroots level reinforced the FCDA's national civil defense preparedness program. Nevertheless, the national program to protect all American citizens was a lie. The way in which the Truman administration went about its emergency planning excluded large percentages of the American polity.

CRISIS PLANNING AND EXCLUSION

If a bomb drops, we don't want regulations that require colored citizens to run ten blocks to a separate racial shelter when one designated "whites only" is just around the corner. We believe that in an attack by an enemy Governor Caldwell would put white supremacy and segregation ahead of the welfare of the citizens the Defense Office is established to protect. Therefore, we urge that his appointment be rejected.[57]

Before the *Brown v. Board of Education* (1954) ruling by the Supreme Court, public policy was fundamentally affected by racial considerations. In the South, state-level planners used race to determine how, where, and in what quantity a wide range of public goods were delivered to citizens.[58] In the North, race and racism were just as much a part of the public policy calculation as in the South. Truman administration officials viewed themselves as defenders of liberal democracy and, with Cold War tensions at the fore of both domestic and foreign policy, U.S. officials used the model of American liberalism as an ideological and political instrument for waging the Cold War. The seeming conflict between the idea of progressive liberalism and legal racism was clear to many in U.S. society, both in and out of the Truman administration.[59] The State Department, for instance, put pressure on the Truman administration to improve the treatment of African American citizens, especially in the South. In the areas of federal emergency planning and national security policy in general, a form of segregationist liberalism held sway among Truman administration policy planners.[60] The result was an interesting, even bizarre, planning structure for nuclear-age civil defense, which pitted urban and suburban sections of the country against one another for emergency services and, at the same time, wove pre–*Brown v. Board of Education* racial policy into overall civil defense disaster planning. Without entering into a complex discussion of political theory, it is plain that there is no intrinsic contradiction between traditional liberalism and systematic legal racial separation.[61] In American history, we do not have to look very hard to find an example of a multifaceted liberalism that accepted racism *in principle*.[62] Not only did *Plessy v. Ferguson* establish a race-based legal structure in the South, but the whole Plessy era is replete with arguments, many quite complex and learned, that support the position that liberalism and segregation are compatible in both theory and practice.[63] As a constitutional scholar has pointed out, "during the *Plessy* era there was no evident disparity between [white] elite and popular attitudes on issues like racial segregation, black disfranchisement, and black jury service. Such a gap may have existed on issues like lynching, but not on the race questions that became subjects of the Supreme Court litigation."[64] In the broadest sense, this observation encapsulates liberal segregationist thinking.

By focusing in this section on the interplay among the Truman administration, the FCDA's first administrator Millard F. Caldwell, Jr., and the

National Association for the Advancement of Colored People (NAACP), I hope to show how the Truman administration not only accepted the idea of segregationist liberalism but also incorporated this idea into its emergency policy planning.

Consider a segregated bomb shelter. As harebrained as this idea might sound, such bomb shelters existed. For the most part, planners did not think there was anything wrong with the principle of "separate-but-equal" bomb shelters as long as they were equal in their ability to protect citizens from the effects of nuclear weapons. Given the way race was used to delimit how "goods" were delivered during this era, there was no "equality" regarding civil defense protection. In fact, the NAACP mobilized a protest against the Truman administration on this issue. Only within the liberal segregationist political and ideological regime of the early 1950s could FCDA planners go about their work as if there were nothing wrong with protecting a political order based on two-tiered citizenship. More to the point, as *public policy* Cold War mobilization conflated almost all domestic policy with overall national security policy, often limiting an expansive liberalism in favor of the more restrictive segregationist liberalism.

Publicly, FCDA civil defense plans called for the protection of "all citizens"; in practice, however, large groups of people were ignored, not only for operational reasons but also for racial and geographic ones. In planning for home-front survival, FCDA planners used racial demographics and geography as delimiting factors for determining which groups of citizens would receive maximum consideration in an emergency and which groups would, in effect, have to fend for themselves.[65] In theory, FCDA planning would have reestablished the contemporary social order of the early 1950s in a post-nuclear era with one fundamental difference: The post-attack demographic reality that civilian defense planners used resembled de Tocqueville's homogenous America of the 1830s, not the country of the early 1950s.[66]

Civil Defense, Administrative Discretion, and the NAACP

Just before the FCDA was created, there was significant concern in Congress about how to evacuate cities in a war. Evacuation planning (civilian and industrial) was the most important analysis of the NSRB's civil defense arm, the OCDP. Uneasiness about evacuation planning broke along sectional lines in Congress. During the debate concerning the enactment of the Civil Defense Act of 1950, representatives from southern and rural states were concerned about central-state expansion through the FCDA. One can imagine the anxiety of representatives from the Midwest when they contemplated the relocation of, say, Brooklyn, New York, to southern Illinois. More seriously, even intrastate mass relocation held the potential for social disruption—and if we add to the mix the issue of race and the place of African Americans in American society in 1950, the potential for political conflict was high.[67] President Truman, fully aware of the consequential political role southern Democrats played on key congressional committees, appointed a southern Democrat and ex-governor of Florida, Millard F. Caldwell, Jr., as the first administrator of the FCDA.[68] If one lived in the urban core or in the South where Jim Crow norms remained part of the legal structure, the appointment of Caldwell to head the FCDA substantially affected public policy planning for civil defense.[69]

Imagine a "community" bomb shelter in Georgia where, if a nuclear attack took place, black and white Americans would have to live together for an extended time in horrific conditions. In 1953, black Americans and white Americans in Georgia were not even allowed to drink out of the same water fountain—and yet, in theory, they were to be protected equally by a federal agency if war came. FCDA considerations on race relations and preservation of the social order were whipsawed by the politics of southern states' rights, de facto northern segregation patterns, and the exigencies of operational planning. Specifically with regard to the issue of states' rights, congressional concerns focused on the tremendous discretionary political power that accrued to the *unelected* FCDA administrator in an emergency.

Briefly, if the FCDA administrator himself were to survive an attack on the United States, he would have carte blanche with respect to relocating evacuees around the country. This enormous discretionary power was part of the original civil defense legislation in 1950, specifically Title III of the Civil Defense Act, "Emergency Power."[70] As Representative Dewey Short of Missouri noted during the floor debate concerning the civil defense legislation, "In case of an atomic attack the power of the Administrator would be almost unlimited."[71] The Title III powers established a disaster-planning regime where evacuees would be shifted arbitrarily to "safe zones" around the country with federal protection if local command and control broke down. Also, the administrator would be able to declare martial law in areas that were without civilian or military command and control structures. The potential power of the FCDA administrator became a source of concern for southern Democrats and rural Republicans, who viewed refugee problems and FCDA evacuation planning schemes as a likely means of central-state expansion.[72]

President Truman acted quickly to calm congressional concerns with Caldwell's appointment. A staunch supporter of states' rights, Caldwell backed Truman in 1948, when many other southern Democrats bolted the party, and to some extent his appointment was a payback by the president.[73] A "moderate" when compared to other southern governors, nevertheless, he was deeply committed to the separate-but-equal system that developed in the American South under Jim Crow. For Caldwell, as for many in the South, his heartfelt commitment to states' rights simply overpowered any reflective impulse to interrogate the jurisprudential theory on which Jim Crow rested or its long-term effects on citizenship rights.[74] Therefore, even though Truman was able to protect his political flank within the party—as the remarks on the Caldwell appointment by Rep. Dewey Short of Missouri illustrate: "a good, loyal Florida Democrat and...he is a great American"— the Caldwell appointment was an affront to African Americans.[75] Although the NAACP began to organize a high-level lobbying campaign to block Caldwell's appointment as early as December 1950, it found little support in official Washington. The next move that the NAACP took was to try to develop a popular mobilization against Caldwell's confirmation.[76] The director of the Washington branch of the NAACP, Clarence Mitchell, remarked that "this [Caldwell's] appointment was an insult to the colored people, because it was an action on the part of the President (Mr. Harry S. Truman) and the Democratic Party which gave aid and comfort to what was popularly called the Dixiecrat wing of the Democratic Party."[77] The Truman administration, true to form on this particular issue, ignored the NAACP and its constituency when it came to issues of national security.

As administrator, Caldwell proposed a comprehensive national civilian defense system of "hardened" community bomb shelters. Known as the "Caldwell Shelter Program," it sought to alleviate the logistical and political problems of mass emergency evacuation by advancing a federally funded, deep underground, and locally administered mass-community bomb shelter system. As policy, the program represented a philosophical shift in disaster planning that emphasized "digging in" rather than "running" if war came. It also had the immediate and brief effect of moving overall planning discussion and operations away from the politically hot issue of evacuation to intrastate, city, and suburban emergency planning. The Caldwell Shelter Program would have allowed each state and locality to control the bomb shelter issue at the politically less sensitive state and local level. Thus, in the American South, community bomb shelter programs could be developed within a framework of Jim Crow legal structures and, equally important, with a minimum of central-state expansion and oversight. By 1953, southern civil defense planning produced both segregated bomb shelters and a segregated civil defense corps.[78] The sociology of disaster planning was not an exclusively southern issue, however. The problem of what kind of "sociological mix" was optimal in community bomb shelters was appraised by municipal governments in all locales; for example, housing studies in New York and other core industrial areas used the delimiting analytical device of "white" and "non-white" when studying housing and emergency billeting.[79] As public policy, the Caldwell Shelter Program failed because of its immense cost, estimates of which reached a staggering 300 billion in 1950 dollars. With the program's failure, FCDA emergency planning switched back to evacuation planning with all of its potential sociological and logistical problems.

The political exigencies of operational planning also exposed the geographic bias in FCDA planning, which affected African Americans as well as citizens living in most large urban centers of the country. Because operational planning for the urban core was too expensive and logistically futile, FCDA planning favored suburban and rural sections of the country over urban industrial areas. From a public policy implementation perspective, only in suburban localities did the minimal physical and architectural requirements exist for individual small bomb shelters and small community evacuation areas. This obvious fact becomes clear in considering emergency operational planning at the state and community level. In comparing operational civil defense plans for a city such as Chicago in 1950 and 1951 with suburban and rural operational plans, it is clear that urban centers could not hope to protect their inhabitants. Alternatively, in suburban civil defense plans at least the possibility existed that people could be evacuated and billeted for a time—even though most evacuees would die, slowly and horribly, in the post-attack environment that the FCDA planners actually modeled between 1952 and 1956.[80]

Local-level FCDA programs that were aimed at suburban homeowners also fit Caldwell's political belief about the primacy of states' rights and local control over centralized federal control. Under Caldwell's direction, viewing comprehensive, national civil defense as an individual, local problem achieved two important corollary objectives: Local management was favored over federal administration, and the Truman administration was able to foster the illusion that the postwar suburban middle classes would survive during and after a nuclear war. For domestic political reasons, both the Truman and later the Eisenhower administrations viewed this constituency as vital for developing and nurturing the Cold War domestic political consensus.[81] These new middle-class, first-generation, mostly white suburbanites had to be unequivocally convinced that the government could do something to protect them if the worst happened.

NAACP Resistance and the Truman Administration's "Negro Problem"
The Truman administration was remarkably silent about the racialized nature of its civil defense planning, even though social scientists working for

the FCDA produced analyses that asserted the social order would collapse if war came. Panic prevention was connected to planning a post-attack social order that would not exacerbate "intergroup tensions."[82] While the Truman administration was silent, the NAACP was not. Hearing of Caldwell's appointment in 1951, the NAACP's national committee responded not only at the confirmation hearings for Caldwell but also by directly writing President Truman. Walter White, executive secretary of the NAACP, blasted the appointment as utterly inconsistent with the FCDA's central reason for being: the protection of all American citizens in the event of war.

> The Board expressed its shock that you would appoint as director of the civil defense [sic] one who is unwilling to observe even the simplest amenities in writing to American citizens who do not happen to be white. [Caldwell] told the committee bluntly that, "I reserve the right to address any person, whether he be a citizen of my state or any other state in such manner as I please and in accordance with my own views." We believe this is a measure of Mr. Caldwell's hostile attitude towards Negroes or anyone else he personally refuses to recognize as a citizen entitled to the same respect and protection guaranteed by our Constitution and laws. The Board of Directors was equally shocked when it was announced that Mr. Caldwell's chief qualification for the job as director of civil defense was his experience in working out interstate compacts. The interstate compact that Mr. Caldwell has been most prominently identified is [sic] is the one in which he and other southern governors attempted to defeat decisions of the U.S. Supreme Court...with the creation of the so-called "southern regional plan."... [T]he National Association for the Advancement of Colored People, in the interest of national unity, urges his removal as the Chief of Civil Defense.[83]

The NAACP response reflected a regional outrage as well. In a letter to President Truman, Dr. Errold Collymore, president of the New York branch of the NAACP, wrote:

> We urge his removal in the interest of national unity, and because of his well known hostility to the Negro, and his consistent advocacy of total racial segregation. His well known attitude toward Negro citizens is a factor that would destroy any sense of security to Negro citizens throughout the country in the event of a common disaster caused by possible atomic attack upon our country.[84]

Dr. Collymore's concern about the protection of all citizens is clear in his letter to President Truman. It also signals a suspicion of civil defense planning and operations that was well founded and long-lasting.[85] To Dr. Collymore and other African Americans, it was clear that any post-attack social order conceived by Caldwell would recreate a two-tiered citizenship structure. For example, it was well known to both national and local members of the NAACP that, as governor of Florida, Caldwell had openly denounced the 1944 Supreme Court ruling in *Smith v. Allwright* that citizens could not be barred from voting in primary elections because of race or color.[86] As Dr. Collymore implied in his letter, how could any African American gain any sense of security when the president has entrusted national protection to Millard Caldwell? M. E. Diggs, secretary of the Norfolk branch of the NAACP—which was heavily involved in politics over the integration of the U.S. Navy—also wrote President Truman with concern about Caldwell: "His open defiance of the Constitution, the decisions of the U.S. Courts and resistance thereto, and brutal advocacy of 'white supremacy by any and all means,' utterly unfits [*sic*] him for the office he holds or any office within our national government."[87]

Grassroots Resistance

A two-pronged strategy was developed by the NAACP to overturn President Truman's appointment of Caldwell: a high-level approach to seek the impeachment of Caldwell and a grassroots protest that included a low-level form of civil disobedience calling for African American civil servants and citizens to refuse to take part in civil defense training programs. The first plan failed: Congress was not prepared to impeach Caldwell. In 1951, contrary to some interpretations of how the Cold War and the Truman administration propelled the rise of a "progressive" civil rights movement, African Americans did not exactly have a Congress brimming with allies.[88]

The second strategy had some success at the grassroots level; at the same time, it caused tension within the NAACP because national security policy was such a potent and politically risky issue on which to base a public protest. Some NAACP members believed that the organization should not pick a fight around this *type* of national security issue. Many believed that patriotism dictated that national security (except in the area of the integration of the armed services) *was not* the issue on which to protest the Truman administration's racial policies (especially while fighting the Korean War):

> First, all civil service employees such as teachers, fireman, policeman are pledged to civilian defense. Also doctors and nurses are pledged to the same thing. I can picture the criticism heaped upon us, if we urge these people not to cooperate with their white co-workers. On the other hand I can see nothing that would please Mr. Caldwell more, than to have a lily white civilian defense setup. I would rather see Negroes in every branch of this defense program, working to see that there is no discrimination in any form. In this way, we could much more effectively harass Mr. Millard Caldwell and also Pres. Truman, who made this very inept appointment.[89]

However, even with this internal debate underway, the NAACP launched an "Oust Caldwell Campaign" in which a substantial number of NAACP chapters took part (see Table Four).

African Americans who were mobilized were asked to protest against FCDA civil defense alerts and ignore training exercises (to do so was illegal at the time). The mobilization effort was located primarily in big cities and organized through churches and by way of pamphlets posted in and around African American neighborhoods (see Figure Four). The organizing effort was labor intensive; passionate in their anger at the Truman administration's choice to lead the FCDA, the posters were clearly designed and reproduced by hand. Although this passion did not translate into huge protests, it did diminish participation on the part of many African Americans in civil defense programs, at least in the core industrial cities.

African Americans understood well what was going on, and more than anecdotal evidence suggests that FCDA programs were less than successful at mobilizing them. For example, the FCDA produced an enormous quantity of public relations literature that was disseminated through national newspapers.[90] Yet there is little evidence in independent African American newspapers that FCDA education was being redistributed (as was planned by the FCDA) through the African American media.[91] *The Michigan Chronicle*, a "New Deal" African American independent newspaper based in Detroit, ran stories about how few African Americans participated in civil defense training compared to white involvement in the same kinds of programs. The city of Detroit was a primary target, according to the FCDA, so one might assume that there would be interracial, or at least segregated, involvement in civil defense training. The auxiliary firefighters (an all-white organization) in Detroit pleaded with African Americans through *The Michigan Chronicle*: "Only a handful of Negro citizens have responded to the appeal of the Auxiliary Fire Fighters for Civil Defense." In an appeal to *The Michigan Chronicle*, Harold C. Reinelt said: "Negroes' contribution to defense in case of enemy attack, sabotage, or conflagration has been practically negligible." The article ends with a lamentation: "Is a nine hour investment in the safety of everything we all value asking too much of our citizens?"[92] In Detroit, Michigan, at least, the answer was an unequivocal yes. The same kind of African American concern about fairness and sincerity was prevalent in New York City as well, where the civil defense programs failed in Harlem even as they were quite successful in other areas of the city and the region. Under the subheading of "Harlem a Sitting-Duck," the African American periodical *Our World* found FCDA concern about urban America deficient, even though *Our World* tended, in the early 1950s, to support FCDA training programs.[93] Although there may have been numerous rea-

Table Four
NAACP Branches Responding to the
"Oust Caldwell Campaign"

City/Town/County	State
Downington	Pennsylvania
Boston	Massachusetts
Boyle County	Kentucky
Albany	New York
Southern Pines	North Carolina
Willow Grove	Pennsylvania
Detroit	Michigan
Decatur	Illinois
Santa Cruz	California
Alemeda County	California
Lagrange	Texas
White Plains	New York
Richmond	California
Lansing	Michigan
Newark	New Jersey
Hartford	Connecticut
Richmond	Virginia
Providence	Rhode Island
Indiana State Branch	Indiana
New England Regional Branch	New England
Hollidaysburg	Pennsylvania
New York City	New York
Washington, DC	District of Columbia

Source: Compiled from Papers of the NAACP, Part 18: Special
Subjects, General Office File.

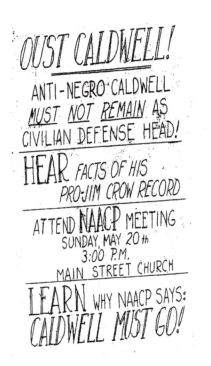

sons why African Americans did not participate in civil defense training in cities, one important reason was that they knew that FCDA strategies for post-attack recovery were framed by the social norm of racial segregation.

What was the Truman administration's reaction to African American concerns about the FCDA and Millard Caldwell? Caldwell made an attempt to meet some members of the NAACP, but since he would not address key members of the NAACP by their professional titles during his confirmation hearings before Congress (and continued his refusal to do so), this attempt at negotiation failed, with NAACP leaders refusing the meeting. The Truman administration made it clear that the issue of race would not be a concern for the FCDA. More important, it would do nothing to compromise the primacy of Cold War national security planning.

The Post-Attack Social Order?

Suppose a strategic nuclear war had taken place in the early 1950s. Using FCDA models under the Caldwell regime, what would the post-attack social order look like? As FCDA literature and public education syllabi regularly suggested, if the citizens practiced civil defense drills, nuclear war, like conventional war, could be successfully managed without serious consequence to the American social order. In the post-attack world, people would go back to work, the government would continue to function, and the country would "prevail" as it always did in war.

However, the real demographics of nuclear war, which were well known, configured how the FCDA actually planned for the ultimate emergency. Writing in 1963, but using data drawn mainly from the 1950 census, FCDA studies, and studies from the FCDA's successor agency, the OCDM, sociologists Robert Dentler and Phillips Cutright prepared a "demographic effects" study using FCDA planning models. The results of their analysis remain stunning: Seventy-two million U.S. citizens would have died outright in the scenario modeled on a 2,000-megaton attack on seventy urban areas.[94] Using the FCDA's own civil defense urban analysis of 1953, we can see what the post-attack environment would have looked like from a ethnographic perspective. We can establish that, for example, the religious composition of the United States would have been fundamentally reconstituted. Killed outright would have been 93 percent of all Jews, 65 percent of all Catholics, and 33 percent of all Protestants. The reason for these kinds of casualties is obvious. In the early 1950s, the target cities all had large numbers of these ethnic and religious groups residing in them. We can infer as well that large segments of first- and second-generation southern and eastern European ethnic groups and the increasingly large African American population that resided in the major target city areas would also have perished.

Further, FCDA publications and government planners made a point of discussing, at least in public education and information, that "continuity of liberal-democratic government" in a post-attack world would be maintained and there would be a "functioning" government body. FCDA planning for "continuity of government" is highly classified to this day, but we can make some inferences. Using the demographic analysis of the Dentler and Cutright study on the effects of nuclear attack on regional Standard Metropolitan Areas (SMAs), we get a picture of the hypothetical regional and ideological makeup of a post–nuclear attack Congress.[95] The FCDA planned for a Congress that was highly sectionalized and devoid of the "problems" of a heterogenous society.[96] The post-attack U.S. government would have consisted mainly of southern Democrats and rural Republicans (the postwar segregationist coalition), and the population of the United States would have been composed primarily of white southerners and economically disadvantaged African Americans from the rural agricultural "Black Belt" of the deep South.[97] Structurally, we can say that FCDA plans for the continuity of government looked a lot like a return of the antebellum southern United States to power, even though those plans were framed around an idealized notion of the middle-class American social order of the early 1950s.

Atomic-Age "Rosies": Gender and the FCDA

The FCDA predicated many of its local mobilization procedures on a specific view of the division of labor between men and women within three stages of national crisis: the pre-attack period, the attack period, and the post-attack recovery period. The centrality of the role of women in civil defense preparedness is quite interesting, for it was simultaneously linked to the theory that the home, properly managed, could literally save one's life or, conversely, kill one. Women's role in the management of the home was not simply a domestic function. It is true that FCDA instructions for "home exercises" at times addressed women's roles in a "traditional" fashion. For example, home-protection exercises depicted the suburban middle-class home with a well-stocked bomb shelter; some home exercises pictured women preparing and storing foodstuffs and material as well as sometimes "decorating" the bomb shelter. But these "traditional" depictions of a woman's role in managing the nuclear crisis were not the central themes in these home exercises, and they were not, by any means, the only kinds of jobs that women were *expected* by the FCDA to do during an emergency. Even before the FCDA was created in December 1950, the NSRB's OCDP considered the vital role of women in an overall national civil defense program. The policy that was derived from this consideration of human resources did not produce a domesticated and paternalistic view of women; instead, it saw women as essentially genderless human resources. William A. Gill, who headed the OCDP, had this to say in 1950 about women and the possibility of training women to handle the attack and post-attack environment: "In considering the role of women in mobilization, the Resources Board has in the past usually treated the question of manpower without regard to sex. Recognition has been given to the principle that a woman can do almost any wartime task for which men are capable, on the assumption that women are given the same amount of training or have equivalent backgrounds of experience."[98] This view of, for want of a better term, generic human resource mobilization and training carried over into FCDA organizational plans in 1951. Consequently, community civil defense mobilization *was not* based on a paternalistic and stultifyingly domesticated function for women. On the contrary, in the FCDA's world of nuclear war, women were expected to take on roles that made "Rosie the Riveter" pale in comparison.

Historian Elaine Tyler May offers the most cogent interpretation of the FCDA as an example of the state's hegemonic paternalism during the early Cold War.[99] However, there is a paucity of evidence for this popular interpretation of the FCDA and its relationship to women. May argues that the central state reproduced the traditional domestic role for women in its civil defense program; in fact, just the opposite is the case. The state's line agency, the FCDA, produced numerous training guides that envisioned women as firefighters, emergency medical technicians, and members of the transportation corps. The advertising campaign of the Alert America program ubiquitously used a poster of a woman driving a Mack truck in a post-attack scenario and imploring her fellow citizens to "Join the Transportation Service." This was anything but the "homemaker" at war.[100] Furthermore, the FCDA was used as a conduit for recruiting women into the Ground Observer Corps, where, as in World War II Great Britain, they were to be used in filtering centers. Finally, there were roles for women's organizations to participate at the local level in civil defense programs.[101]

A different and more complete interpretation of why the FCDA gendered its program in the way that it did would consider that puzzle within an institutional framework and thus attend to the organizational model on which the FCDA based its program to mobilize women. In the case of civilian defense mobilization, FCDA bureaucrats used the institutional model for mobilization employed by the OCD during World War II. In the FCDA plans for community mobilization we see, again, organizational *continuity* between early Cold War preparedness training within the FCDA and the same kinds of home-front preparedness training undertaken by agencies such as the OWI and the OCD during the war. This is exactly what William

Gill of the OCDP meant in 1950 when he commented on the relationship between war mobilization and human resources.

In the fanciful world of nuclear war-fighting, then, FCDA literature regarded human resources (men and women) as tools for the efficient employment of a labor force and instruments for the management of nuclear terror in all three crisis conditions.[102] In this FCDA view of human resource mobilization and gender, women were envisioned as the "atomic" Rosie the Riveters.

CONCLUSION

In the early 1950s, the FCDA successfully mobilized large segments of the population into its community civil defense apparatus. In reality, the FCDA had written off the large cities in favor of marketing its invention of the survivable nuclear war to suburban communities. Middle-class metropolitan suburbia was the key constituency that had to be convinced by both the Truman and, later, the Eisenhower administrations that the government would protect them if the worst happened.[103] Actual FCDA civil defense planning gave the lie to its national-level civic education program that everyone could be and would be protected if war came. In fact, the protection of cities was a logistical nightmare that could not be solved. One of the "logistical" problems was race and, to a lesser extent, ethnicity and the "problems" that inhere in a social order that accepts separation as the norm. The FCDA's main goal was to promote an illusion of protection to a select but important political constituency: mostly white, middle-class, suburban America. Real civil defense would have had to establish a means by which the industrial and urban centers of the nation would be protected or, in the language of strategic planners, "hardened." This was too expensive and probably impossible.

By using its institutional ties to academia, private sector and quasi–private sector organizations such the Ad Council and BBD&O, and large government bureaucracies such as HEW, the FCDA deployed a sophisticated, direct sales marketing campaign to achieve three main goals. The first was marketing a specific illusion about the post-attack world in which the suburban ideal and the social order are left intact. Second, the illusion of post-attack normalcy would be used by FCDA civic education as a grassroots recruitment tool. This local-level recruitment process would reestablish the home-front mobilization scheme that was successful during World War II for the OWI and OCD. Third, the FCDA sought through its warden services and other types of local programs to manage nuclear terror and panic through routinized training that was designed to militarize civilian life.

This FCDA process of civic education based on dissimulation simultaneously established new nontraditional roles for suburban homemakers and totally ignored the issue of race in its public training literature. The fundamental inconsistencies in FCDA programming and public policy indicate that its primary goal was not real civil defense, but national Cold War "civic education." The expansion of the state into the community in the guise of the FCDA and the rationalization of institutions for domestic propaganda and "civic education" were consequences of the Truman administration's policy of continuous Cold War mobilization. Ultimately, the effect of internalizing security policies—and in large part this was the institutional role of the FCDA—was to normalize emergency planning and the Cold War crisis. The normalization of crisis planning as public policy had consequential institutional, legal, and administrative effects on postwar American political development.

Chapter 5

EMERGENCY PLANNING AND AMERICAN POLITICAL DEVELOPMENT

Perpetual apprehension of war keeps the accent upon the consideration of power measured as fighting potential. The common goal of maintaining national freedom from external dictation is perceived as requiring the appraisal of all social values and institutional practices with state-power considerations in view. Economic values and institutions are drawn into the preparation of weapons and thereby subordinated to power. Scientific skill and education are requisitioned for research and development. Public health is fostered by programs designed to conserve the human resources that figure in military potential. Family and ecclesiastical institutions are given encouragement so long as they interpose no ideological or behavioral obstacles to national security. Institutions of social class and caste are remodeled to the extent that national vulnerability is believed at stake.

—*Harold D. Lasswell, 1962*

In this chapter, I examine the consequences for American political development of the Truman administration's emergency preparedness policy from a slightly more theoretical standpoint than in the previous chapters. In a liberal democracy, continual emergency planning had consequences for civil liberties and the meaning of citizenship, broadly conceived. In the language of the time, "the crisis of defense" demanded that individuals act according to the standards of Cold War patriotism of the early 1950s.

To begin with, I present a brief overview of the theoretical relationship between emergency planning and central-state power with reference to the writings of Harold Lasswell, Clinton Rossiter, and the reactionary German legal theorist Carl Schmitt. Schmitt's critique of liberalism rests in part on his theory of "the emergency" and its potential consequences for sustaining fundamental bases of liberal democracy. His observations about the tie between emergency power and its effects on liberal democracy were relevant in the late 1940s when the Truman administration was grappling with the issues of internal security, continuity of government, and emergency planning.[1] Additionally, Schmitt identified key problems at the intersection of liberal jurisprudence and emergency power that do not lend themselves to easy resolution, even today, and thus his observations are germane to this project.[2]

After this overview, and with the Truman administration's FCDA emergency planning designs as a backdrop, I reconsider the garrison-state thesis. While the United States did not become a police garrison state, the Truman administration systematically internalized its external national security policy and set in motion a process that did have garrisonlike effects on the domestic polity. Then I examine how the garrisoning process affected postwar American political development. Specifically, I explore the causal logic behind the internalization of national security policy by the Truman administration, with emphasis on the way domestic emergency planning conflated internal and external security, thereby creating the conditions in which crisis planning became normalized.[3] A by-product of the internalization process was the reestablishment of wartime-like standards for both loyalty and citizenship, but with one very significant difference: There was no foreseeable end to the Cold War.

IN THE SHADOW OF CARL SCHMITT: HAROLD D. LASSWELL, CLINTON ROSSITER, AND THE "CRISIS OF DEFENSE"

Building on the foundation of Harold D. Lasswell's underexamined concept of a civic garrison state, we can conceptualize the problem of early Cold War mobilization along three dimensions. First, the functional problem: How did the liberal-democratic United States prepare for long-term, low-level mobilization and balance the requirements of a liberal-democratic social order against the requirements for mobilization? Second, how did the state penetrate society so as to garner the necessary consensus to support a policy that was, at least theoretically, fraught with risks? Finally, what were the consequences of successfully tending to the first two problems—mobilization and penetration of society? It is within the third dimension that the liberal-democratic state can become Harold Lasswell's militarized society.[4] Lasswell's contemporary, historian Clinton Rossiter, who also had a keen interest in how internal and external emergencies affect constitutional democracies, was more systematic than Lasswell in his analysis of the postwar "crisis of defense."

In his now classic essay "The Garrison State," Lasswell argued that war mobilization and preparedness planning fundamentally impact state formation.[5] He hypothesized that the world (c. 1939–1941) was being transformed into a world of "garrison states," in which the modern nation-state is controlled by the "specialists on violence" who take advantage of technological innovation and change for purposes of war making. It is a world in which the garrison state is continually preparing for war, where continuous war mobilization becomes a way of life encompassing the institutions of both state and society. Furthermore, "for those who do not fit within the structure of the state there is but one alternative—to obey or die. Compulsion, therefore, is to be expected as a potent instrument for internal control of the garrison state."[6] In the Lasswellian garrison state, civil society and any notion of a private sphere collapse as the central state moves inexorably to total war mobilization.

After World War II, Lasswell expanded the original construct of a police garrison state (which should be conceived of as an ideal type) to include the development of what he called a "civic" garrison state. His idea of a democratic civic garrison state is a tantalizing and underdeveloped attribute of Lasswell's original garrison-state hypothesis.[7] Lasswell argued that democracies, in all probability, would not create the kind of garrison state that was constructed under Stalinist communism or German fascism. Focusing specifically on the postwar American experience, his *National Security and Individual Freedom* is rich in references to what he called "the American garrison." The reader is left, however, wondering what the institutional bases were for the so-called American civic garrison; Lasswell's conceptual apparatus, firmly embedded within the postwar behavioralist tradition, offers us nothing about how a "garrisoning" process was transmitted to society at large. For Lasswell, the American garrison was necessary because of the Cold War emergency and the "crisis of defense." What concerned him was how to *balance* the functional requirements for mobilization against the fundamental good of maintaining a liberal-democratic social order. But the institutional agencies and mechanisms by which the process actually unfolded are left unclear in his analysis:

> The present crisis of defense is likely to be with us for years. Public alarm about the danger of war will rise and fall with the headlines, but the danger will probably continue. No one needs to be told that a third world war would devastate man and his works on scale without precedent. A more insidious menace is that even if we avoid a general war, continuing crisis may undermine and eventually destroy free institutions.[8]

Lasswell seemed to place the garrisoning process in an institutional, political, and ideological domain somewhere between the police state and the liberal-democratic state. Here we must speculate, but perhaps Lasswell was suggesting that we consider the process of civilian mobilization and preparedness within the context of democratic structures as safer than, for example, a more drastic wartimelike mobilization process. If this speculative analysis is correct, then the garrisoning process that Lasswell discusses is tempered by democratic institutions and processes: Not a police garrison state but something else develops, the *civic garrison*. Unfortunately, Lasswell left this profoundly interesting concept dangling within his analysis, without a clear-cut institutional or administrative appraisal for the reader to get any purchase on.

In contrast to Lasswell's preliminary and underdeveloped formulation of a civic garrison, Clinton Rossiter posited a more systematic answer to the Cold War emergency: under certain circumstances, a constitutional dictatorship. Rossiter argued explicitly (even though he understood and lamented the consequences for individual liberty) for an expansive positive state to handle Cold War mobilization. Rossiter posed the following question in *Constitutional Dictatorship*: "Can a democracy fight a successful total war and still be a democracy when the war is over?" His answer was yes, but he also saw a more centralized state as the logical outcome of war-making and war mobilization:

> For who in this year 1948 would be so blind as to assert that the people of the United States, or of any other constitutional democracy, can afford again to be weak and divided and jealous of the power of their elected representatives? The Bomb has settled once and for all the question of whether the United States can go back to what Harold Laski had labeled (a little too contemptuously) a "negative state." You can't go home again; the positive state is here to stay, and the accent will be on power, not limitations.[9]

In Rossiter's view, then, the crisis of the Cold War demanded the centralization of power in the Executive branch (legitimized in the name of emergency planning) and the normalization of the emergency within the general public. The public had an important democratic role in electing the proper representatives, especially the Executive, but once that was done the "guardians" would lead. According to Rossiter, the crisis of the Cold War in the atomic age left little time for the day-to-day politics of parliamentary debate: The stakes were too high. In a worst-case situation, Rossiter, systematically applying the logic of his case for "constitutional dictatorship," argued clearly and consistently that:

> In sum, the basic assumption of constitutional dictatorship would seem to be this: constitutional democracy is eminently worth saving, and if temporary dictatorship—that is *suspension* of constitutional democracy—is the only way to save it, then we should by all means submit to temporary dictatorship. The more clearly we see this truth and the more resolutely we acknowledge it, the more certain we can be that such a dictatorship will in fact be temporary and limited in purpose.[10]

His logic is quite clear: Under the rubric of the Cold War emergency, crisis planning demanded that the state take measures to prepare itself and its citizens for long-term confrontation with the Soviet Union.[11]

Perhaps most intriguing is the way both men seemed to be steering toward an illiberal theory of crisis mastery and state survival. In this sense, both Lasswell and Rossiter were asking the same kinds of questions about liberalism, constitutionalism, and emergency planning that political theorist Carl Schmitt considered in the early 1920s. The idea of the "state of emergency" or, as Schmitt put it when he developed his reactionary critique of German liberalism during the Weimar Republic, the *Ausnahmezustand* (the "state of exception") is apropos insofar as both Lasswell and Rossiter were both concerned with the potential opposition between long-term crisis planning and the cumbersome, highly politicized, and torpid nature of American democracy. In the Schmittian epistemology (which is profoundly antiliberal), extraconstitutional measures are the essential tools of the state in an emergency. Schmitt understood well that political leaders who declare emergencies or act under emergency rule accrue tremendous power—"Sovereign is he who decides on the state of exception."[12] Drawing on this view of legal decisionism, Schmitt elaborated his argument that during periods of emergency there is no room for parliamentary discussion, the trappings of liberal civility, and the balancing of the interests of political parties.[13] When state survival is weighed against liberal constitutional protection of the individual, individual rights, and political parties, state survival supercedes all constitutional protection. In other words, liberal-democratic structures are the antithesis of what a government requires to master crises and control states of emergency. Lasswell and Rossiter both saw the incommensurability between long-term mobilization and liberal democracy even as they tried to work out the problem in such a way as to minimize the illiberal facets of Cold War mobilization. They failed. Ultimately, there was no way to avoid the creation of a garrisoning process that had concrete consequences for American society. Postwar American political development clearly fit the quotation that appears at the beginning of this chapter. In postwar America, the "remodeling" of institutions on the basis of fear and perceptions of vulnerability fundamentally influenced postwar political, institutional, and ideological development.

THE INWARD TURN: THE STATE AND THE NORMALIZATION OF EMERGENCY

Between 1946 and the early 1950s, the institutions of the American state reflected the process of "garrisonization." Congress created committees to investigate and expose "subversives," the definition of which expanded as fear of war and Soviet omnipotence gripped the nation after the 1948 Berlin crises, the 1949 atomic weapons test by the Soviet Union, and the outbreak in June 1950 of the Korean War. After the National Security Act of 1947 was enacted in July of that year, the Executive branch began to focus intensively on the problem of "internal security," as evidenced by the vigorous enforcement of the Truman loyalty program (enacted by presidential order in March 1947);[14] the creation of the NSRB and its civil preparedness arm, the OCDP; the creation of the National Security Council's (NSC) internal security directive series 17 and 23, which linked domestic political activity with foreign policy; and the creation between 1947 and 1951 of new, highly insulated executive agencies such as the PSB. NSC planners conceived of the last agency as a "mental CIA" charged with *external* "political warfare" but, ultimately, the PSB shared its information about propaganda techniques and information management with agencies concerned with domestic affairs, such as the FCDA.[15] Additionally, Congress or the Executive branch suffused all the agencies noted here with high levels of discretionary power. In typical fashion, Congress legislated very vague guidelines for agencies associated with Cold War mobilization. In oversimplified terms, Congress passed laws that basically declared, "protect the country," leaving to the "experts" the specifics as to how this charge should be carried out. As Theodore Lowi has keenly argued, vague legislation and discretionary power can undermine, at times, liberal-democratic procedures; at minimum, the internal surveillance procedures between 1946 and 1954 in the United States are a fine example of the dangers that inhere in bureaucratic discretionary power.[16]

Concurrent with the development of agencies to manage internal and external security policy, the wartime links forged from 1941 to 1945 between the state, the research university system, and the national press were also institutionalized by the early 1950s. These ties were cemented as the Cold War was treated as a type of real war, establishing institutional continuity for the continuation of the home-front mobilization program that would not only produce political support for postwar policies but would also redefine what it meant to be a "good" citizen during the early years of the Cold War. After the 1948 Berlin crises, there was a clear sense among officials in Washington and within the general public, as well, that the developing Cold War portended a long-term crisis requiring the "normalization" of long-term emergency planning.[17] As the Cold War intensified, the concepts of patriotism, loyalty, and thus citizenship were viewed by the general public, as well as by officials in Washington, in a narrow wartime tradition. Additionally, the very definition of "national security planning" became part of the immediate postwar public discourse, resulting in public support for the reconfiguration of the national security bureaucracy. As Lasswell's 1962 retrospective analysis of the garrison state argued, mobilization for Cold War produced a causal logic for internalizing national security policies. One effect was that under headings such as "subversive" or "disloyal," alternative political perspectives and points of view were grouped together and then dismissed or prosecuted as treasonous.[18]

Within the Truman administration the perception of an internal threat was not some abstract philosophical notion debated by policy intellectuals, but was *acted* upon by the president and other members of his administration. The NSC considered the issues of internal security and linked them with postwar grand strategy in the same way that internal security is linked to high military strategy during a real war.[19] One consequence of the normalization of emergency planning in the United States was that the narrow definition of "loyal citizenship" established principles by which "good" citizens came to understand that their loyalty and patriotism were integrally connected to anticommunism and domestic national security. In other words, the idea of what constituted the "loyal" citizen was defined by and contrasted to an expansive definition of the "subversive" citizen.[20] As early as May 1946, FBI director J. Edgar Hoover was writing about "an enormous Soviet espionage ring in Washington operating with the goal of obtaining all information possible with reference to atomic energy." Additionally, Cold War patriotism and the malleable standards on which this construction rested permitted individuals to identify "potential spies," persons who were, in the words of Hoover, "termites gnawing at the very foundation of American society," and make reports to the authorities in the same way that citizens reported enemy agents during real war.[21]

By the late 1940s and especially after the beginning of the Korean War, the government established standards to codify what constituted loyalty and patriotism. Again, the FCDA was but one of many agencies that reproduced and disseminated these standards in its training and mobilization programs.[22] As the Cold War "crisis of defense" was normalized into daily life, the Truman administration established legal principles by which it could evaluate the "good" Cold War citizen and the ever-prepared Cold War citizen-soldier: If one was not the prepared, loyal, and "good" citizen, then one was the Cold War "subversive."[23] If an individual or a group was considered subversive, there was legal recourse for the state to take action against those so labeled. Clearly, one could fight in court and win against the state if a false accusation was made, but in reality one's life was essentially ruined if one was accused of subversive behavior: It was easier to conform rather than lose job, friends, and a lot of money to fight the U.S. government in a court of law in 1952.

As I argued in chapter One, the very idea of Cold War citizenship changed as Cold War liberalism took hold within the body politic and narrowed what was acceptable political discourse and political action.[24] As a solid Cold War consensus behind U.S. postwar policy became important to the Truman administration, agencies such as the FCDA maintained, managed, and even maneuvered the public so that the consensus on which Cold War policy rested remained steadfast and bipartisan. In the United States, early Cold War mobilization produced a state and society relationship that did not amount to a *totalitarian* garrison state, but it was a civic garrison that produced a politically constrained Cold War liberalism. The American garrison was not the "functional weak state" that benignly and, in some sort of innocent, ad hoc fashion, won the Cold War; nor was it a Soviet-style police state.[25] In contrast to a militaristic state, a police state, or a state that relies solely on market incentives and disincentives to mobilize for war, the postwar national security state—statist, democratic, and, most important, dependent on an educated public—was the result of the struggle to balance war mobilization and democratic principles. The process of garrisoning the general public became more than an interaction between institutions and agencies of the state. As Lasswell pointed out, the American garrison rested on *both* institutional and psychological bases. In order for the institutional bases of the postwar national security state to be established in the United States, there had to be the broad-based political and ideological will to establish a framework for such a state. The willingness to carry forth a Cold War program of long-term mobilization ultimately did not depend on whether President Truman or James Forrestal thought the United States should engage in a particular type of mobilization project (we can take as a given they were committed to such a project), but whether the citizenry was committed. The process of garrisoning the populace created necessary and sufficient conditions—politically, institutionally, and psychologically—to allow the Truman administration to turn national security policy inward.[26] Ideally, individuals in the civic garrison internalize the security needs of their society so thoroughly that neither market incentives nor outright (physical) coercion by the state is necessary for general compliance in the mobilization effort. The Truman administration's FCDA was very much part of the process that helped to internalize the Cold War crisis in the United States.[27]

Additionally, the conflation of internal security with external security obscured the distinction between two separate kinds of policy planning; thus, with respect to Cold War legislation as well as overall planning, both internal and external national security policy were treated as one and the same. This interpenetration of internal and external security policy is exemplified in the way the FCDA tried to militarize civilian life in the early 1950s.

Civilian defense policy planning required both a legal and a social framework within which to function efficiently. Mobilization of the home front in the early 1950s required that federal and local agencies have the *legal* capability to ratchet up, with increasingly painful levels of sanction, the coerciveness of the central state. The jurisprudential structure of the early 1950s thus fundamentally shaped the essential *social legitimacy* that was required to engage the early Cold War mobilization project. The political underpinning of the "American garrison" was thus sustained by Cold War jurisprudence, which, for the most part, had rational connections with overall national security policy planning.[28]

Many agencies that participated in Cold War national security policy planning were politically, organizationally, and administratively insulated within the EOP. The Truman administration sought to achieve the normalization of emergency planning *without* creating the totalitarian garrison state by maneuvering most national security legislation through Congress in a highly public fashion, thereby establishing a procedure for security-related lawmaking. However, Cold War legislation was purposely discretionary in form, and thus the administrative architecture and the agencies within that architecture were insulated within the EOP, rooting early Cold War mobilization firmly within a statist tradition. The Truman administration's approach to home-front mobilization was systematically centralized when it came to planning key facets of the Cold War mobilization. Policy implementation, however, was integrated into the constitutional structure so that the federal system of decentralized power was not totally undermined; however, because policy implementation was adapted to federalism and some facets of private enterprise, this does not mean that free-market, liberal-democratic anti-statism triumphed over more traditional centralized modes of war mobilization. The United States avoided the totalitarian experience for many reasons, although primarily because of its democratic institutions; however, the United States did not and could not avoid the consequences of the centralization of power and the garrisoning process that *must* accompany any long-term project of war mobilization.

The National Security Act of 1947 and its establishment of the NSRB to handle home-front mobilization is a stark example of this process. For example, consider how Ferdinand Eberstadt viewed the importance of institutional and political insulation of national security agencies with the EOP when he was considering the role of the NSRB in the Cold War mobilization project: "In NSRB the Statute has put at the President's disposal an organization which, without public fanfare—and to a considerable degree without further implementing legislation—he can use as he deems proper to aid this Country in carrying the present heavy national security burdens and to move promptly and effectively into full civilian-industrial mobilization should this prove necessary."[29] As we established in Chapter Two, national security planners and President Truman genuinely tried to avoid undermining American economic and political structures when they put the United States on a program of low-level continuous war mobilization.[30] In the indeterminate world of the Cold War, striking an equal balance between the preservation of the American economic and political order on the one hand and the requirement to engage in continuous war mobilization on the other hand ultimately was impossible. The cost to society of Cold War mobilization was the slow but inexorable erosion of institutions and procedures that provided a level of protection for liberal-democratic politics. In the end, an all-encompassing notion of national security became the key legitimating ideology that propelled the garrisoning process in the early 1950s. Thus the Truman administration was only partially successful in simultaneously mobilizing for the Cold War and protecting American society from a process that created the cannibalistic "mean season" of domestic Cold War politics.

Civil Defense and Civil Society

The FCDA offers an example of how continuous, low-level war mobilization configured policy planning and, most important, how civil society was viewed by planners during the early years of the Cold War. The operational antinomies manifested internal contradictions in FCDA planning, which offer a window through which we can view how the general population was perceived. On one level, the agency was created within a democratic process to promote civil defense as the ultimate instrument for the protection of the American social order if war came. On a second level, however, FCDA planners and national security elites viewed the Cold War as the principle challenge to the U.S. economic, political, and strategic position in the postwar period. In this view, it was vital to garner the support of the American people to shoulder the potential burdens of long-term Cold War mobilization. As we have seen before, the American people had to accept the viewpoint that the Cold War was a new type of war where the war "emergency" was open-ended and thus extremely dangerous, threatening both internal and external national security. The Truman administration had to convince the polity that the Cold War was not some abstract concept put together by defense intellectuals and Washington elites; instead, the public had to accept Cold War preparedness as a high-stakes patriotic responsibility on par with any other war in which the United States had engaged. The open-ended nature of the Cold War crisis is what presented Truman administration planners with the conundrum of how to *continually* maintain a national state of alert and preparedness without being accused of "crying wolf." Through the process of continuous, low-level war mobilization and preparedness training, national security planners tried to normalize the Cold War crisis. FCDA civil defense mobilization, in particular, helped to internalize the Cold War emergency by turning the issue of national security into an active domestic concern.[31] Through its national and community civic education programs, the FCDA taught the general public that the American social order could be protected only if all citizens *willingly* accepted (and participated in) the militarization of parts of both their private and public lives.

Truman-era civic education about Cold War mobilization had two important effects for the development of a civic-garrisoning process: The first was an impressive expansion of central-state directives regarding Cold War preparedness into the most personal spheres—the home, the church, and the workplace. This expansion of the Cold War "pedagogical state" helped to establish the early Cold War culture of preparedness planning. As Theodore Lowi has cogently argued, this preparedness culture was a credible and important facet of postwar American political development: "The Cold War Culture is the widely inculcated belief that your adversary is prepared for war and is ready to commit aggressive and hostile acts the moment your guard is down. If war doesn't happen, that is proof that your preparations prevented it."[32] The second effect was that the civic education program outlined a set of easily understandable criteria for preparedness behavior, thus producing the competent, loyal, "atomic-age" Cold War citizen. The FCDA marketed its conception of the Cold War citizen—ever vigilant and ready for battle against communist slavery—in the familiar contractual rhetoric of loyalty and citizenship: "The Congress, The Cabinet, Federal officials generally, and State and city officials, country-wide, must face the facts of modern warfare. Civil defense is national defense. Civil defense and good citizenship are one. A public organized to protect its communities, keep the wheels of industry turning and to preserve the liberties of a free nation is essential to the future of America."[33] By FCDA standards, the prepared citizen was transformed into *Homo Atomicus:* Looking out the window of one's suburban home at the vaporized remains of the nearby city, the prepared citizen calmly invokes FCDA training. One immediately attends to the family in a systematic and rational fashion—perhaps burying some members, amputating limbs of others, putting out fires, and taking care of hygiene. Atomic-age citizens do not show signs of panic and uncontrollable fear, for they have been trained and readied for this very event. Patriotic citizens were ready, in the worst case, to fight and win a war against communist slavery and, in the best case, to *deter* it by being prepared and taking civil defense seriously:

To the extent that we can prepare our citizens against the mental as well as the physical hazards of any eventuality, we will have rendered a very great service.... This whole mobilization cannot be achieved unless every man, woman, and child knows exactly what he, she or they should do in the event of an emergency. Each one of us, every individual should be physically, mentally, and above everything else spiritually prepared to meet any possible crisis.... The preparation that will assure security and impress a potential enemy is a preparation which indicates that the average American citizen is aware of the facts of life, is not afraid and is prepared to do his or her part.[34]

Thus understood, Cold War citizenship in the United States was tied to a definition of patriotism that stemmed in large part from the strategic concerns discussed in Chapter Two. The political and military vulnerability of the United States to "fifth-column" political influence or outright military attack was high on the list of concerns for postwar policy planners who feared an "atomic Pearl Harbor."[35] The Truman administration was explicit in a 1946 memo: "The impact of initial surprise assaults which will involve new weapons such as the atomic bomb and which will be accompanied by widespread sabotage may cripple the mobilization of the nation for war and at the same time result in a large demand for defense resources."[36] In 1948, the Truman administration categorized these policy concerns in NSC-17:

2). We cannot establish an effective internal security system unless we completely understand the nature of the hostile forces with which we are confronted. It matters not if it is some ancient form of tyranny, shattered Fascism, modern brutality or Communism under the guise of "new democracy." To understand the enemy, his thought, practices and objectives, is to be better able to overcome the enemy.

3). There is a hostile force confronting the United States today which is a far greater threat to our existence than any other threat. This hostile force is Communism. World-wide Communism is directed at the very heart of American life.[37]

NSC-17 also noted the importance of a mobilized and prepared citizenry, for success in defeating the communist threat from within depended fundamentally on a universally shared understanding—not just among political elites in Washington, but within the general public as well—of the peculiar nature of the "Communist menace."[38] And, as described earlier in this chapter, this "menace" demanded a redefinition of "citizenship."

After the start of the Korean War in June 1950, the narrow, instrumentally functional definition of "loyal citizenship" established an immanent link between loyalty and patriotism on the one hand and anticommunism and support for internal security policy on the other. This connection between anticommunism and internal security appears in public opinion polls conducted in 1950 (see Tables One and Two). These data dramatically illustrate the degree to which fear can configure public opinion, but they also offered an opportunity for the Truman administration to channel that fear into preparedness training through the FCDA. FCDA syllabi and training helped to disseminate broadly accepted standards that permitted one to distinguish, in a simplistic and uncomplicated fashion, between patriotism and treason.[39] Perhaps the most telling piece of data in the Gallup poll is that only 1 percent of those questioned believed in the individual's right to hold differing political ideas.

The standards by which one understood "loyalty" were defined and contrasted to an expansive definition of what constituted a "subversive" citizen. In the world of the FCDA, an unprepared or uncaring citizen engaged in a form of disloyalty. Within the wider national polity as a whole, however, it was federal agencies like the FBI that, abetted by legislation with extraordinary levels of discretionary power, "decided" what constituted subversive behavior. The idea that loyal citizenship was systematically connected to supporting the Truman administration's *internalization* of its external policies is what I mean by the term "an instrumentally functional" version of Cold War citizenship. Acceptable Cold War behavior on the part of a loyal individual was functional in that it supported the Truman administration's mobilization efforts. The behavior was instrumentalized in that "good" citizenship behavior could be differentiated, by the average person, from "subversive" or "bad" behavior; thus errant citizens could be coerced to behave properly. Furthermore, Cold War citizenship and patriotism and the criteria on which these notions rested permitted individuals to identify "potential spies," Hoover's "gnawing termites," and make reports to the authorities in the same way that citizens reported enemy agents during real war. From the perspective of national security planners, the notion that the Cold War should be conceived of as a type of real war was a given. In retrospect, it is clear that planners, confronted with the requirement to efficiently manage the early Cold War crisis, presided over the rationalization of a garrisoning process that was, at its core, a long-term *statist* war mobilization policy. This expansion of state power was also reinforced by community-level mobilization that accelerated the blurring of the lines between internal and external security policy. The garrisoning of the mind, if you will, resulted in the individual surveillance of one's own behavior. In this way, the internalization of early Cold War norms inculcated the ultimate value of constant preparedness within the general public, a Cold War value captured nicely by the FCDA's popular refrain: "If we are prepared, we will come back fighting."[40]

Table One
Anti-Communist Public Opinion, 1950

What do you think should be done about members of the Communist party in the United States in the event we get into a war with Russia?

Action	Percentage in support of action
Put them in internment camps	22
Imprison them	18
Send them out of the United States, exile them	15
Send them to Russia	13
Shoot them, hang them	13
Watch them, make them register	4
Nothing, everyone is entitled to freedom of thought	1
Miscellaneous	9
No opinion	10

Table Two
American Citizens' Opinions of Communists, 7/14/1950–7/30/1950

Question	Should	Should Not	No Opinion
Do you think all members of the Communist party should or should not be removed now from jobs in United States industries that would be important in war time?	90%	6%	4%
There is a bill now before Congress that would not stop anyone from belonging to the Communist party—but it would require every individual who belongs to the Communist party or Communist organization to register with the Justice Department in Washington. Do you think Congress should or should not pass this bill?	67%	20%	13%

Source: Gallup, George H. *The Gallup Poll: Public Opinion 1935–71*, vol. 2. New York: Random House, 1972, pp. 933–934.

Additionally, the turn inward created an *egalitarian* panopticism: In the United States the panoptic eye was not the central state per se, but your neighbor who, trained within the milieu of the Cold War emergency, is prepared, nay, required, to report subversive behavior.[41]

THE PAST AS PROLOGUE? POLICY HISTORY AND THE COLD WAR LEGACY

> Tension is sure to rise between the need for protection and rights to privacy, something we hold very dear.... [T]hat kind of friction will force unpleasant choices in the near future. We haven't faced up to it yet.
>
> —*Defense Secretary William S. Cohen, quoted in the* New York Times, *December 27, 1998, Section 4, p. 5*

> And the other half of us, somebody would have to diagnose in a hurry and then contain and treat. Otherwise it would be the gift that keeps on giving.
>
> —*President Clinton, on biological weapons threats, quoted in the* New York Times, *January 22, 1999, p. A–9*

Conjuring New Threats

This book argues that the public policy of civil defense and its connection to early Cold War mobilization had fundamental effects on postwar American political development. I focus on one current implication for policy planning that has its roots in Truman-era FCDA planning: the "new" worry about "weapons of mass destruction" (WMD) and the problem of "superterrorism."[42]

For a moment imagine the following: It's 2:00 P.M. on a beautiful Saturday afternoon in a moderate-sized town in the Midwest and most folks are enjoying themselves as they go about their weekend business. By 4:00 P.M., however, the emergency rooms in the town's two hospitals are unusually busy and doctors' pagers are beeping on golf courses all over the area. People of all ages are ill with what at first seems like a localized outbreak of "summer flu." Within the next five days, events spin out of control, as people begin to die at rates reaching 90 percent after they seemed to be getting better. Additionally, the "first responders," the local nurses, doctors, and emergency personnel, have been infected, and they, too, begin to get ill and die in large numbers. The governor of the state declares an emergency; the president of the United States does the same. The Centers for Disease Control (CDC) and the Federal Emergency Management Agency (FEMA) mobilize all their resources to respond to the growing emergency. Within five days, it becomes clear to the experts that an act of superterrorism with an unknown, infectious biological agent has taken place.

As FEMA activates a civil defense plan and the CDC mobilizes its medical experts, the government attempts to contain mass panic. Unfortunately for FEMA's plans for managing panic, the general public has been glued to its television sets for the last three days, getting a minute-by-minute analysis by the "experts" on twenty-four-hour news programs detailing the gruesome effects of biological weapons. What does civil defense mean under such circumstances in the affected town and surrounding areas? Not very much, at least not very much that is good. The national public gets its first taste of civilian defense against superterror: martial law, quarantines, and perhaps even mass hospices where people will be given palliative treatment as they await slow and agonizing death.

Is this hypothetical scenario a farfetched possibility? Maybe, but not according to the U.S. government, where in the last eight years the possibility of terrorist attacks using WMD has generated an enormous amount of attention and policy analysis. In his 1998 commencement address at the Naval Academy, President Clinton told the graduates and the American public that the country must begin to stockpile vaccines against biological weapons. National security specialists and scholars writing in academic journals are warning that the country must prepare for a terrorist attack (either home-grown or foreign) using "weaponized" biological agents, chemical agents, and fissile materials in the form of crude radioactive weapons or even small nuclear weapons. Of late, we are being told it is not a matter of whether or not an attack will take place, but a matter of when.[43] The president and his national security specialists do have grounds for concern, for we have seen attempts, both successful and—thankfully—unsuccessful, at biological and chemical terrorism: The Aum Shinriko cult in Japan and its attack on Japan's subway system come to mind. Once again civil defense is in vogue, but with a warning by national security specialists that we may miss the "good old days" of the balance of terror with the Soviet Union.

Current discussion about the "new" threat facing the United States is replete with worst-case scenarios. The potentially devastating consequences of such an attack have led to the justification, mainly by academic specialists, for the creation of even more complex agencies for civil defense, as well as calls from local, state, and federal governments for increased funding for almost every bureaucratic agency that can be remotely related to issues of security.[44] What are we to make of all this? In historical perspective, the lessons of the FCDA and the Truman administration's attempts to handle the same problems are lost on current policy planners. The most obvious problem is the notion that the threat today is new: There is nothing new about biological, chemical, or nuclear weapons—all three were used in war during the long and bloody twentieth century—and there is nothing new about the problems of civil defense and emergency planning. FEMA's institutional, legal, and administrative roots are, without any legislative detours whatsoever, directly linked to the FCDA. Because today's policy debate is ahistorical, it creates the conditions for very bad policy planning and potentially dangerous policy operations.

Today, Congress and national security planners have framed policy related to the prevention of superterrorism in the United States against the backdrop of two seminal events: the World Trade Center bombing in 1993 in New York City and the Oklahoma City bombing in 1995. These two acts of domestic terrorism moved Congress to pass Public Law 104-132, The Antiterrorism and Effective Death Penalty Act of 1996 (ATA).[45] In 1950, the creation of the FCDA was propelled by two key events: the Soviet atomic test of 1949 and the Korean War. Policy planning today for WMD, just like most early Cold War national security legislation, is based on emergency lawmaking: indeterminate in language, infused with enormous discretionary power, and ambiguous with respect to specific bureaucratic jurisdiction. Does this sound familiar? It should: As we have seen, civil defense and home-preparedness legislation of the early 1950s were framed by a jurisprudence rife with rationalizations for eroding individual civil liberty in the name of state survival, the direct result of emergency lawmaking.

The early Cold War period was, for the United States, a historical moment in which domestic emergency planning was shaped by the realities of the postwar international system. As we know, the Truman administration developed a broadly conceived national security objective on which it premised almost all of the U.S. domestic and international policies, namely, the containment of the Soviet Union. This led to a process that garrisoned civil society and created politically insulated national security institutions that functioned with a minimal amount of congressional oversight. Similarly, in the early post–Cold War era, we are confronted with changes in the international system that shape the way planners define national security: the end of Cold War bipolarity and its replacement by regional powers (multipolarity) and a single superpower, as well as globalization issues and the question of democratization. In both time periods, policy planning for domestic emergencies was in various stages of flux because national security planners were evoking new threats or new permutations of old threats as a way to cover all possible contingencies in a new, uncertain period. Just as the Truman administration viewed civilian preparedness as part of its overall deterrence strategy and, more specifically, as a tool to manage public concerns about nuclear weapons and a superpower nation-state, so too did both

the Bush and Clinton administrations resurrect national civilian preparedness and emergency planning as a means for what President Clinton hopes
will be "the perfect defense" against non-nation-state actors.[46]

The data on how to control panic and the theories about mass behavior
on which FCDA civil defense programs were based are the exact same data
being used today by the Department of Justice (DOJ), FEMA, the CDC, and
the DOD. Current concerns about preparedness for superterror with WMD
also focus on "band-aid approaches" tied to "first responders" in order to
offer an illusion of civil defense, just as the FCDA did in the early 1950s.
What is not made public is that for logistical reasons the federal government
and its agencies have the same exact problem that the government and the
FCDA had in the early 1950s: A successful WMD attack will so disrupt the
social order that *post-attack* civil defense becomes highly problematic. This
post-attack problem raises two important questions: Why have any civil
defense planning at all, and what is the ultimate purpose of this planning if
post-attack civilian defense against superterror would be so difficult? In a
slightly different way, these two questions arose in the Truman administration, especially during the FCDA's first full year of operation in 1952.[47] Today,
emergency-management planners answer both questions in the same way as
did their early 1950s counterparts. Post-attack civilian defense serves primarily as a tool for managing panic. Thus, civil defense functions as an instrument
for emotion management. As a result, the civil defense policy becomes very
public: Various agencies carry out civil defense training and preparedness
drills and issue press releases about them; representatives from key agencies
give public interviews to spark public interest and to show the general public
that specialized expertise is being brought to bear on the problem.

The answer to the second question about the ultimate purpose of emergency planning intersects with a less public (in terms of open discussion and
press) goal of policy planners in both the recent past and in the present: to
plan and deploy a civilian defense apparatus aimed at *preempting* an attack.
As public policy, this approach to emergency management raises issues for
civil liberties. Preventive defense entails, at the very least, a highly rationalized interagency relationship among various kinds of organizations that, by
their very nature, are less oriented to the protection of individual civil rights.
The same kind of arrangements between internally and externally oriented
security policy that occurred during the early Cold War era are more probable in the post–Cold War world where non-nation-state actors are viewed by
national security planners as a primary menace to the civilian population.
Given this type of threat assessment, a bureaucracy such as DOD, DOJ, and
first-response agencies such as FEMA and the CDC will have to conflate, in

an even more concrete fashion than did the FCDA in the early 1950s, both internal and external security in the name of antiterrorism.

One of the lasting legacies of Cold War mobilization is the institutional and administrative capacity to carry out internal surveillance. Additionally, this institutional capacity has become more potent with the advent of modern computer technology. Today's civil defense planning against superterror is following the same two-track policy the FCDA developed almost fifty years ago in its attempt to mobilize the public for nuclear war. As we have seen, the Cold War served the Truman administration as the structure that framed policy planning. Today, it is the new, evolving war against superterrorism that focuses attention in almost the same way the Cold War did fifty years ago. In both time periods, planners used the language of impending war to define civilian defense threats and policies as if the worst-case scenario was a foregone conclusion: That is, not *if* a disaster is to happen but *when* it will happen. Ultimately, the logic of this kind of planning drives central-state planners to conceive of the military as the key to *internal policing* under emergency circumstances; the evidence is clear that the Clinton administration resurrected this policy option.[48] Although the Clinton administration's plans for military policing were reported in the popular press as something new, they are not. Extensive planning took place throughout the early Cold War period to use the military, under certain circumstances, in a policing role.[49]

The second track for civil preparedness planning is bit more fateful than using the armed forces to "help out" in a national emergency. Preventive civil defense means finding a systematic way in which to identify potential threats. The term "potential" is significant because in bureaucratic planning this requires high levels of discretionary power in order to allow "experts" to decide who and what are potential threats. It is within an opaque domain of organizing for "possible," "potential," threats of superterrorism that civil liberties can be undermined. Just as the terms "communist" and "subversive" took on specific meanings in the late 1940s and early 1950s, so too does the term "potential terrorist." The means by which security is defined *must* be left up to experts with special knowledge regarding disaster planning and WMD. Thus civilian defense planning in FEMA, DOD, and DOJ is especially vulnerable to what is sometimes referred to as "mission creep"; that is, discrete facets of civilian mobilization and defense become expansive projects. This happened with the FCDA, and it looks as if it might happen again. The reason is that this second track of civil defense mobilization is not really about "cleaning up" after an attack; it is about preempting an attack. As public policy, preventive civil defense falls within the jurisdiction of politically insulated national security agencies that do three important things: define standards by which national security threats can be identified, define the parameters of the threat, and plan for and engage in preventive measures against these threats.

Just as in the early Cold War period, today's antiterrorist lawmaking, civil defense preparedness, and disaster planning have two ominous interrelated features that bode ill for the protection of individual civil liberties and pave the way for a regarrisoning of civil society: enormous discretionary power and cumbersome jurisdictional overlap among agencies charged with emergency management.[50] If the policy history outlined in this book confirms anything, it is that crisis lawmaking in the United States will result in highly discretionary and ambiguously written legislation.[51] Antiterrorist legislation such as the ATA is a prime example of this kind of swift, crisis-driven legislation: It is broad in scope, its language is indeterminate, and it is filled with fuzzy guidance and discretionary power. As Max Weber, F. A. Hayek, and Theodore Lowi have eloquently argued (at different times and under different circumstances), emergency lawmaking often leads to bad laws because "reactive" lawmaking is often amorphous in terms of intent and general guidance. In a liberal democracy equivocal and unclear lawmaking often result in two outcomes for the polity: First, diffuse legislative language cultivates bureaucratic growth, as line agencies fight for legitimacy, jurisdiction, and funding, and second, the potential for the illiberal expansion of central-state power emerges out of the proliferation of bureaucratic line agencies. The legacy of the Cold War model for legislating emergency planning has not only survived but also flourished in the post–Cold War era. By any standard, today's planning for civil defense against WMD is the most bureaucratically laden system one can imagine. Even when compared to the policy history of the Cold War era, the bureaucracy engaged in today's planning for superterrorism is nothing short of astonishing (see Figure One).

Considering this kind of organizational structure, one is left wondering if all these different agencies could possibly function efficiently if there were an actual emergency. If there is any validity to the bureaucratic politics model of Graham Allison, then the ad hoc nature of today's civil preparedness structure indicates that current legislation has made a lot of money available for civil defense planning—hence the explosion of line agencies—but it is doubtful, at best, that this kind of administratively top-heavy planning structure can do what it is charged with doing in an emergency.[52] In classic Cold War style, contemporary policy planning has produced the hydra-headed bureaucratic planning structure illustrated in Figure One, which *will*, given the high level of discretion available to each agency, undermine civil liberties in the name of trying to prevent terrorism.

Figure One
Organizational Chart for Federal Emergency Preparedness.

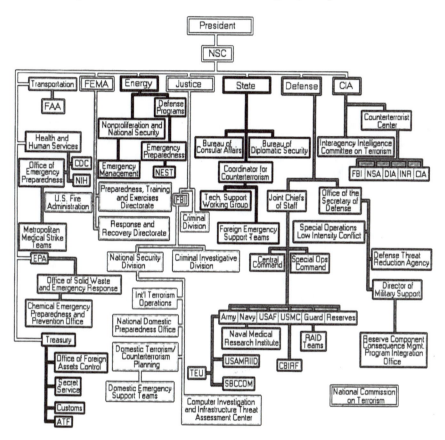

Source: Monterey Institute of International Studies: Center for Nonproliferation Studies.

Current plans for "preventive civil defense" mean a return to the kind of relationship that existed in the early 1950s between internal and external security agencies. All of these capabilities are in place—the institutional legacy of the Cold War—with a dangerous twist: the use of modern computer technology to centralize surveillance apparatuses, to collect and collate data on citizens domestic and foreign, and ultimately to deploy security forces to enforce preventive measures. Fifty years ago, the same kind of aggressive jurisprudence was used to "root out" suspected communist subversives within the United States. The results of this exercise in Cold War internal security are well known: Some spies were caught, and many, many other people had their lives ruined because they held views that were deemed by national security bureaucrats as subversive. In this sense, the reestablishment of a civic garrison is but one terrorist action away, and the problem is that policy planners do not want to examine the long and mixed history of the postwar civic garrison as a referent for current policy planning. In the end, this is potentially as dangerous to a liberal democracy as a terrorist bomb.

CONCLUSION

In the United States, the aim of civilian defense planning and education, and home-front mobilization in general, was to manage and control the process by which the general public was informed about issues of nuclear weapons and the politics of postwar national security. The NSRB's plans and the FCDA's civil defense programs served as instruments of social control, the prime objective of which was to prevent the American public from becoming so terrified over the effects of nuclear weapons as to erode the domestic political consensus for postwar grand strategy. In particular, they were concerned about the various collective security arrangements that U.S. foreign policy planners implemented in the decade following the end of World War II. Civil defense education attempted to carry out this objective in several ways: It "domesticated" nuclear weapons and sought to explain their role in America's arsenal by selling their deterrent value and U.S. collective security arrangements.[53] It communicated to the public at large the message that if they became overly fearful or exhibited panic concerning nuclear issues, they would undermine U.S. national security by calling into question the country's national will. Finally, civil defense education reinforced the Manichaeanism of the era by demonizing not only the Soviet Union but also alternative political views *inside* the United States. An important characteristic of the civic garrison, of which the FCDA was an institution, was the collapse of the distinction between internal and external national security.

For a liberal-democratic state, institutions must derive their political and legal legitimacy from a domestic political consensus achieved through democratic means. In the case of the early Cold War mobilization project, there is little evidence that *undemocratic* political activity was institutionalized, but there is abundant evidence that moments of illiberalism were accommodated by the Truman administration and the general public as a price that had to be paid for Cold War mobilization. It would not be until the public mobilizations of the mid-to-late 1960s that a negative public reaction arose over the requirements for the postwar grand strategy of the United States to contain Soviet power on the one hand and the social effects of the rationalization of national security policy and the internalizing of that policy on the other. Moreover, even though there is a substantially different relationship today between American citizens and their government when compared to the early 1950s, the institutional capacity of the state to reestablish a garrisoning process remains not only intact but also enhanced. Perhaps this is one consequence of winning the Cold War, for in 1989 the United States did not dismantle the institutional capacity or the standing agencies that functioned within the highly discretionary world of national security policy. Almost fifty years of Cold War mobilization tied to the management of the postwar Pax Americana not only centralized state power, but did so in the familiar fashion of European states. The United States did not manage its Cold War mobilization as a totalitarian garrison state, nor was the Cold War mobilization process the result of a functional weak state. In the end, the United States became a type of national security state: a civic garrison. Not only did the civic garrison rationalize the institutional and administrative capacity of a democratic society, but the consequences of that process, which was often illiberal and always statist, also affected American political development. Just as important, because the process of early Cold War mobilization was well documented, it offers us a robust policy history that should not be ignored, for the stakes are always high in a liberal democracy that cherishes individual civil liberties.

NOTES

Preface

1. On the numerous Operation Alerts and their sociological effects, see Guy Oakes, *The Imaginary War: Civil Defense and American Cold War Culture* (New York: Oxford University Press, 1994), pp. 84–96.

2. See Janice Gross Stein, Thomas Risse-Kappen, et al., "Symposium: The End of the Cold War and Theories of International Relations," *International Organization* 48 (Spring 1994):155–278; Michael J. Hogan, ed., *The End of the Cold War: Its Meaning and Implications* (New York: Cambridge University Press, 1992); and idem, *A Cross of Iron: Harry S. Truman and the Origins of the National Security State, 1945–1954* (New York: Cambridge University Press, 1997).

3 On the rationalization of national security policy and the role of the National Security Act of 1947, see Secretary of State George Marshall's comments in *Foreign Relations of the United States, 1947*, vol. 1, pp. 712–715. For the sweeping law itself, see Public Law 253, 80th Cong., 1st Session, July 26, 1947, *U.S. Statutes at Large*, LXI, pp. 495–510.

4. Aaron L. Friedberg, *In the Shadow of the Garrison State: America's Anti-Statism and Its Cold War Grand Strategy* (Princeton, NJ: Princeton University Press, 2000).

5. See Azza Salama Layton, *International Politics and Civil Rights Policies in the United States, 1941–1960* (New York: Cambridge University Press, 2000); and Philip A. Klinkner with Rogers M. Smith, *The Unsteady March: The Rise and Decline of Racial Equality in America* (Chicago: University of Chicago Press, 1999), pp. 202–241. For an exceptionally cogent study of the relationship between the Cold War and the civil rights movement, see Mary L. Dudziak, *Cold War Civil Rights: Race and the Image of American Democracy* (Princeton, NJ: Princeton University Press, 2000).

6. Two often-cited works in this vein are G. William Domhoff, *Who Rules America?* (Englewood Cliffs, NJ: Prentice Hall, 1967), pp. 115–138; and C. Wright Mills, *The Power Elite* (New York: Oxford University Press, 1956).

7. Elaine Tyler May, *Homeward Bound: American Families in the Cold War* (New York: Basic Books, 1988), pp. 92–113.

Chapter 1: Framing the Problem

1. Guy Oakes, *The Imaginary War: Civil Defense and American Cold War Culture* (New York: Oxford University Press, 1994), p. 6.

2. See "Report on Social Science Research in Cold War Operations," Papers of Harry S. Truman (PHST), Psychological Strategy Board (PSB), Box 1, Social Science Research Folder 2 of 2; "Information and Training for Civil Defense," National Archives (NA), National Security Resources Board (NSRB), Records Group (RG)-304, Box 19, Project East River Folder. See also "Funds Obligated for Social Science Research in Fiscal 1952,"

PHST, President's Secretary's Files (PSF), PSB, Box 1, Social Science Research Folder 2 of 2. Finally, see Roger L. Geiger, *Research and Relevant Knowledge: American Research Universities since World War II* (New York: Oxford University Press, 1993); and the essays in Christopher Simpson, ed., *Universities and Empire: Money and Politics in the Social Sciences during the Cold War* (New York: The New Press, 1998).

3. The term "nuclear fear" refers to public apprehension not only about the effects of nuclear weapons but also about all aspects of nuclear power. The term is taken from the title of a book on this subject written by Spencer R. Weart, *Nuclear Fear: A History of Images* (Cambridge, MA: Harvard University Press, 1988).

4. With regard to early civilian defense analysts and intellectuals, see Fred Kaplan, *The Wizards of Armageddon* (New York: Simon and Schuster, 1983); Gregg Herken, *Counsels of War* (New York: Oxford University Press, 1987), pp. 3–122. On the idea of a nuclear revolution, see Robert Jervis, *The Meaning of the Nuclear Revolution* (Ithaca, NY: Cornell University Press, 1989); Michael Mandelbaum, *The Nuclear Revolution: International Politics before and after Hiroshima* (New York: Cambridge University Press, 1981).

5. In the late 1940s and early 1950s, a disaster literature developed that focused on the human effects, physical and psychological, of World War II. These studies were an effort by civilian defense analysts and academics to develop working models to prepare for nuclear war. See the following examples: Fred C. Iklé, *The Social Impact of Bomb Destruction* (Norman: University of Oklahoma Press, 1958); idem, "The Social Versus the Physical Effects from Nuclear Bombing," *The Scientific Monthly* 78 (1954):182–187; Irving L. Janis, *Air War and Emotional Stress* (New York: McGraw Hill, 1951); idem, "Problems of Theory in the Analysis of Stress Behavior," *Journal of Social Issues* 10:3 (1954):12–25; idem, "Psychological Problems of A-Bomb Defense," *Bulletin of Atomic Scientists* 6 (August/September 1950):256–262.

6. See, for example, Lynn Eden, "Oblivion Is Not Enough: How the U.S. Air Force Thinks about Deterrence, Nuclear War, and Nuclear Weapons" (unpublished paper, 1989); Robert Jervis, Richard Ned Lebow, and Janice Gross Stein, *Psychology and Deterrence* (Baltimore, MD: Johns Hopkins University Press, 1989); Richard Ned Lebow, *Between Peace and War* (Baltimore, MD: Johns Hopkins University Press, 1981); Jervis, "Deterrence Theory Revisited," *World Politics* 41 (January 1989); and especially idem, *The Illogic of American Nuclear Strategy* (Ithaca, NY: Cornell University Press, 1984), pp. 56–58.

7. See Scott D. Sagan, *Moving Targets: Nuclear Strategy and National Strategy* (Princeton, NJ: Princeton University Press, 1989), pp. 4–9. See also Steven Kull, *Minds at War: Nuclear Reality and the Inner Conflicts of Defense Policymakers* (New York: Basic Books, 1988); Erik Yesson, "Strategic Make-Believe and Strategic Reality: Psychology and the Implications of the Nuclear Revolution," *International Security* 14 (Winter 1989/90):182–193; Carol Cohn, "Sex and Death in the Rational World of the Defense Intellectual," *Signs* 12 (Summer 1987):687–718.

8. On October 30, 1953, National Security Document number 162-2, "Basic National Security Policy," supplanted NSC-68 as the basis for U.S. nuclear strategy. It provided the guidance for a grand political and military strategy that fulfilled the requirements of NSC-68, but without destroying the economy of the United States. In the opening paragraph of the document, concern about the political economy of America's strategic commitments is made plain. The paragraph stated that the basic problem of national security policy was: "(a) To meet the Soviet threat to U.S. security and (b) in doing so, to avoid seriously weakening the U.S. economy or undermining our fundamental values and institutions." The whole document is reprinted in full in The Gravel Edition, *The Pentagon Papers*, vol. 1 (Boston: Beacon Press, 1971), pp. 412–429. On this issue of the political economy of American strategic commitments, see National Security Council Document 5501, in Marc Trachtenberg, ed., *The Development of American Strategic Thought*, vol. 4 (New York: Garland Publishing, 1987), pp. 91–115; Glenn Snyder, "The New Look of 1953," in

Strategy, Politics and Defense Budgets, ed. Warner R. Schilling, Paul Y. Hammond, and Glenn H. Snyder (New York: Columbia University Press, 1962); Lawrence Freedman, *The Evolution of Nuclear Strategy,* 2nd ed. (New York: St. Martin's, 1989), pp. 81–84; Marc Trachtenberg, "A 'Wasting Asset': American Strategy and the Shifting Nuclear Balance, 1949–1954," *International Security* 13 (Winter 1988/89):32–44; Melvyn P. Leffler, *A Preponderance of Power: National Security, The Truman Administration, and the Cold War* (Stanford, CA: Stanford University Press, 1992); and Stephen Ambrose, *Eisenhower,* vol. 2 (New York: Simon and Schuster, 1984), pp. 171–173, 224–226. For a different tack, see R. H. Brands, "The Age of Vulnerability: Eisenhower and the National Insecurity State," *American Historical Review* 94 (October 1989):963–989.

9. For a helpful discussion of the doctrines of "defense" and "deterrence" and the way these concepts have often been confused, see Scott D. Sagan and Kenneth N. Waltz, *The Spread of Nuclear Weapons: A Debate* (New York: W.W. Norton, 1995), pp. 1–47.

10. A superb work on the gradual blurring of distinctions between civilians and combatants is John Keegan's *The Face of Battle* (New York: Viking Penguin, 1976). That the military was slow to recognize the differences between conventional and nuclear weapons is apparent in early American war plans that treated atomic weapons as if they were large conventional weapons. See, for example, Stephen T. Ross, *American War Plans 1945–1950* (New York: Garland Publishing, 1988); David Alan Rosenberg, "The Origins of Overkill," *International Security* 7 (Spring 1983):3–71.

11. See Benjamin O. Fordham, "Economic Interests, Party, and Ideology in Early Cold War Era U.S. Foreign Policy," *International Organization* 52 (Spring 1998):359–396; Peter Trubowitz, *Defining the National Interest: Conflict and Change in American Foreign Policy* (Chicago: University of Chicago Press, 1998).

12. See *Nuclear Diplomacy and Crisis Management,* ed. Sean Lynn-Jones, Steven E. Miller, and Stephen Van Evera (Cambridge, MA: MIT Press, 1990), pp. 3–158.

13. This internationalist strategy came under political attack by the isolationist wing of the Republican party in the late 1940s and early 1950s. See, for example, Lynn Rachele Eden, "The Diplomacy of Force: Interests, the State, and the Making of American Military Policy in 1948" (Ph.D. diss., University of Michigan, 1985); Robert A. Pollard, *Economic Security and the Origins of the Cold War* (New York: Columbia University Press, 1985); John Lewis Gaddis, *Strategies of Containment: A Critical Appraisal of the Postwar American National Security Policy* (New York: Oxford University Press, 1982); and Robert Latham, *The Liberal Moment: Modernity, Security, and the Making of Postwar Order* (New York: Columbia University Press, 1997), pp. 96–137.

14. Between 1947 and 1989 U.S. strategy shifted between two strategies of containment: global and finite. For an analysis of these two concepts and their implementation, see Stephen M. Walt, "The Case for Finite Containment: Analyzing U.S. Grand Strategy," *International Security* 14 (Summer 1989):5–49.

15. An exception is Ira Katznelson and Kenneth Prewitt, "Constitutionalism, Class, and the Limits of Choice in U.S. Foreign Policy," in *Capitalism and the State in U.S.-Latin American Relations,* ed. Richard R. Fagen (Stanford, CA: Stanford University Press, 1979), pp. 25–40. Of interest as well is Theodore Lowi's concept of oversell in his *The End of Liberalism: The Second Republic of the United States,* 2nd ed. (New York: W.W. Norton, 1979), pp. 139–145. See also Stephen Krasner, "United States Commercial and Monetary Policy: Unravelling the Paradox of External Strength and Internal Weakness," in *Between Power and Plenty: Foreign Economic Policies of Advanced Industrial States,* ed. Peter J. Katzenstein (Madison: University of Wisconsin Press, 1978), pp. 151–188; David A. Lake, "The State and American Trade Strategy in the Pre-Hegemonic Era," *International Organization* 42 (Winter 1988):33–58; Gregory Hooks, *Forging the Military-Industrial Complex: World War II's Battle of the Potomac* (Urbana: University of Illinois Press, 1991); Gregory Hooks and Gregory McLaughlan, "Institutional Foundation of Warmaking:

Three Eras of U.S. Warmaking," *Theory and Society* 21 (1991): 257–288; and Brian Waddell, "Economic Mobilization for World War II and the Transformation of the U.S. State," *Politics and Society* 22 (June 1994):165–194.

16. Postwar foreign policy was by no means a matter of universal agreement. For example, in Congress there were two opposing views with regard to how the United States should structure its postwar foreign policy. The main point of contention between these two camps centered on exactly what kind of international role the United States should pursue. This political battle between "business nationalists" and "internationalists" helped to shape the larger debate about what kind of force structure the U.S. military should develop in the postwar atomic era. The former were unilateralists who favored a strong nuclear-equipped Air Force. The latter were interested in collective security arrangements that depended on both nuclear and conventional deterrence and ultimately rested on the logic of finite containment. See Trubowitz, *Defining the National Interest*, esp. pp.1-30, 235–246. See also idem, "Diplomacy of Force"; Eden, "The End of U.S. Cold War History?" *International Security* 18 (Summer 1993):174–207.

17. This process entailed the "selling" of a set of Cold War legitimating ideologies; the attendant development of a domestic consensus based on these ideologies and the ability to plan were dealt with successfully overall by the United States within the first decade after the end of World War II. However, problems of consensus development, strategic planning, and political legitimacy are highly contentious issues in a democratic state and thus a premium is placed on institutional capacity, political insulation, and broad-based acceptance and legitimacy from the general public for any new grand strategic policy. For analyses that focus on different aspects of these issues, see Robert W. Rieber and Robert J. Kelly, "Substance and Shadow: Images of the Enemy," in *The Psychology of War and Peace: The Image of the Enemy*, ed. Robert W. Rieber (New York: Plenum Press, 1991), pp. 3–39; Bruce D. Porter, *War and the Rise of the State: The Military Foundations of Modern Politics* (New York: Free Press, 1994), pp. 286–296; John Mueller, "The Impact of Ideas on Grand Strategy," in *The Domestic Bases of Grand Strategy*, ed. Richard Rosencrance and Arthur A. Stein (Ithaca, NY: Cornell University Press, 1993), pp. 48–62; and Ernest R. May, "The U.S. Government, a Legacy of the Cold War," in *The End of the Cold War: Its Meaning and Implications*, ed. Michael J. Hogan (New York: Cambridge University Press, 1992), pp. 217–228.

18. See, for example, Robert Higgs, *Crisis and Leviathan: Critical Episodes in the Growth of American Government* (New York: Oxford University Press, 1987). See also Barry D. Karl, *The Uneasy State: The United States from 1915–1945* (Chicago: University of Chicago Press, 1983), pp. 34–49, 205–223.

19. See Aaron L. Friedberg, *In the Shadow of the Garrison State: America's Anti-Statism and Its Cold War Grand Strategy* (Princeton, NJ: Princeton University Press, 2000), pp. 9–33; Samuel P. Huntington, *Political Order in Changing Societies* (New Haven, CT: Yale University Press, 1968), pp. 93–139.

20. Theda Skocpol, "Bringing the State Back In," in *Bringing the State Back In*, ed. Peter Evans, Dietrich Rueschemeyer, and Theda Skocpol (New York: Cambridge University Press, 1985), p. 17; Theda Skocpol and Kenneth Finegold, "State Capacity and Economic Intervention in the Early New Deal," *Political Science Quarterly* 97 (Summer 1982):225–278.

21. Friedberg, *In the Shadow of the Garrison State*, pp. 9–33, 340–351.

22. A superb example of how placing American political development in a comparative historical context generates a more thorough and robust analysis of the American state is Karen Orren, *Belated Feudalism: Labor, the Law, and Liberal Development in the United States* (New York: Cambridge University Press, 1991).

23. See Aristide R. Zolberg, "How Many Exceptionalisms?" in *Working-Class Formation: Nineteenth-Century Patterns in Western Europe and the United States*, ed. Ira Katznelson and Aristide R. Zolberg (Princeton, NJ: Princeton University Press, 1986), pp. 397–455. As

an example of how comparisons can be useful for a more robust analysis of American political development, see John Brewer, *The Sinews of Power: War, Money and the English State 1688–1783* (New York: Knopf, 1989), pp. 137–218.

24. See, for example, Elizabeth Sanders, *Roots of Reform: Farmers, Workers, and the American State, 1877–1917* (Chicago: University of Chicago Press, 1999).

25. This is not to suggest, as some have, that U.S. political leaders have never thought strategically about foreign policy. On the contrary, U.S. foreign policy historically has been isolationist, which has determined the strategic structure of its foreign policy. Policy orientation was connected to the protection of the Western hemisphere and the maintenance and protection of sea lanes for purposes of trade. Thus U.S. foreign policy was particularistic—local, economic, and linked to the international system only insofar as sea lanes and other key avenues to trade remained unhindered, which allowed for empire building but did not articulate a grand strategy in the European sense of the term. See Richard Franklin Bensel, *Sectionalism and American Political Development, 1880–1980* (Madison: University of Wisconsin Press, 1984), pp. 60–103; Marc Egnal, *A Mighty Empire: The Origins of the American Revolution* (Ithaca, NY: Cornell University Press, 1988); Robert W. Tucker and David C. Hendrickson, "Thomas Jefferson and Foreign Policy," *Foreign Affairs* 69 (Spring 1990):135–156. For a provocative alternative point of view, see William Appleman Williams, *Empire as a Way of Life* (New York: Oxford University Press, 1980).

26. See Eden, "Diplomacy of Force"; Michael J. Hogan, *A Cross of Iron: Harry S. Truman and the Origins of the National Security State, 1945–1954* (New York: Cambridge University Press, 1997), pp. 119–158.

27. See Trubowitz, *Defining the National Interest.*

28. In the case of the post–World War II period, recent scholarship suggests that the Cold War consensus was forged through a benign relationship between state and society, resulting in programs that were carefully adapted to the American economic and political system. For an analysis that takes a different tack, see my "Atomic Fantasies and Make-Believe War: The American State, Social Control, and Civil Defense Planning, 1946–1952," *Political Power and Social Theory* 9 (1995):91–120.

29. Oakes, *The Imaginary War.*

30. Laura McEnaney, *Civil Defense Begins at Home: Militarization Meets Everyday Life in the Fifties* (Princeton, NJ: Princeton University Press, 2000); and Margot A. Henriksen, *Dr. Strangelove's America: Society and Culture in the Atomic Age* (Los Angeles: University of California Press, 1997), pp. 11–38, 87–112.

31. See, for example, Charles Tilly, "War Making and State Making as Organized Crime," in *Bringing the State Back In*, pp. 169–191. For a classic theoretical analysis of bureaucratic discretionary power, see Max Weber, *Economy and Society*, vol. 2, ed. Gunther Roth and Claus Wittich (Berkeley: University of California Press, 1978). See also Lowi, *End of Liberalism*, pp. 92–124, 295–310.

32. See especially Hogan, *A Cross of Iron*, pp. 23–68.

33. During World War I mass propaganda and war advertising were used by the Wilson administration to sell the war to the American people; World War II was not the first time such techniques were used, and no doubt the experience of World War I helped to shape how information was managed. What I claim here is that during World War II these techniques were refined and institutionalized, so that when the war ended in 1945, the idea of "communication science" became, as historian Christopher Simpson has argued, a type of "science of coercion" that was not dismantled after the war. On World War I, see Ronald Schaffer, *America in the Great War: The Rise of the War Welfare State* (New York: Oxford University Press, 1991). On the notion of communication science and its rationalization, see Christopher Simpson, *Science of Coercion: Communication Research and Psychological Warfare 1945–1960* (New York: Oxford University Press, 1994).

34. Herbert N. Foerstel, *Secret Science: Federal Control of American Science and Technology* (Westport, CT: Praeger, 1993), p. 3.

35. See, for example, Denis W. Brogan, *Democratic Government in an Atomic World: A Lecture Delivered Under the Auspices of the Walter J. Shepard Foundation, April 24, 1956* (Columbus: Ohio State University Press, 1956).

36. Colin Grey, "Strategy in the Nuclear Age: The United States, 1945–1991," in *The Making of Strategy: Rulers, States, and War*, ed. Williamson Murry, MacGregor Knox, and Alvin Bernstein (New York: Cambridge University Press, 1994), pp. 589–601; Alastair Iain Johnston, "Thinking about Strategic Culture," *International Security* 19 (Spring 1995):32–64.

37. The long-term effects of the formation of a U.S. civic garrison in the early Cold War period are detailed in Chapter Five, where Lasswell's ideas are reconsidered with specific reference to the militarization of civilian life and the FCDA. On Lasswell and the civic garrison state, see Harold D. Lasswell, "Does the Garrison State Threaten Civil Rights?" *The Annals of Political and Social Science* 275 (May 1951):111–116; idem, "The Garrison State Hypothesis Today," in *Changing Patterns of Military Politics*, ed. Samuel Huntington (Glencoe, IL: The Free Press, 1962), pp. 51–70. See also Arthur E. Naftalalin, "Political Freedom and Military Necessity," in *The Garrison State: Its Human Problems* (Minneapolis: University of Minnesota Press, 1953), pp. 28–42; Brogan, *Democratic Government in an Atomic World*. Thanks also to Yagil Levy, who helped me to clarify the three-dimensional conceptual apparatus that I employ here.

38. On Truman administration war-planning and morale, see Barry H. Steiner, *Bernard Brodie and the Foundations of American Nuclear Strategy* (Lawrence: University Press of Kansas, 1991), pp. 46–75. On the development of early U.S. nuclear strategy, see Grey, "Strategy in the Nuclear Age," pp. 579–613.

39. Grey, "Strategy in the Nuclear Age," p. 588. See also Cohn, "Sex and Death in the Rational World of the Defense Intellectual."

40. For a fine example of scholarship that does make the connection between social order and war, see Peter T. Manicas, *War and Democracy* (Cambridge, MA: Basil Blackwell, 1989). Now that the Cold War has ended, the strategic literature has changed as evidenced by the new vogue in international relations theory, "democratic peace theory," which, of course, focuses precisely on the important connection between social order and war-making. See, for example, John M. Owen, "How Liberalism Produces Democratic Peace," *International Security* 19 (Fall 1994):87–125; and for an opposing perspective, Christopher Layne, "Kant or Cant: The Myth of Democratic Peace," *International Security* 19 (Fall 1994):5–49.

41. Herman Kahn, *On Thermonuclear War* (Princeton, NJ: Princeton University Press, 1960), p. 86.

42. See, for example, Kull, *Minds at War*.

43. The idea of "bringing the state back in" has not gone unchallenged. In part, the whole notion of "rediscovery" of the state has been somewhat contentious, especially within American political science. For example, Gabriel Almond's critique of contemporary research suggests that the recent scholarship does not give enough credit to early work in state theory, both Anglo-American and—especially—German. Almond's subtext holds that "state theory" has been done by the earlier scholars (of his generation in particular) and done better and more comprehensively than the new state theorists; see his "The Return to the State," *American Political Science Review* 82 (September 1988):853–874 and the responses in the same. Also see Evans, Rueschemeyer, and Skocpol, *Bringing the State Back In*.

44. Otto Hintze, *The Historical Essays of Otto Hintze*, ed. Gilbert Felix (New York: Oxford University Press, 1975); and Weber, *Economy and Society*, vol. 2. For an excellent recent treatment of European state formation in historical context, see Thomas Ertman, *Birth of the Leviathan: Building States and Regimes in Medieval and Early Modern Europe* (New York: Cambridge University Press, 1997), pp. 1–19, 48–88.

45. Weber, *Economy and Society*, vol. 2, pp. 980–1005.

46. Ibid., pp. 901–940.

47. See, for example, Tilly, "War Making and State Making as Organized Crime," pp. 169–191. Also see idem, *Coercion, Capital, and European States, AD 990–1990* (Cambridge, MA: Basil Blackwell, 1990).

48. For other important works that focus on the United States and war-making from the same war-making/state expansion perspective, see Hooks, *Forging the Military-Industrial Complex*; and Hooks and McLaughlan, "The Institutional Foundation of War-Making."

49. For more on the normalization of emergency and its effects on democracy, citizenship, and military strategy in the postwar era, see Allan Silver, "Democratic Citizenship and High Military Strategy: The Inheritance, Decay, and Reshaping of Political Culture," *Research on Democracy and Society* 2 (1994):317–349.

50. See Morris Janowitz, *The Reconstruction of Patriotism: Education for Civic Consciousness* (Chicago: University of Chicago Press, 1983).

51. See, for example, Aaron L. Friedberg, "Why Didn't the United States Become a Garrison State?" *International Security* 16 (Spring 1992):109–142.

52. For a classic analysis of discretionary power and its potential consequences for liberal-democratic processes and American political development, see Lowi, *The End of Liberalism*.

53. See Henriksen, *Dr. Strangelove's America*.

54. This is not the same thing, however, as saying that nuclear weapons revolutionized *how* the U.S. military was actually used, in, for example, Korea, Vietnam, or the Gulf War. The argument here is first an existential claim: that nuclear weapons changed the way humankind understood its place in a world of nuclear weapons—that it could utterly destroy itself, perhaps causing its own extinction—and second, that Truman administration planners charged with managing postwar national security policy did conceive of nuclear weapons as revolutionary in the sense that they believed doctrinal changes tied to the integration of nuclear weapons into the armed forces did have consequences for the state and society. Consider Colin Grey's point that the "promotion of the United States to a superpower was coincidental with, not a product of, the success of the Manhattan Project. Nuclear weapons rendered some of the negative tasks in statecraft easier than before, but once other powers acquired them they also introduced a new set of limitations upon the use of force, the ultima ratio of powers greater than other powers." "Strategy in the Nuclear Age," pp. 579–613, quotation on p. 582. Also see John E. Mueller, *Retreat from Doomsday: The Obsolescence of Major War* (New York: Basic Books, 1989).

55. See Ross, *American War Plans 1945–1950*.

56. For an interesting and important study that ties the "liberal tradition" to the militarization of the postwar world order, see Latham, *The Liberal Moment*. On "security internationalists," see Herman M. Schwartz, *States versus Markets: History, Geography, and the Development of the International Political Economy* (New York: St. Martin's Press, 1994), p. 210.

57. For an extremely helpful analysis on how a "relatively" weak state can maneuver—within a liberal-democratic/pluralist framework—and shape consensus development within a domestic polity, see Eric Nordlinger, *The Autonomy of the Democratic State* (Cambridge, MA: Harvard University Press, 1981).

58. I want to thank Guy Oakes for his counsel with respect to conceptualizing the process this way. The idea was essentially his, and he has graciously allowed me to use it in my book. See too Oakes's *The Imaginary War*, which frames the process in this fashion as well.

59. In using these terms, I cast the net widely and am fully aware that I do not provide a detailed analysis of the class and institutional backgrounds of these influential individuals. As used here, the term "national security elites" refers to a group of decision-makers and advisors that includes the president; a group of civilian defense analysts who were primarily academics, foreign-policy specialists, and career diplomats, such as the so-called "wise men of foreign affairs"; members of the armed services; and key members of Congress. For the period 1946–1954, I have in mind people such as Bernard Brodie, Arnold Wolfers,

Frederick Dunn, Grayson Kirk, Harold Sprout, William Borden, Klaus Knorr, Edward Teller, Paul Nitze, General George Marshall, Navy Secretary James Forrestal, Admiral Arthur Radford, General Curtis Lemay, Dean Acheson, Senator Arthur Vandenberg, David Lilienthal, Admiral Lewis Strauss, John Foster Dulles, Allen Dulles, George Kennan, and John McCloy. For an examination of class and its connection to elite thinking and American foreign policy, see Gabriel and Joyce Kolko, *The Limits of Power: The World and United States Foreign Policy 1945–1954* (New York: Harper and Row, 1972). For more on the so-called "wise men," see Walter Isaacson and Evan Thomas, *The Wise Men: Six Friends and the World They Made* (New York: Simon and Schuster, 1986); Robert D. Schulizinger, *The Wise Men of Foreign Affairs: The History of the Council on Foreign Relations* (New York: Columbia University Press, 1984). Finally, for an overview of how the national security elite functioned in the immediate postwar period, see Herken, *Counsels of War*, pp. 3–122.

60. See Stuart W. Leslie, *The Cold War and American Science: The Military-Industrial-Academic Complex at MIT and Stanford* (New York: Columbia University Press, 1993), pp. 14–188; Kim Geiger and Andrew Grossman, "Preparing for Cold War: The Politics of Home-Front Mobilization, 1946–1952," Center for Studies of Social Change, Working Paper No. 202 (November 1994). Also see Peter M. Hass, "Introduction: Epistemic Communities and International Policy Coordination," *International Security* 46 (Winter 1992):1–36.

61. Leslie, *Cold War and American Science*, pp. 1–44, 188–233; Foerstel, *Secret Science*, pp. 1–49; Herken, *Counsels of War*, pp. 60–122.

62. An example is Associated Universities, Inc., of New York. For more on this confederation of major research universities, see Chapter Three and the discussion of the Project East River civil defense study.

63. See Chapter Three for details on war advertising and the role of the Ad Council. On the relationship between the Ad Council and the government in general, see John Vianney McGinnis, "The Advertising Council and the Cold War" (Ph.D. diss., Syracuse University, 1991); and Robert Griffith, "The Selling of America: The Advertising Council and American Politics, 1942–1960," *Business History Review* 57 (1983):338–412.

Chapter 2: The Never-Ending Threat

1. See Michael Sherry, *Preparing for the Next War: American Plans for Postwar Defense, 1941–1945* (New Haven, CT: Yale University Press, 1977).

2. See Robert Gilpin, *The Political Economy of International Relations* (Princeton, NJ: Princeton University Press, 1987), pp. 65–116; idem, *War and Change in World Politics* (Cambridge, Cambridge University Press, 1981); Paul Kennedy, *The Rise and Fall of the Great Powers* (New York: Random House, 1987), esp. pp. 194–413; Karl Polanyi, *The Great Transformation: The Political and Economic Origins of Our Time* (Boston: Beacon Press, 1957).

3. See for example, John Gerard Ruggie, "International Regimes, Transactions, and Change: Imbedded Liberalism in the Postwar Economic Order," in *International Regimes*, ed. Stephen Krasner (Ithaca, NY: Cornell University Press, 1983), pp. 195–231; Charles S. Maier, "The Politics of Productivity: Foundations of American International Economic Policy after World War II," in *Search for Stability*, ed. Charles S. Maier (Cambridge: Cambridge University Press, 1987), pp. 121–152; G. John Ikenberry, "Rethinking the Origins of American Hegemony," *Political Science Quarterly* 104 (Fall 1989):375–400; and Polanyi, *The Great Transformation*.

4. For a historical overview of the symbolism of "Red Fascist" imagery and its effects on American national security planners and the general population, see Thomas G. Patterson, *Meeting the Communist Threat: Truman to Reagan* (New York: Oxford University Press, 1988), pp. 3–17.

5. The argument that liberal-democratic systems and structures produce "soft" polities is systematically analyzed in Samuel Huntington's classic *The Soldier and the State: The Theory and Politics of Civil-Military Relations* (Cambridge, MA: Harvard University Press, 1957), pp. 143–162. The so-called wise men of foreign policy assumed a type of "Hamiltonian" democracy in which high limits were placed on democracy. In this form, democracy limits participatory action through institutional political insulation, formal procedure, restrictive norms, and elite discretionary power. In short, the "wise men" would be the guardians of postwar Western principles of democracy and freedom. For a memorable statement that defines the idea of "guardianship democracy," i.e., illiberal democracy, see David Truman's introduction to the second edition of his classic work on pluralism, *The Governmental Process: Public Interests and Public Opinion*, 2nd ed. (New York: Alfred A. Knopf, 1971), pp. xvii–xlviii.

6. For a general overview of this point, see Melvyn P. Leffler, *A Preponderance of Power: National Security, the Truman Administration, and the Cold War* (Stanford, CA: Stanford University Press, 1992), pp. 5–9. With regard to the elite thinking, see George Kennan's February 22, 1946, "Moscow Embassy Telegram # 511 [The Long Telegram], reprinted in *Containment: Documents on American Policy and Strategy, 1945–1950*, ed. Thomas H. Etzold and John Lewis Gaddis (New York: Columbia University Press, 1978), pp. 50–63; George F. Kennan, *Memoirs: 1925–1950* (Boston: Little, Brown, 1967), pp. 292–295; and Clark M. Clifford and George M. Elsey's 1946 secret report to President Truman, "American Relations with the Soviet Union: A Report to the President by the Special Counsel to the President" (also known as the "Clifford–Elsey Report"), reprinted in Etzold and Gaddis, pp. 64–71. With regard to the later (1950) notion that democracies could be considered "soft spots," see "Memorandum by the Secretary of the Army (Pace), the Secretary of the Navy (Mathews), and the Secretary of the Air Force (Finletter) to the Secretary of Defense (Johnson), August 1, 1950, reprinted in *Foreign Relations of the United States (FRUS)*, 1950, vol. 1 (Washington, DC: GPO), pp. 353–357. James Forrestal took very seriously the idea that the philosophy of communism, as he understood it, was a real threat to U.S. interests. See Edward F. Willitt's two analyses of Soviet philosophy and ideology undertaken at Forrestal's request. The first analysis, dated January 14, 1946, is titled "Dialectical Materialism and Russian Objectives"; the second, dated January 22, 1946, is titled "Communist versus Christian Concepts of Man." John Vincent Forrestal Papers (JVFP), Miscellaneous Files, Box 18, Psychological Background of Soviet Foreign Policy Folder, Seely–Mudd Library, Princeton University. For an interesting analysis of how George Kennan and John Foster Dulles conceived the relationship between American capitalism and the type of citizenry it produces, see Guy Oakes, "The Cold War Ethic: National Security and National Morale," *International Journal of Politics, Culture and Society* 6 (Spring 1993):390–401.

7. For example, in 1946, when plans for a massive demobilization program were getting underway, there was tremendous resistance by individuals like John Foster Dulles and Forrestal. They were concerned with the "national drift toward a state of not only physical but also mental demobilization." This worry was directly related to the issue of whether the United States was prepared to battle the "crusading spirit" of the Soviet Union. See Daniel Yergin, *Shattered Peace: The Origins of the Cold War and the National Security State* (Boston: Houghton Mifflin, 1977), pp. 193–220, quotation on p. 218. Also see James Forrestal's comments concerning postwar planning and its integral link to a strong, mobilized, domestic political and industrial base. This view was at odds with the public's view of postwar demobilization. JVFP, Miscellaneous Files, Box 44, 1947 Folder, "Statement by James Vincent Forrestal before the President's Air Policy Commission," December 3, 1947, esp. p. 5. Finally, see Guy Oakes and Andrew Grossman, "Managing Nuclear Terror: The Genesis of American Civil Defense Strategy," *International Journal of Politics, Culture, and Society* 5 (Spring 1992):361–404.

8. Quoted in Will Brownell and Richard C. Billings, *So Close to Greatness: A Biography of William C. Bullitt* (New York: Macmillan, 1987), pp. 289–291, emphasis added.

9. These early war mobilization programs were highly disorganized. See Albert A. Blum, "Birth and Death of the M-Day Plans," in *American Civil-Military Decisions: A Book of Case Studies*, ed. Harold Stein (Birmingham: University of Alabama Press, 1963), pp. 63–96; U.S. Civilian Production Administration, *Industrial Mobilization for War: History of the War Production Board and Predecessor Agencies, 1940–1945*, vol. 1 (New York: Greenwood Press, 1969), pp. 3–17, 857–966; Calvin Lee Christman, "Ferdinand Eberstadt and the Economic Mobilization for War, 1941–1943" (Ph.D. diss., Ohio State University, 1971).

10. Two events crystallized this concern: the seizing of the Baltics and the deliberate delaying of the invasion of Poland in order to allow the retreating Nazis to destroy the Polish underground. See Yergin, *Shattered Peace*, pp. 169–171.

11. On the way that the Soviet threat was interpreted by both civilian and military advisors and the interplay between these two very important groups of advisors and experts, see Sherry, *Preparing for the Next War*, pp. 159–190.

12. Ibid., pp. 169–190.

13. For a fine example of how domestic sectional politics buffeted postwar planning, see Peter Trubowitz's *Defining the National Interest: Conflict and Change in American Foreign Policy* (Chicago: University of Chicago Press, 1998). Unlike Trubowitz, however, I argue that the key strategic issue regarding the Soviet Union and the circumscribing of its power was not an issue that was hotly contested.

14. The popularization of the concept and strategy of containment can cause some confusion. Much Cold War scholarship has canonized George Kennan's famous 1947 "X" article in *Foreign Affairs*. This public articulation of the containment thesis was an abridged version of Kennan's 1946 "Long Telegram" (see n. 6), an analysis of Soviet ideology, politics, and postwar grand strategic objectives and possible U.S. responses to those objectives. No doubt, the secret telegram was an important document that influenced policy planning. From the point of view of periodizing Cold War history, however, I think the *Foreign Affairs* article is overrated in its importance. Periodizing the "containment policy" of the United States around the 1947–1949 period and using as evidence the *Foreign Affairs* essay is, I believe, facile. Containment, as most people use the term, was a strategic concept that key civilian and military advisors agreed on by 1944. Strategically, one can argue that it is a commonsensical doctrine that was neither new nor a profound change, historically, in U.S. foreign policy. See "Mr. X" [George F. Kennan], "The Sources of Soviet Conduct," *Foreign Affairs* 25 (July 1947):566–582; "Moscow Embassy Telegram # 511" [The Long Telegram], *FRUS*, 1946, vol. VI, pp. 696–709. For an in-depth examination of Kennan's view on containment, see David Mayers, "Containment and the Primacy of Diplomacy: George Kennan's Views, 1947–1948," *International Security* 11 (Summer 1986):124–162. On various ways that scholars have conceived the strategic significance of containment policies, see Stephen M. Walt,"The Case for Finite Containment: Analyzing U.S. Grand Strategy," *International Security* 14 (Summer 1989):5–49. For a contrary argument, see Robert Pollard, "The National Security State Reconsidered: Truman and Economic Containment, 1945–1950," in *The Truman Presidency*, ed. Michael J. Lacey (New York: Cambridge University Press, 1989), pp. 205–234.

15. Written to his friend Palmer Hoyt, the editor of the *Denver Post*. See Walter Millis, ed., *The Forrestal Diaries* (New York: Viking Press, 1951), p. 14. See also Townsend Hoopes and Douglas Brinkley, *Driven Patriot: The Life and Times of James Forrestal* (New York: Knopf, 1992).

16. See Averell Harriman to James V. Forrestal, April 4, 1945, in James Vincent Forrestal Diaries, Seely–Mudd Library, vol 2., Box 1, February 10, 1945–August 30, 1945, p. 3. The telegram concerned the penetration of the Western Allies by Soviet agents planted within the

Communist party structures. The whole telegram, however, is an interesting artifact in that it concisely sums up how a "hardline" consensus concerning the Soviet Union was taking shape by the end of the war. Most important, it indicates the swiftness with which moderate views would be marginalized. For more on the development of the anticommunist-Soviet containment consensus, see Yergin, *Shattered Peace*, pp. 221–272; Hoopes and Brinkley, *Driven Patriot*, pp. 246–259.

17. See Robert Latham, *The Liberal Moment: Modernity, Security, and the Making of Postwar International Order* (New York: Columbia University Press, 1997), pp. 142–195; Lynn Rachele Eden, "The Diplomacy of Force: Interests, the State, and the Making of American Military Policy in 1948" (Ph.D. diss., University of Michigan, 1985), pp. 83–126. The term "the gospel of national security" is Yergin's, *Shattered Peace*.

18. See, for example, postwar planning document SWNCC-282 (State-War-Navy Coordination Committee). This top secret document dealt with the formulation of U.S. military policy and was written in September 1945. The plan itself was not adopted, but was supplanted by a more aggressive formulation as relations with the Soviet Union deteriorated. See Etzold and Gaddis, *Containment*, pp. 39–44.

19. Millis, *The Forrestal Diaries*, p. 100.

20. On the importance of domestic economic concerns, the postwar international political economy in Europe, and American national security planning, see Leffler, *A Preponderance of Power*, pp. 1–24, 55–99. Ultimately (by 1948) ideological and political plans of action were systematically integrated into overall American national security strategy. See, for example, the NSC-7 and NSC-20 series in *FRUS*, 1948, vol. 1, pp. 545–550, 589–624.

21. See "Report by F. Eberstadt to Arthur M. Hill, Chairman of the National Security Resources Board, 4, June 1948" (*The Eberstad Report*), PHST, White House Central Files (WHCF), Box 27, NSRB, Folder 1 of 10, p. 33.

22. I take the term "military-economic synthesis" from Alan S. Milward, *War, Economy and Society, 1939–1945* (Berkeley: University of California Press, 1977), pp. 20–54. For Baruch's reference to the atomic bomb, see Gregg Herken, *The Winning Weapon: The Atomic Bomb in the Cold War, 1945–1950* (New York: Knopf, 1980), p. 5.

23. On the "politics of sacrifice," on the home front during World War II, see Mark H. Leff, "The Politics of Sacrifice on the American Home Front in World War II," *Journal of American History* 77 (March 1991):1296–1318.

24. It is important to note that this was a *perception* of vulnerability. For an analysis and historical overview of how political leaders, citizens, and members of the press have perceived the vulnerability of the United States, see John A. Thompson, "The Exaggeration of American Vulnerability: The Anatomy of a Tradition," *Diplomatic History* 16 (Winter 1992):23–43.

25. For example, in late 1945, cartographic displays dealing with U.S. national security changed dramatically. Civilian and military advisors began to speak of a new "air frontier" in which the United States was depicted as wide open to future attack by aircraft, via new polar routes. On this point, see Yergin, *Shattered Peace*, p. 39. Also see the Social Science Research Council's study on the problem of U.S. vulnerability to atomic attack in Ansley J. Coale, *The Problem of Reducing Vulnerability to Atomic Attack* (Princeton, NJ: Princeton University Press, 1947). Finally, influential academics also discussed the issue of U.S. vulnerability in the atomic age, perhaps the most important work being Frederick A. Dunn, Bernard Brodie, Arnold Wolfers, Percy E. Corbett, and William T. R. Fox, *The Absolute Weapon* (New York: Harcourt, Brace, 1946).

26. See memo from Forrestal and Patterson to President Harry S. Truman, "Determination of the Agencies Responsible for Civil Defense and Anti-Sabotage Activities," November 29, 1946, p. 1, Papers of Harry S. Truman (PHST), President's Secretary Files (PSF), Box 117, General File–Civil Defense Folder.

27. Operations Crossroads consisted of two atomic tests on July 1 and July 26, 1946. The first test, code named ABLE, was intended to ascertain the effects of an air burst of a Nagasaki-

type bomb on a fleet of Navy ships. The second test, code named BAKER, attempted to determine the effects of an underwater atomic explosion on a fleet of warships. A third test, code-named CHARLIE, was canceled for reasons that were not revealed.

28. *Enclosure "A," The Evaluation of the Atomic Bomb as a Military Weapon*, June 30, 1947, PHST, PSF, Box 202, NSC–Atomic Crossroads Folder, pp. 1–37. The conclusions noted in the text can be found on pp. 10–12. Also see Coale, *Problem of Reducing Vulnerability to Atomic Attack*.

29. See Leffler, *A Preponderance of Power*. See also Michael J. Hogan, *A Cross of Iron: Harry S. Truman and the Origins of the National Security State* (Chicago: University of Chicago Press, 1998), especially pp. 69–118; Trubowitz, *Defining the National Interest*; Lynn Eden, "The End of Cold War History?" *International Security* 18 (Summer 1993):174–207; John Lewis Gaddis, *The Long Peace: Inquiries into the History of the Cold War* (New York: Oxford University Press, 1987); idem, *Strategies of Containment: A Critical Appraisal of Postwar American National Security Policy* (New York: Oxford University Press, 1982); idem, "International Relations Theory and the End of the Cold War," *International Security* 17 (Winter 1992/93):5–58; "Symposium" in *Diplomatic History* 15 (Fall 1991); and 16 (Winter 1992).

30. Leffler, *Preponderance of Power*, p. 145.

31. Public Law 253, 80th Cong., 1st Session, July 26, 1947, *U.S. Statutes At Large*, LXI, pp. 495–510. With respect to the rationalization of national security policy and the role of the National Security Act of 1947, see Secretary of State George Marshall's comments in *FRUS*, 1947, vol.1, pp. 712–715. See also PHST, Papers of Ralph N. Stohl, Box 1, National Security Act of 1947 folder.

32. See Trubowitz, *Defining the National Interest*.

33. Although they were not reestablished during the early Cold War period, I have in mind World War II agencies such as the War Production Board, the Office of War Mobilization and Reconversion, and the Office of War Information. Even though these presidential agencies received their share of criticism during the war and after, they represented a model for a centralized and structured relationship among the central state, the industrial sector, and the civilian sector that was understood as a requirement for swift mobilization planning in a world with weapons of mass destruction. See Yergin, *Shattered Peace*, pp. 215–217; Hoopes and Brinkley, *Driven Patriot*, p. 373.

34. See Robert J. McMahon, "Credibility and World Power: Exploring the Psychological Dimension in Postwar American Diplomacy," *Diplomatic History* 15 (Fall 1991):455–472. On the historical significance of psychology in the planning of national security and foreign policy, see Richard H. Immerman, "Psychology," in *Explaining the History of American Foreign Relations*, ed. Michael J. Hogan and Thomas G. Patterson (New York: Cambridge University Press, 1991), pp. 151–164.

35. *Enclosure "A," The Evaluation of the Atomic Bomb as a Military Weapon*, point 10, p. 12.

36. On the importance of mobilization readiness and modern warfare, see Martin van Creveld, "The Origins and the Development of Mobilization Warfare," in *Strategic Dimensions of Economic Behavior*, ed. Gordon H. McCormick and Richard E. Bissell (New York: Praeger, 1984), pp. 26–43.

37. See Oakes and Grossman, "Managing Nuclear Terror" pp. 361–403.

38. This was a running theme in popular magazines such as *Life* and *Collier's*. Also see "Defense Lack Seen as Pearl Harbor," *New York Times*, October 10, 1949, p. 9; "Baruch Is Critical of Defense Plans," *New York Times*, October 31, 1949, p. 41; U.S. Congress, Joint Committee on Atomic Energy, *Hearings, Civil Defense Against Atomic Attack*, 81st Congress, 2nd sess., 1950, pp. 140–150. Also see Thomas J. Kerr, *Civil Defense in the U.S.: Bandaid for a Holocaust?* (Boulder, CO: Westview Press, 1983), p. 24.

39. See Abe Fortas to Truman, September 26, 1945, "The Atomic Bomb and Atomic Energy," PHST, PSF, Box 112, Atomic Bomb Folder, p. 2. Regarding General Leslie Groves's incorrect estimate that it would take the Soviet Union as long as a generation to develop an atomic capability, see Memo, Franklin A. Lindsay to Bernard M. Baruch, September 12,

1946. Papers of Bernard M. Baruch, Unit X, Section 1, Box 56, Seely–Mudd Library. See also Marc Trachtenberg, "A 'Wasting Asset': American Strategy and the Shifting Nuclear Balance, 1949–1954," *International Security* 13 (Winter 1988/89):5–49.

40. This issue became more significant in the 1947–1948 period. However, President Roosevelt's postwar concept of the "four policeman" envisioned the United States as the sole nuclear power. See Sherry, *Preparing for the Next War*, p. 27. For more on nuclear diplomacy and its relationship to foreign policy and postwar crisis management, see *Nuclear Diplomacy and Crisis Management*, ed. Sean M. Lynn-Jones, Steven E. Miller, and Stephen Van Evera (Cambridge, MA: MIT Press, 1990); and Allan M. Winkler, *Life under a Cloud: American Anxiety about the Atom* (New York: Oxford University Press, 1993), pp. 57–83. For a history of the early years of the American nuclear arsenal, see David Aaron Rosenberg, "The Origins of Overkill: Nuclear Weapons and American Strategy, 1945–1960," *International Security* 7 (Spring 1993):1–71. On the policy implications for the loss of the nuclear monopoly, see Trachtenberg, "'Wasting Asset'"; Bernard Brodie, "A Commentary on the Preventive War Doctrine," in *The Development of American Strategic Thought*, vol. 3, ed. Marc Trachtenberg (New York: Garland Publishing, 1987), pp. 131–148.

41. See Spencer Weart, *Nuclear Fear: A History of Images* (Cambridge, MA: Harvard University Press, 1988), pp. 103–269; Oakes and Grossman, "Managing Nuclear Terror," pp. 368–371. See also Michael J. Yavendetti, "American Reactions to the Use of the Atomic Bombs on Japan, 1945–1947" (Ph.D. diss., University of California, Berkeley, 1970); Social Science Research Council, *Public Reaction to the Atomic Bomb and World Affairs: A Nation Wide Survey of Attitudes and Information* (Ithaca, NY: Cornell University, 1947); Gabriel A. Almond, *The American People and Foreign Policy* (New York: Praeger, 1960), pp. 106–115.

42. See Guy Oakes, "The Cold War Conception of Nuclear Reality: Mobilizing the American Imagination for Nuclear War in the 1950's," *International Journal of Politics, Culture and Society* 6 (Spring 1993):339–364; idem, *The Imaginary War: Civil Defense and the Genesis of American Cold War Culture* (New York: Oxford University Press, 1994). With regard to strategic thinking and civil defense, see U.S. Office for Civil Defense Planning, *Civil Defense for National Security* (Washington, DC: GPO, 1948) (*Hopley Report*); U.S. National Military Establishment, Office of the Secretary of Defense, War Department Civil Defense Board, *A Study of Civil Defense* (Washington, DC: GPO, 1948); and Wayne Boyce Blanchard, "American Civil Defense, 1945–1975: The Evolution of Programs and Policies" (Ph.D. diss., University of Virginia, 1980), pp. 26–100.

43. James Forrestal, in a 1945 statement to the House Military Affairs Committee, advocated universal military training. This plan failed; nevertheless a component of his statement touched on the link between deterrence and credibility. He noted in part: "The world must know with equal conviction that, much as we hate war, we are ready to wage swift and effective war against any nation which tries to overthrow rule by law and justice, replacing it with rule by force. We should make the determination clear—by deeds as well as words—to any dreamer anywhere who may be scheming for world dominion." See JVFP, Miscellaneous Files, Box 44, 1945 Folder, "Statement by James Vincent Forrestal to the House Military Affairs Committee On H.R. 515 'Universal Military Training,'" November 26, 1945, p. 2. Also see McMahon, "Credibility and World Power," pp. 457–462.

44. See, for example, Hadley Cantril and Gerard B. Lambert to Samuel I. Rosenman, Confidential Report, "Suggested Procedure to Make Administration's Post-War Policy Acceptable to the American Public," November 15, 1943, Franklin Delano Roosevelt Library, Official Files, "Postwar Problems," Box 3, November 1943 Folder, esp. p. 1.

45. Allan M. Winkler, *The Politics of Propaganda: The Office of War Information, 1942–1945* (New Haven, CT: Yale University Press, 1978); Winkler, *Home Front U.S.A.: America during World War II* (Chicago: Harlan Davidson, 1986); Robert Earnest Miller, "The War That Never Came: Civilian Defense, Mobilization, and Morale during World War II" (Ph.D. diss., University of Cincinnati, 1991).

46. See especially Harold G. Vatter, *The U.S. Economy in World War II* (New York: Columbia University Press, 1985), pp. 67–88, 113–145; Richard Franklin Bensel, *Sectionalism and American Political Development, 1880–1980* (Madison: University of Wisconsin Press, 1984); pp. 104–174, 175–255; Winkler, *Politics of Propaganda*; Robert Higgs, *Crisis and Leviathan*: Critical Episodes in the Growth of American Government (New York: Oxford University Press, 1987); idem, "Fifty Years of Arms, Politics, and the Economy," in *Arms, Politics, and the Economy*, ed. Robert Higgs (New York: Holmes & Meier, 1990), pp. xv–xxxii; Gregory Hooks, *Forging the Military-Industrial Complex: World War II's Battle of the Potomac* (Urbana: University of Illinois Press, 1991); Calvin Lee Christman, "Ferdinand Eberstadt and the Economic Mobilization for War, 1941–1943" (Ph.D. diss., Ohio State University, 1971).

47. Vatter, *The U.S. Economy*, p. 87, and esp. pp. 67–88. See also Civilian Production Administration, *Industrial Mobilization for War*, vol. 1; Herman Miles Somers, *Presidential Agency OWMR: The Office of War Mobilization and Reconversion* (Cambridge, MA: Harvard University Press, 1950).

48. On the importance placed on the recruitment of social scientists, especially those who were doing new research into the measurement of public opinion, see Memo of Philleo Nash, July 7, 1942, PHST, Papers of Philleo Nash, Box 3, OWI–General Folder, pp. 1–4. On the recruitment of academics within the "hard sciences" and evolving weapons technology, see Michael Sherry, *The Rise of American Air Power: The Creation of Armageddon* (New Haven, CT: Yale University Press, 1987). On the role of the universities from World War II into the Cold War, see Stuart W. Leslie, *The Cold War and American Science: The Military-Industrial-Academic Complex at MIT and Stanford* (New York: Columbia University Press, 1993), pp. 1–13, 188–211. On the relationship between epistemic communities and the state in general, see Peter M. Hass, "Introduction: Epistemic Communities and International Policy Coordination," *International Organization* 46 (Winter 1992):1–36; with regard to postwar American policy, see G. John Ikenberry, "A World Economy Restored: Expert Consensus and the Anglo-American Postwar Settlement," ibid., pp. 289–322. On organizational planning derived from experts within the business sector, see especially Jeffrey M. Dorwart, *Eberstadt and Forrestal: A National Security Partnership, 1909–1949* (College Station: Texas A&M University Press, 1991), pp. 3–11, 30–171; Hoopes and Brinkley, *Driven Patriot*; and Somers, *Presidential Agency*.

49. The Office of War Information managed domestic propaganda by building strong links among popular press outlets, Hollywood, community organizations, association and trade groups, and the federal government. The OWI also engaged in a sophisticated public opinion analysis that depended on the input of social scientists and statisticians working in the Office of Facts and Figures, which was folded into the OWI. The OCD worked closely with the OWI when it instituted its morale-building campaigns. During the early Cold War, the roles of the OWI and the OCD were folded into one program. For an interesting and thorough history of the OWI, see Winkler, *Politics of Propaganda*. See also Clayton R. Koppes and Gregory D. Black, *Hollywood Goes to War: How Politics, Profits, and Propaganda Shaped World War II Movies* (New York: The Free Press 1987); Richard W. Steele, "Preparing the Public for War: Efforts to Establish a National Propaganda Agency," *American Historical Review* 75 (October 1970): 1640–1653. On the OCD, see especially Miller, "The War That Never Came"; Miller, "Combating Complacency on the Home Front: The Office of Civilian Defense, Voluntarism, and Wartime Morale, 1941–1945," paper delivered at the annual meeting of the American Historical Association, Washington, DC, 1993; James Edward Tobin, "Why We Fight: Versions of the American Purpose in World War II" (Ph.D. diss., University of Michigan, 1986).

50. Political sociologists interested in institutional development and institutional capacity have begun to examine in more detail the way in which the United States organized for war mobilization between 1941 and 1945. For example, Gregory Hooks argues that the institutional arrangements and experience of social planning from the New Deal period were

folded into the war-making project of the 1940s and then carried forward into the Cold War. Hooks, *Forging the Military-Industrial Complex*, pp. 225–276. Economic historian Harold Vatter also illustrates the links between the war effort and postwar institutional continuity, especially the macroeconomic consequences of U.S. victory in World War II. *U.S. Economy in World War II*, pp. 145–70.

51. Martin van Creveld, "Origins and Development of Mobilization Warfare." John Ohly, Ferdinand Eberstadt, and John R. Steelman were all recruited into the government during World War II to help in the mobilization and war-fighting efforts. Eberstadt was a close friend of James Forrestal and an extremely successful Wall Street investment banker and lawyer who pioneered the development of mutual funds. Eberstadt was at Princeton with Forrestal and worked with him at the Wall Street firm of Dillon Read during the 1920s. He held positions in the War Production Board and acted as an advisor on national security organizational planning throughout the Cold War until his death in 1969. For a meticulous examination of the Forrestal/Eberstadt relationship and in particular each man's view that an enlightened corporatism was the best model for postwar national security mobilization, see Dowart, *Eberstadt and Forrestal*. John R. Steelman was Assistant to the President from 1946 to 1953. He headed the Office of War Mobilization and Reconversion and later the NSRB. John Ohly was perhaps the most important individual involved in organizing postwar mobilization planning. He was essentially a "behind-the-scenes" organizational specialist. He held the position of Assistant Secretary of War, 1940–1946; Special Assistant to the Secretary of Defense, 1947–1949; and Assistant Director for Programs and Deputy Director for Plans and Programs, Mutual Security Agency, 1951–1958. One thing that all four of these very influential advisors had in common was the view that the United States had to remain fully engaged in international affairs and that postwar national security policy ultimately depended on an integrated domestic mobilization readiness plan. In the early postwar years, this viewpoint was at odds with the popularly held wish for swift postwar demobilization.

52. See Eberstadt's 5/15/48 diary entry on this issue in Ferdinand Eberstadt Papers (FEP), Seely–Mudd Library, Box 113, NSRB Diary Entries Folder. Eberstadt was concerned that a lack of a rationalized postwar mobilization plan linked to a reorganized national security establishment would lead to the chaotic planning that occurred between World War I and mid-1942. For more on the early mobilization plans and their shortcomings, see William L. O'Neill, *A Democracy at War: America's Fight at Home and Abroad in World War II* (New York: The Free Press, 1993), pp. 75–103.

53. Memo by the Deputy Director of the Office of European Affairs (Hickerson) to the Director of the Office of European Affairs (Matthews), *FRUS*, 1947, vol. 1, pp. 715–716.

54. The concept of "defense-in-depth" mobilization was applied and put into operation during World War II. The official history of the World War II superagency, the War Production Board, discussed the concept in the following way: "Industrial mobilization in World War II required a 'defense in depth' that reached from the individual homes and factories to the battlefronts abroad." The NSRB adopted this concept, especially in its home-front mobilization plans. See U.S. Civilian Production Administration, *Industrial Mobilization for War*, p. 969.

55. See *The Eberstadt Report*, pp. 7–8. For an analysis of the implications and politics of the report see Dowart, *Eberstadt and Forrestal*, pp. 90–108.

56. See FEP, NSRB Chronological Files, Box 113, *Summary of Special Presentation to the President and Members of the Board, by the Staff of NSRB*, December 10, 1948, NSRB Doc. 97, "The Principles of Mobilization Planning," p. 2.

57. The NSRB's plans for state survival in time of war clearly illustrate this point. Top priority was assigned to planning for systematic industrial dispersal (most of which ultimately was not implemented), a domestic industrial "security policy" (which was implemented in conjunction with the FBI), and continuity of government after atomic attack, plans for which remain highly classified and mostly inaccessible to researchers. See for example, "Basic

Principles and Assumptions Governing Preparation of the Long-Range Plan for the Security of the Nation's Capitol," NA, NSRB, RG-304, Box 94, Folder E4-12; James T. Martin to V. B. Lamoureux for Norvin C. Kiefer, Director Health Resources Division, December 30, 1949, assignments 80–94. NA, Office of Civil Defense Mobilization, RG-304, Box 12, Civil Disaster in Wartime Folder E4-13. On industrial plant security and relocation, see Frank M. Shields, Director, Productions Office, to Stuart Symington, "Industrial Security," July 20, 1950, NA, OCDM, Box 11, Industrial Security and Plant Relocation File E4-7.

58. See NSRB Doc. 76, August 19, 1948, "Preliminary Statement on Guiding Principles and Program Framework for Mobilization Planning," PHST, WHCF, Box 27, NSRB Folder 1. War mobilization planning within the NSRB reflected one view of modern war, the rationalization of postwar national security policy, and postwar international relations with the Soviets. The NSRB plans were grounded on the basic premise, to which the Air Force was also committed, that warfare was revolutionized by atomic weapons. Modern war would take the form of global nuclear war, dependent on rapid mobilization and air power. The only enemy would be the Soviet Union. This view of modern war was contested by key diplomats such as George Kennan. Kennan claimed that the Soviets did not want global war with the United States; he argued that they would try to achieve their grand strategic goals through political and ideological means. See, for example, "Resume of World Situation," PPS/13 (George Kennan), *FRUS*, 1947, Volume 1, pp. 770–777. With regard to early worst-case-scenario war-planning, see Steven T. Ross, *American War Plans, 1945–1950* (New York: Garland Publishing, 1988); David Alan Rosenberg, "U.S. Nuclear War Planning, 1945–1960," in *Strategic Nuclear Targeting*, ed. Desmond Ball and Jeffrey Richelson (Ithaca, NY: Cornell University Press, 1986), pp. 35–56.

59. In 1948, the NSRB produced a detailed prospectus for a comprehensive, national civil defense program. The report, which was met with election-year resistance and heartfelt skepticism by some, nevertheless became the basic document on which the civil defense program of the early 1950s was based. The report clearly outlined how the central state would manage civilian defense operations. Key to this outline was the creation of a relationship between the federal government and state and community governments that gave the illusion of minimal central state expansion. See *Hopley Report*. On the use of World War II as the baseline experience for civilian mobilization within the NSRB, see PHST, Confidential File, Box 27, NSRB Document 116/2, NSRB Folder 3 of 10, dated 11/25/49.

60. This was the ill-received *Hopley Report*. See also Memorandum, Forrestal to Truman, November 8, 1948, PHST, OF, Box 1651, Office of Civil Defense Planning Folder; Assistant Secretary of Defense John S. Gorman to Forrestal, November 23, 1948, PHST, Papers of John W. Snyder, Box 5, Civil Defense–General 1948 Folder, pp. 1–5. For a detailed history of the different civil defense studies undertaken from 1946 to 1948, see Nehemiah Jordan, *U.S. Civil Defense before 1950: The Roots of Public Law 920*, Study S–212 (Washington, DC: Institute for Defense Analyses Economic and Political Studies Division, May 1966).

61. *Hopley Report*, p. 13.

62. Regarding civil defense plans in the U.S., see Oakes and Grossman, "Managing Nuclear Terror," pp. 376–382. On the curious but common phenomenon of conceptualizing nuclear weapons as powerful conventional weapons, see Hans Morgenthau, "The Fallacy of Thinking Conventionally about Nuclear Weapons," in *Arms Control and Technological Innovation*, ed. David Carlton and Carlow Schaef (New York: Wiley, 1976), pp. 256–264; and Robert Jervis, *The Illogic of American Nuclear Strategy* (Ithaca, NY: Cornell University Press, 1984).

63. United States National Security Resources Board, NSRB Doc. 130, *Survival Under Atomic Attack* (Washington, DC: GPO, 1950), cover page and p. 4.

64. See, for example, the *Hopley Report*; "Progress Report on Civil Defense Planning Under the N.S.R.B. March 3, 1949–March 3, 1950," NA, NSRB, RG-304, Box 94, Folder E4-12. See also Oakes and Grossman, "Managing Nuclear Terror," pp. 361–403; Jordan, *U.S. Civil Defense before 1950*; Lyon G. Tyler, "Civil Defense: The Impact of the Planning Years, 1945–1950" (Ph.D diss., Duke University, 1967); and Kerr, *Civil Defense in the U.S.: Bandaid for a Holocaust?*

65. See "Remarks of Russell J. Hopley Before the First Army Advisory Committee," May 26, 1948, PHST, OF, Box 1651, Office of Civil Defense Planning, Folder 1285M, p. 6. Hopley was making the case for comprehensive, national civil defense in his report to James Forrestal. Interestingly, Hopley was not aware of the top-secret evaluation of the Crossroads test, which indicated contamination of wide areas around the test sites, undermining his claim for an absolutely "safe" and benign atomic weapons test in the South Pacific in 1946. For more on the importance of mass education to garner support for continuous mobilization planning and civil defense, see *The Eberstadt Report*, p. 33.

66. On the discovery of the Soviet atomic device and its ramifications, see memorandum, Hoyt Vandenberg to Truman confirming the Soviet atomic bomb test as taking place sometime between August 8 and August 29, 1949, in PHST, PSF, NSC–Atomic Bomb, Box 199, Atomic Bomb Long Range Detection Program Folder. See also Jess Larsen, Administrator of the General Services Administration to Stuart Symington, Chairman NSRB, August 17, 1950 in NA, OCDM, RG-304, Box 12, Wartime Disaster Relief Folder. For more on the overall political effects of the discovery in Washington and the way national security planners reacted, see Walter Isaacson and Evan Thomas, *The Wise Men: Six Friends and the World They Made* (New York: Simon and Schuster, 1986), p. 480. For an analysis of the strategic ramifications of the Soviet atomic capability and its effects on U.S. Cold War policy, see Leffler, *Preponderance of Power*, pp. 9, 369–370; Randall B. Woods and Howard Jones, *Dawning of the Cold War: The United States' Quest for World Order* (Athens: University of Georgia Press, 1991), pp. 248–255. For a chilling analysis of how war fear drove policy planners at the highest levels of the American government to seriously consider a preemptive atomic attack on the Soviet Union, see Trachtenberg, "'A Wasting Asset.'" Finally, for provocative treatment of the "war scare" of 1948, see Frank Kofsky, *Harry S. Truman and the War Scare of 1948: A Successful Campaign to Deceive the Nation* (New York: St. Martin's Press, 1993).

67. According to a Gallup Poll conducted in August 1950, 57 percent felt World War III was underway. In an earlier Gallup Poll conducted in January 1950, 70 percent believed the Soviet Union was "out to take over the world." By November 1950 (five months after the start of the Korean War), 81 percent polled thought the Soviets were seeking world conquest. See *Gallup Poll of Public Opinion, 1935–1971*, vol. 2 (New York: Random House, 1972), pp. 949, 993.

68. Cannon to Truman, August 17, 1950. PHST, OF, Box 1671, Folder 1591, p. 4. The letter dealt with using community organizations to supplement the civil defense programs.

69. See Trachtenberg, "'A Wasting Asset,'" pp. 5–18.

70. See Oakes, "The Cold War Ethic," pp. 385–390; Oakes and Grossman, "Managing Nuclear Terror," pp. 362–371; Winkler, *Life Under a Cloud*, pp. 109–135; and *Survival Under Atomic Attack*.

71. Quoted in Etzold and Gaddis, *Containment*, p. 442. The Korean War and the advent of Soviet atomic capability inspired fundamental changes in national security policy in the United States. The result was a reformulation of postwar U.S. grand strategy and a massive reorganization of national security policy. The key document here is NSC-68. On the domestic scene, the internalization of the Cold War emergency and its dictates produced the McCarthyite "Red Scare" and the illiberal behavior of the House Un-American Activities Committee. On NSC-68, see Etzold and Gaddis, pp. 385–442; Samuel F. Wells,

"Sounding the Tocsin: NSC–68 and the Soviet Threat," *International Security* 4 (Fall 1979):116–158; Gaddis, *Strategies of Containment*; Paul Hammond, "NSC-68: Prologue to Rearmament," in *Strategy, Politics, and Defense Budgets*, ed. Warner Schilling, Paul Hammond, and Glenn Snyder (New York: Columbia University Press, 1962); and Tractenberg, "'Wasting Asset,'" pp. 111–118.

72. See, for example, *FRUS*, 1950, vol. 1, pp. 324–347.

73. Civil Defense Act of 1950, Public Law 920, 81st Congress, 2nd session. See, too, *Congressional Record*, 81st Congress, 2nd session, pp. 16825, 16841–16843. For a complete text of the original Federal Civil Defense Act and the various amendments that were attached over the years, see Federal Civil Defense Administration, "The National Plan for Civil Defense against Enemy Attack" (Washington, DC: GPO, 1956), pp. 77–103.

74. There was complete organizational continuity between the NSRB and the FCDA. The OCDP was folded whole into the FCDA, which then operationalized OCDP plans. See the NSRB plan for the transfer of civil defense operations in United States National Security Resources Board, NSRB Doc. 128, *United States Civil Defense* (Washington, DC: GPO, 1950). For more detail on the transfer of duties and institutional continuity, see Tyler, "Civil Defense of the Impact of the Planning Years"; and Kerr, *Civil Defense in the U.S.*

75. An example of the relationship between the Ad Council and the FCDA can be seen in the radio and television civil defense promotion programming. These media mobilization projects, which are discussed in more detail in Chapter Three, usually were managed by the Ad Council under the guidance of the FCDA's public affairs office. In one week, April 9–15, 1951, NBC, ABC, and CBS ran promotional campaigns for civil defense on both radio and television on the hour and half hour. See NA, FCDA, RG-304, Survival Manual Plans Folder, FCDA, Bulletin No. 15, "Radio Industry Promotion on Air Raid Instruction Cards." On the use of film, see PHST, internal memorandum, "The Federal Civil Defense Audio-Visual Program," Files of Spencer R. Quick, Box 5, Civil Defense Correspondence Folder.

76. See U.S. Federal Civil Defense Administration, *Annual Report for 1951* (Washington, DC: GPO, 1951), esp. pp. 5–28.

77. As has been noted, it was in the area of developing a program for panic prevention that both the NSRB and the FCDA used their extensive links to the academic community and agents of the popular media to develop the basic framework for selling an imaginary conception of atomic war. The influential civil defense study, *Project East River* (published in 1952), is an example of the mobilization of these societal links. See "Information and Training for Civil Defense," *Project East River*, Part IX. NA, NSRB, RG-304, Box 19, Project East River Folder. See specifically "Panic Prevention and Control," Appendix IXB of *Project East River*, Part IX, pp. 55–65. On the interesting and important role of the Ad Council, especially with regard to the phenomenon of constructing an alternative reality, in this case a mythical nuclear reality that is then sold by the central state and quasi-private sector organizations such as the Ad Council to the general population, see Frank W. Fox, "Advertising and the Second World War: A Study in Private Propaganda" (Ph.D. diss., Stanford University, 1973); idem, *Madison Avenue Goes to War: The Strange Military Career of American Advertising, 1941–1945* (Provo: University of Utah Press, 1975); Robert Griffith, "The Selling of America: The Advertising Council and American Politics, 1942–1960," *Business History Review* 57 (Autumn 1983):338–412; and John Vianney McGinnis, "The Advertising Council and the Cold War" (Ph.D. diss., Syracuse University, 1991). Finally, for an overview of the cultural effects of the "domestication" of atomic weapons on American society as a whole, see Paul Boyer, *By the Bomb's Early Light: American Thought and Culture at the Dawn of the Atomic Age* (New York: Pantheon, 1985).

78. See Chapter Four for an analysis of the use of the public school system by the FCDA. The famous "duck-and-cover" campaign used a cartoon character dubbed "Bert the Turtle" to teach school-age children to protect themselves in an atomic attack. See JoAnne Brown, "A Is for Atom, B Is for Bomb: Civil Defense in American Public Education, 1948–1963," *Journal of American History* 75 (June 1988):68–90.

Chapter 3: From Civic Education to Social Control

1. U.S. National Security Resources Board, NSRB Doc.128, *United States Civil Defense* (Washington, DC: GPO, 1950), p. 7 (hereafter, the *Blue Book*).

2. The theory that fear could be used to channel the emotions of large groups emerged from military-strategic studies undertaken during World War II that were primarily concerned with the emotional and economic effects of warfare, specifically massive strategic bombing of cities and its effect on national morale. For example, both NSRB emergency war-planning and the FCDA operations used U.S. Strategic Bombing Surveys in their analyses of the emotional effects of strategic bombing and its effects on morale. These surveys, whose conclusions, in retrospect, are suspect on a number of levels, were nevertheless taken quite seriously. The surveys were "after-action" studies of the bombing campaigns undertaken by the Allies during World War II against Germany and Japan and represented some of the best available data on this issue at the time. They furnished planners with detailed analyses of the cumulative social, political, and economic effects of strategic bombing. In the early 1950s, a civilian defense analysis entitled *Project East River* offered a study of all aspects of civilian defense in the atomic age, placing great emphasis on the idea that panic prevention could be handled by channeling fear through routinization and training. On morale and the strategic bombing surveys, see "The Effects of Strategic Bombing on German Morale," *The United States Strategic Bombing Survey*, vols. I and II (Washington, DC: GPO, 1946); "Overall Report (European War)," *The United States Strategic Bombing Survey* (Washington, DC: GPO, 1945), pp. 95–105. For a concise overview of the surveys and their importance, see Gordon Daniels, ed., *A Guide to the Reports of the United States Strategic Bombing Survey* (London: Royal Historical Society, 1981), pp. xvi–xxvi. With regard to *Project East River*, see especially National Archives (NA), National Security Resources Board (NSRB), Records Group-304 (RG), Box 19, Project East River Folder, "Information and Training for Civil Defense," *Project East River*, Part IX, specifically, "Panic Prevention and Control," Appendix IXB, pp. 55–65.

3. See especially Hans J. Morgenthau, "The Fallacy of Thinking Conventionally about Nuclear Weapons," in *Arms Control and Technological Innovation*, ed. David Carlton and Carlo Schaerf (New York: Wiley, 1976), pp. 255–264. Also see Solly Zuckerman, *Nuclear Illusion and Reality* (New York: Viking Press, 1982), esp. pp. 15–78. The view that nuclear war was just another kind of warfare and could be planned for as if it were essentially a con-ventional war was standard operating procedure within the U.S. military as well. See David Alan Rosenberg, "U.S. Nuclear War Planning, 1945–1960," in *Strategic Nuclear Targeting* ed. Desmond Ball and Jeffrey Richelson (Ithaca, NY: Cornell University Press, 1986), pp. 35–56; Desmond Ball, "The Development of the SIOP, 1960–1983, ibid., pp. 57–83.

4. For an analysis of technological innovation, war, and the inexorable blurring of distinctions between civilians and combatants, see John Keegan, *The Face of Battle* (New York: Viking Penguin, 1976); Martin van Creveld, *The Transformation of War* (New York: The Free Press, 1991); and idem, *Technology and War: From 2000 B.C. to the Present* (New York: The Free Press, 1989), pp. 153–311. On the salient arguments surrounding the development of early nuclear strategy and deterrence theory, see Frederick A. Dunn, Bernard Brodie, Arnold Wolfers, Percy E. Corbett, and William T. R. Fox, *The Absolute Weapon* (New York: Harcourt Brace, 1946); Bernard Brodie's essays in *The Development of American Strategic Thought*, vol. 3, ed. Marc Trachtenberg (New York: Garland Publishing, 1987), pp.1–148; idem, "The Development of Nuclear Strategy," *International Security* 3 (Spring 1978):65–83; Jacob Viner, "Implications of the Atomic Bomb for International Relations," in Trachtenberg, vol. 2, pp. 1–6; Alexander L. George and Richard Smoke, *Deterrence in American Foreign Policy* (New York: Columbia University Press, 1974); Lynn Eden and Steven E. Miller, eds., *Nuclear Arguments: Understanding the Strategic Nuclear Arms and Arms Control Debates* (Ithaca, NY: Cornell University Press, 1989); Lawrence Freedman, *The Evolution of Nuclear Strategy* (New York: St. Martin's Press, 1989); Robert Jervis, Richard Ned Lebow, and Janice Gross Stein, *Psychology and Deterrence* (Baltimore, MD: Johns Hopkins University Press, 1989).

5. *Enclosure "A," The Evaluation of the Atomic Bomb as a Military Weapon*, June 30, 1947, PHST, President's Secretary's Files (PSF), Box 202, NSC–Atomic Crossroads Folder, p. 11 (hereafter "Enclosure A"). Also see Marc Trachtenberg, "'A Wasting Asset': American Strategy and the Shifting Nuclear Balance, 1949–1954," *International Security* 13 (Winter 1988/89):5–49.

6. Quoted in Fred Kaplan, *The Wizards of Armageddon* (New York: Simon and Schuster, 1983), p. 10.

7. The original three members who began Yale's Institute of International Studies in 1935 were Nicholas Spykman, Arnold Wolfers, and Frederick Dunn. They were subsequently joined by Bernard Brodie, Jacob Viner, William T. R. Fox, and Klaus Knorr. For more on the history of the institute and its members' contributions to postwar strategic thinking in the United States, see ibid, pp. 19–23.

8. For two excellent but competing interpretations of how "revolutionary" nuclear war was, see John Mueller, "The Escalating Irrelevance of Nuclear Weapons," and Colin Gray, "Nuclear Weapons and the Revolution in Military Affairs," both in *The Absolute Weapon Revisited: Nuclear Arms and the Emerging International Order* ed. T. V. Paul, Richard J. Harknett, and James J. Wirz, (Ann Arbor: University of Michigan Press, 1998), pp. 73–98, 99–136.

9. On nuclear diplomacy, its relationship to foreign policy and postwar crisis management, deterrence, and the home front, see Sean M. Lynn-Jones, Steven E. Miller, and Stephen Van Evera, eds., *Nuclear Diplomacy and Crisis Management* (Cambridge, MA: MIT Press, 1990); Allan M. Winkler, *Life Under a Cloud: American Anxiety about the Atom* (New York: Oxford University Press, 1993), pp. 57–83; and Jervis, Lebow, and Stein, *Psychology and Deterrence*. For a history of the early years of the American nuclear arsenal, see David Aaron Rosenberg, "The Origins of Overkill: Nuclear Weapons and American Strategy, 1945–1960," *International Security* 7 (Spring 1993). On the policy implications for the loss of the nuclear monopoly, see Trachtenberg, "'Wasting Asset'"; Bernard Brodie, "A Commentary On The Preventive War Doctrine," in Trachtenberg, *Development of American Strategic Thought*, vol. 3, pp. 131–148.

10. On this "social dimension" of nuclear strategy and the importance of national morale in deterrence theory, see Philip Bobbitt, *Democracy and Deterrence: The History and Future of Nuclear Strategy* (New York: St. Martin's Press, 1988), pp. 3–19, 110–133; Charles Reynolds, "Explaining the Cold War," in *Deconstructing and Reconstructing the Cold War*, ed. Alan P. Dobson (Aldershot, Great Britain: Ashgate Publishing, 1999), pp. 44–66.

11. See Nehemiah Jordan, *U.S. Civil Defense before 1950: The Roots of Public Law 920* (Washington, DC: Institute for Defense Analyses, 1966), pp. 1–78.

12. See Ansley J. Coale, *The Problem of Reducing Vulnerability to Atomic Attack* (Princeton, NJ: Princeton University Press, 1947). On the theoretical relationship between communication and deterrence, see especially Thomas C. Schelling, *Arms and Influence* (New Haven, CT: Yale University Press, 1966); Jervis et al., *Psychology and Deterrence*, pp. 13–33, 125–152.

13. For more on the psychological presuppositions that inhere in deterrence theory and the potential problems for communication, rationality, and understanding between nation-states during crises, see Jervis et al., *Psychology and Deterrence*, 1–34, 60–125, 203–232.

14. FCDA administrator Millard F. Caldwell, Jr., considered that many people were like ostriches—hiding from the brutal reality of modern war. "If we are going to be prepared for modern war we have got to get rid of our atomic ostrichism." See Millard Caldwell address to the Annual Conference of Mayors, PHST, Papers of Spencer R. Quick, Box 5, Civil Defense Campaign Folder 1, p. 3. Also see Andrew Grossman, "Atomic Fantasies and Make-Believe War: The American State, Social Control and Civil Defense Planning, 1946–1952," *Political Power and Social Theory* 9 (1995): 91–120; Guy Oakes and Andrew Grossman, "Managing Nuclear Terror: The Genesis of American Civil Defense Strategy,"

International Journal of Politics, Culture, and Society 5 (Spring 1992):361–403; and Guy Oakes, "The Cold War Ethic: National Security and National Morale," *International Journal of Politics and Culture* 6 (Spring 1993):391–400. The concept of a "national will" that is then linked to the notion that nation-states have collective personalities, as if they were living organisms, is analyzed in some detail by historian Daniel Pick, *War Machine: The Rationalization of Slaughter in the Modern Age* (New Haven, CT: Yale University Press, 1993), pp. 75–87, esp. p. 85.

15. "Enclosure A," p. 37. For more on the concept of nuclear terror, see Oakes and Grossman, "Managing Nuclear Terror," pp. 365–368.

16. "Enclosure A," p. 36.

17. The idea that political elites view themselves very differently from the populace they govern is not new; it is a Burkean view, if you will, of democracy. This commitment to democracy with very high limits—ultimately illiberal—in its structure, was very much part of George Kennan's world view. See Guy Oakes, *The Imaginary War: Civil Defense and Cold War Culture* (New York: Oxford University Press, 1994), pp. 25–30. Don Herzog's work also offers an excellent philosophical investigation of the "conservative inheritance" that configures the classic elite view of democracy. *Poisoning the Minds of the Lower Orders* (Princeton, NJ: Princeton University Press, 1998).

18. The Research Branch, Information and Education Division of the War Department undertook a series of social-psychological studies that eventually were published in four volumes under the title *Studies in Social Psychology in World War II*. The attempt to scientifically grasp how people understood messages embodied in propaganda films and other forms of mass communication took on great importance during the early Cold War period. See, for example, volume III of the *Studies in Social Psychology*, Carl I. Hovland, Arthur A. Lunsdaine, and Fred D. Sheffield, eds., *Experiments on Mass Communication* (Princeton, NJ: Princeton University Press, 1949). Especially see the series of conference papers presented at the New York Academy of Medicine and the Josiah Macy, Jr., Foundation on February 2, 1951, and November 3–6, 1954, in *Panic and Morale*, ed. Iago Galdston and Hans Zetterberg (New York: International Universities Press, 1958). See Chapter Five for a detailed analysis of how a "strategic" view of morale developed and its consequences for postwar American political development.

19. See Hans Speier, "Morale and Propaganda," in *Propaganda in War and Crisis*, ed. Daniel Lerner (New York: Arno Press, 1972), pp. 3–25, quotation p. 6, emphasis in the original. Also see idem, "The Future of Psychological Warfare," *Public Opinion Quarterly* 12 (Spring 1948).

20. See, for example, Spencer Weart, *Nuclear Fear: A History of Images* (Cambridge, MA: Harvard University Press, 1988), pp. 155–262; Grossman, "Atomic Fantasies and Make-Believe War," pp. 91–120.

21. See, for example, *Panic and Morale*. See also Michael Choukas, *Propaganda Comes of Age* (Washington, DC: Public Affairs Press, 1965), pp. 39–61.

22. See National Security Resources Board, NSRB Doc. 130, *Survival Under Atomic Attack* (Washington, DC: GPO, 1950).

23. On the importance of administrative continuity to World War II, especially in the area of advertising and home front mobilization, see Papers of John T. Gibson, Harry S. Truman Library, Box 2, Advertising Council Miscellaneous 1945–47 Folder.

24. Letter from Arthur Feldman, Director of Special Events, Mutual Broadcasting System, to Jesse Butcher, Chief, Audio-Visual Division, Federal Civil Defense Administration, February 15, 1951, NA, OCDM, RG-304, Box 13, Civil Defense Film File.

25. Series of letters—2/13, 14, 17, 20, 21 (1951)—between NBC, CBS, Jesse Butcher, DeChant re: Caldwell Appearances. NA, RG-304, OCDM, Box 14, "Television Programs File."

26. See NA, FCDA, RG-304, Survival Manual Plans Folder, Federal Civil Defense Administration, Bulletin No. 15, "Radio Industry Promotion on Air Raid Instruction

Cards." Regarding film, see especially PHST, Files of Spencer R. Quick, Box 5, Civil Defense Campaign Correspondence Folder, "The Federal Civil Defense Audio-Visual Program," undated, pp. 1–7.

27. See the letter from photographer Ansel Adams to Mr. Joseph Short, Press Secretary to President Truman, offering his expertise in support of the FCDA and civil defense preparedness training. Ansel Adams to Joseph Short, January 2, 1951, NA, RG-304, OCDM, Civil Defense Contacts and Businesses File. See also the response to Adams' note by John A. DeChant, Public Affairs Division of the FCDA. John DeChant to Ansel Adams, January 12, 1951, NA, RG-304, OCDM, Civil Defense Contacts and Business File.

28. Leslie L. Kullenberg to John G. Bradley, October 18, 1950, memo entitled, "Motion Pictures in Civil Defense," pp. 1–2. NA, OCDM, RG-304, Box 13, Civil Defense Films Folder, E4-31.

29. Although I am in disagreement with his overall thesis about the garrisoning process and its effects on postwar American political development in general, an excellent analysis of how facets of the Cold War mobilization process were parsed out by the Truman administration to private sector businesses can be found in Aaron Friedberg's scholarship. See "Why the United States Did Not Become a Garrison State," *International Security* 16 (Spring 1992):109–142.

30. See letter from Carl Vinson to Millard F. Caldwell, January 25, 1951, NA, OCDM, Box 12, Civil Defense Training, General File. Also see Richard Nixon to Millard F. Caldwell, January 30, 1951, NA, OCDM, Box 12, Civil Defense Training, General File.

31. For background on how the Ad Council came to be, see Frank W. Fox, "Advertising and the Second World War: A Study in Private Propaganda" (Ph.D. diss., Stanford University, 1973), pp. 147–149; John Vianney McGinnis, "The Advertising Council and the Cold War" (Ph.D. diss, Syracuse University, 1991).

32. See the discussion concerning the Ad Council's program for marketing civil defense instruction cards, in PHST, Files of Spencer Quick, Box 1, Civil Defense Program Folder, letter from Edward B. Lyman, Office of Public Affairs, Federal Civil Defense Administration, to Charles W. Jackson, Assistant to the White House, August 3, 1951, pp. 1–2. For a complete picture of the Ad Council's role in the marketing of FCDA programs and literature, see October 23, 1951, memorandum, John A. DeChant to Joseph Short, "Alert America Campaign," PHST, Official File, Box 1671, Folder 1591-C, pp. 1–15.

33. The FCDA's relationship with the Ad Council was often strained. During World War II, the use of sophisticated advertising was part of the overall domestic home-front propaganda program run by the OWI. During this experience there developed serious tensions between bureaucrats and advertising specialists from Madison Avenue. In short, there was basically tremendous distrust of professional admen among some members of the government because they believed that "Madison Avenue" was really out to protect itself—by offering to do government-sponsored work gratis—from wartime emergency controls. This interpretation of why and how "Madison Avenue went to war" was not incorrect. Nevertheless, modern advertising techniques were very useful at making American wartime propaganda highly professional in terms of its aesthetic quality and were ultimately more successful than, for example, the more heavy-handed German war propaganda. For more on the history of the Ad Council and its wartime effort and place in the overall propaganda effort during the war and the postwar period, see Fox, "Advertising and the Second World War"; Frank W. Fox, *Madison Avenue Goes to War: The Strange Military Career of American Advertising, 1941–1945* (Provo: University of Utah Press, 1975); Robert Griffith, "The Selling of America: The Advertising Council and American Politics, 1942–1960," *Business History Review* 57 (Autumn 1983):338–412; McGinnis, "Advertising Council and the Cold War."

34. During World War II this was not just an American enterprise. The British also had a elaborate system of wartime home-front propaganda. The images and messages that were conveyed were almost exactly like those in the United States. See Marion Yass, *This Is Your*

War: Home Front Propaganda in the Second World War (London: Her Majesty's Stationery Office, 1983).

35. PHST, Files of Spencer Quick, Box 1, Civil Defense Program Folder, letter from Edward B. Lyman, Office of Public Affairs, Federal Civil Defense Administration, to Charles W. Jackson, Assistant to the White House, August 3, 1951, p. 2.

36. See especially Fox, "Advertising and the Second World War"; and idem, *Madison Avenue Goes to War.* On the issue of institutional and administrative continuity, see Elmer Davis and Byron Price, *War Information and Censorship* (Washington, DC: American Council of Public Affairs, 1943), esp. pp. 26–28.

37. The analysis of "war advertising" within the framework of ethos, pathos, and didactics is Frank Fox's. Fox notes that war advertising, especially as it related to national morale, was refined during World War II through the development of this framework to market public service and wartime propaganda to the average citizen. I extend his analysis to the Ad Council's Cold War civil defense campaign, as this is exactly the framework in which the home-front mobilization aesthetic was reproduced. See Fox, "Advertising and the Second World War," p. 184. See also Choukas, *Propaganda Comes of Age*, pp. 97–137.

38. In general, see *A Cross of Iron: Harry S. Truman and the Origins of the National Security State, 1945–1954* (New York: Cambridge University Press, 1997), Michael Hogan, pp. 1–22. On a more theoretical level, however, the goal of the Ad Council and Truman administration planners was to have the polity, through both language and practice, internalize the security preparedness programs. In this "Foucauldian" sense, early Cold War political culture was framed by a discursive and emotional regime. See especially Michel Foucault, *The Archaeology of Knowledge: A Discourse on Language* (New York: Pantheon Books, 1972), pp. 21–71, 157–178. For a recent discussion on how this idea of internalizing understanding of reality can effect behavior, see Richard Price, "A Genealogy of the Chemical Weapons Taboo," *International Organization* 49 (Winter 1995):73–104.

39. Some planners were antagonistic to the Ad Council's advice, for they saw it as too slick. On the resistance to the Ad Council's overly packaged approach to mobilization, see Allan M. Wilson, Vice President of the Ad Council, to Charles W. Jackson, memorandum, August 14, 1951, PHST, Papers of Spencer R. Quick, Box 5, Civil Defense Campaign Correspondence Folder.

40. The analysis here on early media coverage and response draws heavily on Oakes and Grossman, "Managing Nuclear Terror," pp. 371–375.

41. By the end of 1945, many of the former Manhattan Project scientists had organized themselves into the Federation of Atomic Scientists, the so-called League of Frightened Men. Concerned over congressional and public indifference to the dangers of atomic power, they advocated an international commission that would control the development and use of atomic energy, a proposal that required the United States to relinquish its monopoly over nuclear weapons and the technology required for their manufacture. Since there was virtually no public support for such a policy, the scientists attempted to terrify the public into action with blunt warnings about the frightful effects of nuclear weapons. See Lawrence S. Wittner, *One World or None: A History of the World Nuclear Disarmament Movement through 1953* (Stanford, CA: Stanford University Press, 1993), pp. 55–79; Alice Kimball Smith, *A Peril and a Hope: The Scientist's Movement in America, 1945–47* (Chicago: University of Chicago Press, 1965). Also see Social Science Research Council, *Public Reaction to the Atomic Bomb and World Affairs: A Nation-Wide Survey* (Ithaca, NY: Cornell University, 1947), p. 27; "Scientists Scare Congress," *Life*, December 31, 1945, p. 18.

42. "A Report to the Secretary of War," *Bulletin of the Atomic Scientists* (May 1946):2.

43. *The Journals of David E. Lilienthal*, vol. II, *The Atomic Energy Years 1945–1950* (New York: Harper and Row, 1964), p. 20, emphasis in the original.

44. U.S. Senate, Special Committee on Atomic Energy, *A Resolution Creating a Special Committee to Investigate Problems Relating to the Development, Use, and Control of Atomic Energy, Hearings Pursuant to Senate Resolution 179*, 79th Congress, 1st Session

(November 30, 1945), Part I, pp. 116–117. On Langmuir's testimony, see *New York Times*, October 9, 1945, p. 9.

45. *Hearings*, pp. 116–117.

46. Dr. Harold C. Urey as told to Michael Armine, "I'm a Frightened Man," *Collier's*, January 5, 1946, p. 18.

47. Ibid., p. 18.

48. The campaign to redefine reality depended on a national domestic education program that took as its baseline model the wartime civic education experience of the early 1940s. The best example here is the demonization of the enemy during the war. The OWI, with the help of Madison Avenue advertising specialists, produced propaganda that sought to define for the public who and what the enemy was. This was part of the overall home-front pro-gram to explain, using the lexicon of the time, "why we fight" to the American people. See John Morton Blum, *V Was for Victory: Politics and American Culture during World War II* (New York: Harcourt Brace, 1976), pp. 45–52.

49. See Brian Balough's observations on the links between the central state and the effects of the Cold War on postwar planning in *Chain Reaction: Expert Debate and Public Participation in American Commercial Nuclear Power, 1945–1975* (New York: Cambridge University Press, 1991), pp. 24–59. On continuous war mobilization and the way it affected the discus-sion of nuclear weapons, see NSRB Doc. 76, August 19, 1948, "Preliminary Statement on Guiding Principles and Program Framework for Mobilization Planning," PHST, White House Central Files, Box 27, NSRB Folder 1; "Basic Principles and Assumptions Governing Preparation of the Long-Range Plan for the Security of the Nation's Capital," NA, NSRB, RG-304, Box 94, Folder E4-12; James T. Martin to V. B. Lamoureux for Norvin C. Kiefer, Director, Health Resources Division, December 30, 1949, assignments 80–94. NA, OCDM, RG-304, Box 12, Civil Disaster in Wartime Folder E4-13.

50. *Survival Under Atomic Attack*, p. 4. When the FCDA was created, it continued to publish the booklet. The FCDA also contracted to have the booklet turned into a civil defense training film aimed at the general public.

51. On this view, see, for example, Griffith, "The Selling of America," pp. 338–412. Specifically regarding the FCDA, see John A. DeChant to Joseph Short, memorandum, October 23, 1951, PHST, Official Files, Box 1671, Folder 1591-C, pp. 2–5.

52. To name just a few of the contributors: Hanson Baldwin, Robert E. Sherwood, Edward R. Murrow, Walter Winchell, Philip Wylie, Arthur Koestler, Senator Margaret Chase Smith, Walter Reuther, Professor Alan Nevins, and GI cartoonist Bill Mauldin. For the complete list of contributors, see *Collier's*, October 27, 1951, pp. 6–8.

53. Ibid., p. 6, emphasis in the original.

54. Ibid., p. 52

55. On the close relationship between the FCDA and Wylie, see The Philip Wylie Collection, Firestone Library, Princeton University, Box 121. Additionally, Robert Sherwood had extensive experience working for the OWI under Elmer Davis during World War II. Philip Wylie, *Tomorrow!* (New York: Rinehart, 1954).

56. Paul Boyer, *By the Bomb's Early Light: American Thought and Culture at the Dawn of the Atomic Age* (New York: Pantheon, 1985).

57. Consensus development is understood here as part of a bargaining strategy between a democratic polity and the central state to effect what H. Richard Friman has labeled "issue redefinition." The premise on which this line of thinking rests is that, at least in the case of the United States, the relative "weakness" of the central state, combined with a decentral-ized democratic political structure, forces state planners to essentially implement programs of domestic civic education in order to set political agendas and, perhaps more important, to *define* for the public the issues at stake. See H. Richard Friman, "Domestic Tactics in Economic Negotiations," *International Organization* 47 (Summer 1993):387–410. A more comprehensive analysis regarding the issue of consensus development within "weak"

democratic state structures is made by Eric Nordlinger, *The Autonomy of the Democratic State* (Cambridge, MA: Harvard University Press, 1981). See also See Balough, *Chain Reaction*, p. 25. Standards of self-censorship and the acquiescence to official censorship for "patriotic" purposes exemplified this institutional relationship between the popular media and the state. See, for example, a set of letters from Jesse Butcher and Jack DeChant of the FCDA public affairs office to Henry Morgenthau III, February 17–20, 1951, NA, OCDM, RG-304, Box 14, Television Programs File.

58. Charles E. Johnson, "Problems of Mutual Concern to PSB and FCDA," *Memorandum of Conversation*, September 10, 1951. PHST, PSB, Box 3, FCDA folder 1 of 2.

59. Ibid.

60. See Christopher Simpson, "U.S. Communication Research, Counterinsurgency, and Scientific 'Reality,'" in *Ruthless Criticism: New Perspectives in U.S. Communication History*, ed. William S. Solomon and Robert W. McChesney (Minneapolis: University of Minnesota Press, 1993), pp. 313–348; idem, *Science of Coercion: Communication Research and Psychological Warfare, 1945–1960* (New York: Oxford University Press, 1994), 31–62.

61. "Panic Prevention and Control," Appendix IXB of *Project East River*, Part IX, p. 55.

62. See Christopher Simpson, ed., *Universities and Empire: Money and Politics in the Social Sciences during the Cold War* (New York: The New Press, 1998).

63. For more on the Cape Cod series, see Gregg Herken, *Counsels of War* (New York: Oxford University Press, 1987), pp. 60–71.

64. "Panic Prevention and Control," Appendix IXB of *Project East River*, Part IX, p. 62.

65. Ibid., p. 57.

66. Ibid., pp. 58–59.

67. Ibid., p. 5.

68. Ibid., p. 7.

69. Ibid.

70. Ibid., pp. 63–69.

71. Ibid., p. 64.

72. Ibid., p. 63.

73. U.S. Federal Civil Defense Administration, *Annual Report for 1951* (Washington, DC: GPO, 1951), p. 15.

74. U.S. Federal Civil Defense Administration, *Annual Report for 1952* (Washington, DC: GPO, 1952), p. 47.

75. See the Ad Council's newspaper advertising order mat AC-6 in PHST, Papers of Spencer R. Quick, Box 5, Civil Defense Campaign Folder 1.

76. See esp. Simpson, *Science of Coercion*, pp. 31–51. Regarding the "informal" relationship and discussions between the PSB and the FCDA, see PHST, PSB, Box 3, FCDA folder 1 of 2. See esp. Charles E. Johnson to George A. Morgan, "PSB and FCDA Relations," October 8, 1952.

77. No official government-sanctioned *formal* ties between the FCDA and the PSB were established, even though FCDA administrator Millard Caldwell requested such an arrangement. Instead, PSB memoranda often noted that its external charge forbid a formal relationship—so the so-called informal relationship was set up. Also, by setting up "interagency committees" the line between formal and informal relations became fuzzy, at best. In any case, the end result for FCDA/PSB relations was as if formal interagency relations had been set up; namely, the sharing of important information on morale, propaganda, and panic. On the informal links between the FCDA and PSB, see PHST, PSB, Box 337, "Staff Meetings 1952–January 1953." On the connections with Project East River, see PHST, PSB, Box 34, "Project East River" Folder. Finally, on epistemic communities, see PSHT, PSB, "Report on DeChant's Second Michigan Study," Box 1, Folder #000.8. On the internalization of these wartime propaganda and communication methods and their consequences, see Simpson, *Science of Coercion*, pp. 94–106.

Chapter 4: Community Mobilization and the FCDA

1. *The Siren* (March–April 1952), p. 15.
2. See Emily S. Rosenberg, "Commentary: The Cold War Discourse of National Security," *Diplomatic History* 17 (Spring 1993):277–284.
3. On public policy and its implementation, see Randall Ripley and Grace Franklin, *Policy Implementation and Bureaucracy* (Homewood, IL: Dorsey Press, 1986), esp. pp. 1–58.
4. U.S. FCDA, *The National Plan for Civil Defense against Enemy Attack* (Washington, DC: GPO, 1951).
5. On regional identification inside the United States I am following the model laid out by Richard F. Bensel, *Sectionalism and American Political Development* (Madison: University of Wisconsin Press, 1984). By 1950, there was a tremendous interest on the part of communities and small-business organizations in civil defense. See National Archives (NA), Records Group 304 (RG-304), Office of Civil Defense Mobilization, Box 5, Civil Defense Comments and Queries File. This was also the case for core industrial states such as New Jersey, where Governor Driscoll had barely gotten that state's civil defense program underway when it was deluged by local organizations offering their services (some for profit) for training and equipping nascent community civil defense corps throughout the state. See the many letters to Governor Driscoll's office in New Jersey State Library, Governor Alfred E. Driscoll Papers, Box 844, Civil Defense Departmental General A–M folder.
6. See NA, RG-304, OCDM, Box 5, Civil Defense Comments and Queries Folders.
7. Modern sales techniques emphasize the importance of the salesperson to identify a "need," even if it has absolutely no basis in fact, and then to spin narratives (sales tracts) to place the "prospect" (the person being "sold to") into the story so that he or she will want to buy whatever product or idea is being pitched. See Guy Oakes, *The Soul of the Salesman: The Moral Ethos of Personal Sales* (Atlantic Highlands, NJ: Humanities Press, 1990), pp. 1–37.
8. The Truman administration's considerable interest in government-funded social science is evidenced by the fact that at the Truman Library there are numerous archives within the President's Secretary's Files dedicated specifically to social science research. The FCDA syllabi for community civil defense mobilization drew not only on the work of psychologists and sociologists but also on the "war advertising" and marketing theory outlined in Chapter Three. See, for example, "Report on Social Science Research in Cold War Operations," PHST, Psychological Strategy Board, Box 1, Social Science Research Folder 2 of 2; "Information and Training for Civil Defense" NA, National Security Resources Board, RG-304, Box 19, Project East River Folder; Kim Geiger and Andrew Grossman, "The Politics of Home-Front Mobilization, 1946–1952," Center for Studies of Social Change Working Paper No. 184 (April 1994).
9. Affecting both the jargon and the imagery of the natural sciences, social scientists during World War II developed strategies for marketing the OWI and the OCD's domestic mobilization as well as "offensive" psychological warfare programs for the Office of Strategic Services and military intelligence. See Franklin D. Roosevelt Library, Official Files 5015, Box 3, Office of War Information, Intelligence Reports 1942–1943 Folder.
10. This figure includes funds for research conducted inside various government agencies. See "Funds Obligated for Social Science Research in Fiscal 1952," PHST, PSF, PSB, Box 1, Social Science Research file 2 of 2. Spending levels for social science research funded by the CIA were expurgated from the document upon its declassification, so this figure necessarily underestimates total government spending. This section is drawn from Geiger and Grossman, "Politics of Home-Front Mobilization."
11. Christopher Simpson, *Science of Coercion: Communication Research and Psychological Warfare, 1945–1960* (New York: Oxford University Press, 1994), p. 4.
12. On the link among the federal government, social science research, and disaster studies, see the series of publications produced by the Committee on Disaster Studies, especially Charles E. Fritz and J. H. Mathewson, "Convergence Behavior in Disasters: A Problem of Social Control," *Committee on Disaster Studies Number 9* (Washington, DC: National

Academy of Science, 1957). See also Roger L. Geiger, *Research and Relevant Knowledge: American Research Universities since World War II* (New York: Oxford University Press, 1993), pp. 30–58; John Tirman, ed., *The Militarization of High Technology* (Cambridge, MA: Ballinger Publishing, 1984); Stuart W. Leslie, *The Cold War and American Science: The Military-Industrial-Academic Complex at MIT and Stanford* (New York: Columbia University Press, 1993); Herbert N. Foerstel, *Secret Science: Federal Control of American Science and Technology* (Westport, CT: Praeger, 1993); and Michael D. Reagan, *Science and the Federal Patron* (New York: Oxford University Press, 1969).

13. Allan M. Wilson, Vice President of the Advertising Council, to Charles Jackson, Assistant to President Truman, August 14, 1951. PHST, Files of Spencer R. Quick, Box 5, Civil Defense Campaign Correspondence Folder.

14. See "An FCDA Mass Consumer Advertising Campaign (undated), PHST, Papers of Spencer R. Quick, Box 5, Civil Defense Campaign–Industrial.

15. For example, the OCD tapped Eleanor Roosevelt and Hollywood stars such as Melvyn Douglas to promote its public relations campaign. There was a backlash against this by some in Congress. See, for example, the comments by Congressman Carl Hinshaw of California concerning the OCD and its hiring of persons such as Douglas to do its public relations work. *Congressional Record*, 77th Cong., 2nd sess., 1942, vol. 88, p. 1028. See also "Progress Report Alert America Campaign," Oct. 15, 1951, PHST, Official File, Box 1671, Folder 1591-C.

16. See Loren Baritz, *The Good Life: The Meaning of Success for the American Middle Class* (New York: Knopf, 1982); Kenneth T. Jackson, *Crabgrass Frontier: The Suburbanization of the United States* (New York: Oxford University Press, 1985).

17. See U.S. FCDA, *Annual Report for 1952* (Washington, DC: GPO, 1952), pp. 46–49. For a contemporary (1952) account of the Alert America campaign, see U.S. FCDA, *The Civil Defense Alert* 1 (May 1952), pp. 1, 3, 4.

18. U.S. FCDA, *Home Protection Exercises* (Washington, DC: GPO, 1953); U.S. FCDA, *Emergency Action to Save Lives* (Washington, DC: GPO, 1951); U.S. FCDA, *Fire Fighting for House-holders* (Washington, DC: GPO, 1951). For an interesting sociological analysis of the home exercise programs, see Guy Oakes, *The Imaginary War: Civil Defense and the Genesis of American Cold War Culture* (New York: Oxford University Press, 1994), pp. 109–113.

19. PHST, Files of Spencer R. Quick, Box 5, Civil Defense Campaign Folder, Order Mat AC-2.

20. U.S. FCDA, *Annual Report for 1952*, pp. 46–49.

21. Ibid., pp. 48–49.

22. PHST, Official File (OF), John A. DeChant to Joseph Short, "Alert America Campaign," October 23, 1951, Box 1671, Folder 1591-C, p. 12.

23. PHST, OF, *Alert America Campaign Progress Report*, October 15, 1951, Box 1671, Folder 1591-C.

24. "A Preliminary Report on Public Attitudes toward Civil Defense 1950–1951," PHST, PSF, Box 144, FCDA Folder. By 1961, the FCDA and the OCDM had published and circulated more than 503 million pieces of literature dealing with civil defense. Of these, more than 400 million pieces were aimed specifically at the general public. This is an enormous quantity of literature, especially when one considers that the total population of the United States in 1960 was 179.3 million.

25. The GOC was a civilian program in which people would search the skies for enemy bombers and report them to "filtering centers" run by the Air Force. It was run by both the Air Force and the FCDA. This program had its roots in similar civil defense programs instituted during World War II. In New Jersey, GOC-run "Operation Skywatches" became part of the local and national civil defense programs. See especially U.S. FCDA, *1954 Annual Report* (Washington, DC: GPO, 1954), p. 97.

26. These figures are based on 1,468 schools in 129 cities with populations larger than 50,000. See U.S. FCDA, *Annual Report for 1952*, p. 66.

27. See PHST, Official File, *Civil Defense Guide for Council and District Planning: Boy Scouts of America*, File 1591. On the organizational structure of the Boy Scouts of America and its use as an overall model for everyday citizens, see esp. pp. 25–31.
28. Clyde W. Meredith, "Civil Defense and the Schools," *School Life* 34 (April 1952):99–100.
29. State of New Jersey Division of Civil Defense, *Civil Defense and the School Principle* (Trenton, NJ: Division of Civil Defense, 1952), p. 9.
30. Ibid., p. 8.
31. Ibid.
32. It was clear to many people, including members of boards of education and individual educators, that the basic lesson plans for teaching civil defense were not objective lessons on how to survive a nuclear war, but lessons on politics, national security, the origins of the Cold War, and the role of the U.S. armed forces in protecting amorphously defined national security interests. As a result, there were questions about the use of the public school system to disseminate what was clearly overt propaganda. But these were muted voices of dissent and, given the tenor of the times, one might say they were rather brave voices of dissent. On this issue, see Michael J. Carey, "The Schools and Civil Defense: The Fifties Revisited," *Teachers College Record* 84 (Fall 1982):115–127; JoAnne Brown, "A Is for Atom, B Is for Bomb: Civil Defense in American Public Education," *Journal of American History* 75 (June 1988):68–90.
33. U.S. FCDA, *Interim Civil Defense Instructions for Schools and Colleges* (Washington, DC: GPO, 1951), pp. 5, 24; quotation on p. 5.
34. The success of using children to deliver the civil defense message to their parents and, more important, to mobilize them is empirically harder to prove than, for example, determining whether an Operation Alert was successful. One obvious question is: How many families actually, in terms of hard numbers, participated in FCDA-sponsored home exercises? I could find no evidence that the FCDA systematically tried to calculate the answer to this question. However, there is good empirical data on how much literature was indeed sent by the FCDA (not including local and state organizations) to families in the form of "home kits." We do know that all schools participated in civil defense exercises. We do know that 40 percent of all publicly aimed FCDA literature (1951–1960) was "home kits" and that the total figure for all FCDA civil defense literature between 1951 and 1960 was 476 million pieces. See Office of Civil Defense and Mobilization, *Annual Statistical Report 1961* (Washington, DC: GPO, 1961).
35. Ibid., pp. 49–50.
36. In a post-screening discussion of an FCDA cartoon for children entitled "Bert the Turtle," in which the now-amusing phrase "duck and cover" was concocted, the official, John C. Cocks, was referring to mental hygiene as it applied to children. However, the mental hygiene approach as conceived by the FCDA was not limited just to children. All of the civil defense literature that was aimed at the general public was packaged within this approach. See, for example, "New Film to Help in Bomb Training," *New York Times*, January 25, 1952, p. 7. See also State of New Jersey, Division of Civil Defense, *Proceedings of the Institute on Mental Hygiene: Aspects of Civil Defense* (Trenton, NJ: Division of Community Services, 1951).
37. The information sheet goes on to detail the information that was to appear on these dog tags: name, next of kin, address, blood group or type, and religion. "Civil Defense Identification Tags," Information Sheet No. 20, *Civil Defense Education Project* (Washington, DC: GPO, May 9, 1955), pp. 1–4. See also New York State Civil Defense Commission, *Civil Defense and the Schools* (Albany: New York State Civil Defense Commission, 1953).
38. *The Siren* (Winter 1960), pp. 1–3.
39. See "Enemy Target No. 1—Civilians," PHST, Papers of Spencer Quick, Civil Defense Campaign–General, Folder 1.
40. On continuity, see FDRL, OF 5051, Box 1, Office of War Information, Jan–July 1942 Folder; FDRL, Wayne Coy Papers, Alphabetical File, Box 2, Committee on War Information Folder and Civil Defense Folder.

41. U.S. Office of Civil Defense Planning, Civil Defense for National Security (Washington, DC: GPO, 1948), p. 150 (hereafter, *Hopley Report*).

42. See Lyon G. Tyler, "Civil Defense: The Impact of the Planning Years, 1945–1950" (Ph.D. diss., Duke University, 1967), pp. 41–64, 113; *Hopley Report*, pp. 150–156; U.S. FCDA, *Civil Defense in Outline: A Study Guide for the National Civil Defense Program* (Washington, DC: GPO, 1951), pp. 1–41. Overall, see "Panic Prevention and Control," Part IXB of the *Project East River*, NA, RG-304, NSRB, Project East River Folder.

43. U.S. FCDA, Publication H-7-1, *Before Disaster Strikes: What to Do Now* (Washington, DC: GPO, 1951), p. 19.

44. New York State Civil Defense Commission, Defense Welfare Services, *Introductory Course in Defense Welfare Services: Instructor's Guide* (New York: New York State Civil Defense Commission, 1952), p. 4.

45. Ibid., emphasis in the original.

46. Ibid., p. 7.

47. See, for example, U.S. FCDA, "The Role of the Warden in Panic Prevention," *Civil Defense Technical Bulletin*, TB-7-1 (Washington, DC: GPO, 1955), pp. 1–3.

48. See U.S. FCDA, *Annual Report for 1951*, pp. 64–65; U.S. FCDA, *Annual Report for 1952*, pp. 87–88; U.S. FCDA, *Before Disaster Strikes*.

49. On the organizational theory that underpinned some of the FCDA's administration of the warden system, see Lawrence B. Mohr, *Explaining Organizational Behavior* (San Francisco, CA: Jossey-Bass, 1982), pp. 106, 204–205. On the internalization of duty and its relationship to social control, see Michel Foucault, *Ethics, Subjectivity and Truth*, vol. 1, ed. Paul Rabinow (New York: The New Press, 1997), pp. 67–71.

50. Auxiliary police and wardens, when on duty, were given "regular" police powers. See *The Siren*, June 1951, p. 7.

51. See U.S. Office for Civil Defense Planning, *Civil Defense for National Security* (Washington, DC: GPO, 1948), p. 4.

52. See "Panic Prevention and Control," Appendix IXB of *Project East River*, Part IX, pp. 56–64.

53. See State of New Jersey Department of Civil Defense, *1952 Annual Report* (Trenton, NJ: Department of Civil Defense, 1952), p. 33.

54. State of New Jersey, Division of Civil Defense, *Manual for Wardens* (Trenton, NJ: Division of Civil Defense, 1952), p. 11.

55. Ibid., pp. 3–4.

56. See *The Siren*, Jan–Feb 1952, p. 10.

57. Clarence Mitchell, Director, Washington Bureau of the NAACP, to Senator George D. Aiken, December 19, 1950. Papers of the NAACP, Part 18: Special Subjects, 1940–1955, Series B: General Office Files, Civil Defense, "Caldwell, Millard issue," 1950–1951.

58. *Brown v. Board of Education of Topeka*, 347 U.S. 483 (1954).

59. See, for example, Azza Salama Layton, *International Politics and Civil Rights Policies in the United States* (New York: Cambridge University Press, 2000), pp. 39–73.

60. Thanks to Glenn Perusek for sharing his ideas on this concept. I borrow the term "segregationist liberalism" from Perusek's forthcoming work *Citizenship in the Industrial Republic: Race, Labor, and Representation in Detroit, 1910–1945*. For more on American liberalism and its impact on American political development, see Louis Hartz, *The Liberal Tradition in America* (New York: Harcourt Brace Jovanovich, 1955); and Rogers M. Smith, *Civic Ideals: Conflicting Visions of Citizenship in U.S. History* (New Haven, CT: Yale University Press, 1997). For a sophisticated and important argument concerning American liberalism and the development of a jurisprudence of separation, see J. David Greenstone, *The Lincoln Persuasion: Remaking American Liberalism* (Princeton, NJ: Princeton University Press, 1993), pp. 3–67. For two sets of comments on the different permutations and interpretations of American liberalism, see Ira Katznelson, "Review of Rogers M. Smith's *Civic Ideals*," *Political Theory* 27 (August 1999):565–570; and Eldon Eisenach, "Liberal Citizenship and American National Identity," *Studies in American Development* 13 (Spring 1999):198–215.

61. Katznelson, "Review," p. 568. See also David F. Ericson, *The Shaping of American Liberalism: The Debates over Ratification, Nullification and Slavery* (Chicago: University of Chicago Press, 1993), pp. 117–135; and Ericson, "Dew, Fitzhugh, and Proslavery Liberalism," in *The Liberal Tradition in American Politics: Reassessing the Legacy of American Liberalism*, ed. David F. Ericson and Louisa Bertch Green (New York: Routledge, 1999), pp. 67–98.

62. A theory of "equalization" versus integration within the framework of a liberal social order was not just a philosophy held by white citizens; see, for example, "Being in the Field of Education and Also Being a Negro...Seems...Tragic: Black Teachers in the Jim Crow South," *The Journal of American History* 87 (June 2000):86–87. See also W. E. B. Du Bois, "A Philosophy of Race Segregation," *Quarterly Review of Higher Education for Negroes* 3 (1936).

63. *Plessy v. Ferguson*, 163 U.S. 537 (1896). See also Michael J. Klarman, "The Plessy Era," in *The Supreme Court Review 1998*, ed. Dennis J. Hutchinson, David A. Strauss, and Geoffrey R. Stone (Chicago: University of Chicago Press, 1999), pp. 303–414.

64. Klarman, "The Plessy Era," p. 306.

65. See U.S. FCDA, *Population Estimates for Survival Planning* (Washington, DC: GPO, 1956).

66. Ibid.

67. *Congressional Record*, 81st Congress, 2nd session, pp. 16825, 16841–16843. See especially the exchange between Representatives Brown of Ohio and Dewey Short of Missouri, p. 16831.

68. See Thomas J. Kerr, *Civil Defense in the U.S.: Bandaid for a Holocaust?* (Boulder, CO: Westview Press, 1983), pp. 46–65. The reaction to the appointment in the African American press was swift and understandably negative. See "Meet Mr. Caldwell," *Crisis* (March 1951):183–184.

69. My use of geographic areas identified as urban core, semi-periphery, periphery (or rural) is drawn from Bensel, *Sectionalism and American Political Development*. The geographic parameters of the South used here follow those of Ira Katznelson, Kim Geiger, and Daniel Kryder, "Limiting Liberalism: The Southern Veto in Congress, 1933–1950," *Political Science Quarterly* 108:2 (1993):284, n. 3. I also consider space in the more traditional short-hand fashion, i.e., urban, suburban.

70. The Civil Defense Act is a classic example of vaguely written legislation that contains enormous discretionary power. On the consequences for liberal democracy of this kind of lawmaking, see Theodore J. Lowi, *The End of Liberalism*, 2nd ed. (New York: W.W. Norton, 1979), pp. 92–123.

71. *Congressional Record*, 81st Congress, 2nd session, p. 16831.

72. See ibid., pp. 16825, 16841–16843. The emergency powers of the administrator of the FCDA were clearly on the minds of many representatives during the debate concerning the Civil Defense Act of 1950. See also B. W. Menke, *Martial Law—Its Use in Case of Atomic Attack* (Washington, DC: Industrial College of the Armed Forces, 1956); and Section 301 of the Civil Defense Act of 1950.

73. On the importance of southern Democratic support for President Truman in 1948, see V. O. Key, *Southern Politics in State and Nation* (Knoxville: University of Tennessee Press, 1986), pp. 329–344; For background on Caldwell as governor of Florida, see pp. 82–105.

74. For Caldwell's position on the role of the South and the states' rights issue, see "Report to the State," p. 11, August 13, 1945, Papers of Millard F. Caldwell, Jr., University of Florida, Gainesville, Speeches Delivered 1942–1946; and in general Box 10, Speeches Delivered Folder 1946–1948. On the beginning of civil rights mobilizations where Caldwell berates the "manipulators of controlled racial groups," see "Report to the State," May 14, 1946, p. 5., ibid.

75. Congressional Record, 81st Cong., 2nd sess., p. 16831.

76. See correspondence, December 8, 1950, between Walter White, Executive Secretary to the NAACP in New York City, and Clarence Mitchell, Director of the Washington Bureau of

the NAACP. Papers of the NAACP, Part 18, Special Subjects 1940–1955, Series B, General Office Files, Civil Defense, Caldwell, Millard issue.

77. Quoted in "Meet Mr. Caldwell." p. 183.

78. The use of segregated bomb shelters has its roots in the experience of World War II. On bomb shelters, see Horace R. Cayton, "Negro Morale," *Opportunity* (December 1945):371–375. On segregated bomb shelters, see Rufus Wells, "What Would Happen if the Bomb Falls?" *Sepia* (January 1962):10–11. On the relationship between national security, war mobilization, and race, see Daniel Kryder, *Divided Arsenal: Race and the American State during World War II* (New York: Cambridge University Press, 2000); idem, "Race Policy, Race Violence, and Race Reform in the U.S. Army during World War II," *Studies in American Political Development* 10 (Spring 1996):130–167. See also Patricia Sullivan, *Days of Hope: Race and Democracy in the New Deal Era* (Chapel Hill: University of North Carolina Press, 1996), pp. 133–168; and Penny M. Von Eschen, *Race against Empire: Black Americans and Anticolonialism, 1937–1957* (Ithaca, NY: Cornell University Press, 1997), pp. 22–43.

79. See Fred C. Iklé and Harry V. Kincaid, *Social Aspects of Wartime Evacuation of American Cities: With Particular Emphasis on Long-Term Housing and Reemployment*, Committee on Disaster Studies, Disaster Study Number 4, Publication No. 393 (Washington, DC: National Academy of Sciences, 1956), pp. 11–39.

80. See especially David M. Heer, *After Nuclear Attack: A Demographic Inquiry* (New York: Praeger Publishers, 1965), pp. 248–327. On city planning, see *Chicago Alerts: A City Plans Its Civil Defense against Atomic Attack* (Chicago: The Chicago Civil Defense Corps, 1950); *Proceedings of Emergency Meeting: League of California Cities* (Sacramento, CA: State Office of Civil Defense, 1951); U.S. FCDA, *Civil Defense Urban Analysis* TM-8-1 (Washington, DC: GPO, 1953). On rural planning, see *Tri-Cities Operational Survival Plan: Tennessee State Civil Defense*, vols. 1 and 2 (State of Tennessee: Office of Civil Defense, 1958), note esp. vol. 2, annexes G–.; U.S. Office of Civil and Defense Mobilization, Region III, *A Special Report on Civil Emergency Planning* (Thomasville, GA: OCDM, 1961). On protecting the "suburban ideal," see Andrew Grossman, "Preparing for Cold War: Home Front Mobilization, State Expansion, and Civil Defense Planning in the United States, 1946–1954" (Ph.D. diss., New School for Social Research, 1996), pp. 153–204.

81. On the correlation between domestic political support and deterrence theory, see Andrew Grossman, "Atomic Fantasies and Make-Believe War: The American State, Social Control and Civil Defense Planning, 1946–1952," *Political Power and Social Theory* 9 (1995), pp. 99–112; Oakes, *The Imaginary War*, pp. 10–30.

82. For example, John Donaldson et al., *An Examination of Psychological Problems during Shelter Confinement Following a Thermonuclear Attack*, Operations Research Office, Home Defense Division, Staff Paper No. ORO-SP-45 (Washington, DC: Department of the Army, 1957); Martha Wolfenstein, *Disaster: A Psychological Essay* (Glencoe, IL: Free Press, 1957); "Information and Training for Civil Defense," *Project East River*; "Panic Prevention and Control," pp. 55–65. For more recent analyses of these issues, see Arthur M. Katz, *Life after Nuclear War: The Economic and Social Impacts of Nuclear Attacks on the United States* (Cambridge, MA: Ballinger, 1982), pp. 69–78; Bruce C. Allnutt, *A Study of Consensus on Social and Psychological Factors Related to Recovery from Nuclear Attack*, OCD, Department of the Army, OCD Contract No. DAHC 20-70-C-038 (Mclean, VA: Human Sciences Resources, 1971).

83. Walter White, Executive Secretary of the NAACP, to President Harry S. Truman, February 21, 1951, PHST, OF, Box 1743, 2965-Misc. Folder, pp. 1–2.

84. Dr. Errold D. Collymore, President, New York Branch, NAACP, to President Harry S. Truman, March 19, 1951, PHST, OF, Box 1743, 2965-Misc. Folder, p. 1.

85. The FCDA and Air Force research studies throughout the 1950s and into the early 1960s often considered "social stress" within a framework that used race, gender, religion, and geography as fundamental principles for framing disaster studies. See, for example, Peter G.

Nordlie and Robert D. Popper, *Social Phenomena in a Post-Nuclear Attack Situation: Synopses of Likely Social Effects of the Physical Damage*, Air Force Office of Scientific Research, Behavioral Sciences Division, Contract No. AF 49(638)-549, Project No. 9779, Task No. 37735 (Arlington, VA: Human Sciences Research, 1961), pp. 12–34; 87–89. Writing in 1963 but drawing on his experiences in the early to mid-1950s, Dr. Nathan Hare of the *Negro Digest* wrote a piece on how, in effect, emergency planning of all sorts gave little consideration to issues of race. See Dr. Nathan Hare, "Can Negroes Survive a Nuclear War?" *Negro Digest* (May 1963): 26–33.

86. *Smith v. Allwright*, 321 U.S. 649 (1944).
87. M. E. Diggs, Secretary, Norfolk Branch, NAACP, to President Harry S. Truman, March 21, 1951, PHST, OF, Box 1743, 2965-Misc. Folder, p. 1.
88. For more on the Cold War as an agent of progressive social change regarding race relations in the United States, see Layton, *International Politics and Civil Rights Policies* Philip A. Klinkner, *The Unsteady March: The Rise and Decline of Racial Equality in America* (Chicago: University of Chicago Press, 1999); and David McCullough, *Truman* (New York: Simon and Schuster, 1992), pp. 569–570, 587–588, 702.
89. Samuel A. Williams, Vice President New Jersey State Conference of the NAACP, to Walter White, Executive Secretary of the NAACP, March 18, 1951. Papers of the NAACP, Part 18: Special Subjects, Civil Defense File, "Caldwell, Millard issue," 1950–1951.
90. For descriptive statistics on the FCDA's national public relations campaign, see Grossman, "Preparing for Cold War," pp. 96–149.
91. An exception was the African American periodical *Our World*. In 1952, the journal ran a series of FCDA-sponsored civil defense instructions and stories. But even in this context, skepticism about how much concern there was for "all citizens" was high among African Americans. *Our World* editors made note in the essay that "where you experience any kind of discrimination write *Our World* immediately." See "Negroes and the Atom Bomb," *Our World* (September 1952): 28–31.
92. See *The Michigan Chronicle*, "Negro Response to City's Appeal for Auxiliary Fighters Negligible," July 26, 1952, p. 2. See also "What Would Happen if the Bomb Falls? Negroes Not Bothering to Build Fallout Shelters–Southern Civil Defense Programs Racially Segregated," *Sepia* (January 1962): 9–11. By the late 1950s, the Rand Corporation did studies on the "problem" of race relations in the New York City subways, which were the designated bomb shelters. The concern was that there would be race riots in the subways.
93. "Harlem and the Hell Bomb," *Our World* 9 (October 1954): 38–42. See also "Say Harlem Failed in Bomb Drill Test," *New York Amsterdam News*, June 25, 1955, pp. 1–2.
94. Robert A. Dentler and Phillips Cutright, *Hostage America: Human Aspects of a Nuclear Attack and a Program of Prevention* (Boston: Beacon Press, 1963), pp. 1–77. See also Heer, *After Nuclear Attack*, pp. 34–174. For a "Strangelovian" analysis of "how to fight" a nuclear war, see Herman Kahn, *On Thermonuclear War* (Princeton, NJ: Princeton University Press, 1961), pp. 3–96, 578–641.
95. It is important to note that this hypothetical post-attack analysis considers these issues *before* the deployment of intercontinental ballistic missiles. After 1960 many rural areas of the United States became prime target areas. However, between 1951 and 1954 FCDA assumptions modeled a primary target list using seventy SMAs, which left areas of rural America, in theory at least, free of attack.
96. For contemporary theoretical consideration of nuclear war and continuity of liberal-democratic governance, see Clinton Rossiter, *Constitutional Dictatorship: Crisis Government in the Modern Democracies* (New York: Harcourt, Brace & World, 1948); idem, "What of Congress in Atomic War," *Western Political Quarterly* 3 (December 1950):602–605; and Denis W. Brogan, *Democratic Government in an Atomic World: A Lecture Delivered under the Auspices of the Walter J. Shepard Foundation, April 24, 1956* (Columbus: Ohio State University Press, 1956), p. 31.

97. See especially the study prepared for the FCDA by the Department of Commerce, Bureau of the Census, *Population Estimates for Survival Planning* (Washington, DC: GPO, 1956). See also the following studies that used data from the early 1950s, including the aforementioned analysis: John Donaldson et al., *An Examination of Psychological Problems during Shelter Confinement Following a Thermonuclear Attack*, Operational Research Office, Home Defense Division, Staff Paper ORO-SP-45, March 1958; William W. Chenault, Richard E. Engler, and Peter G. Nordlie, "Social and Behavioral Factors in the Implementation of Local Survival and Recovery Activities," Human Science Research, Contract DAHC 20-67-C-0102, August 1967, pp. 27–46; Richard Bentz et al., *Some Civil Defense Problems in the Nation's Capital Following Widespread Thermonuclear Attack*, Operations Research Office, Home Defense Division, Passive Defense Group, Staff Paper ORO-SP-1 (Chevy Chase, MD: Johns Hopkins University, 1956).

98. NA, RG-304, OCDM, Box 1, Records Relating to Civil Defense 1949–1953.

99. I am unconvinced by the argument May lays out in her book; nevertheless, my criticism here is aimed only at her fifth chapter that deals with the FCDA, which argues that this agency conceived women in highly domesticated fashion and then tried to reproduce this view of women in all its education and training programs. See Elaine Tyler May, *Homeward Bound: American Families in the Cold War Era* (New York: Basic Books, 1988), pp. 114–134.

100. On the Alert America poster, see the advertising mat in PHST, Papers of Spencer Quick, Box 5, Civil Defense Campaign, Folder 1.

101. The FCDA made a significant effort to mobilize women to take jobs that were traditionally considered male, but on the whole, FCDA statistics show that women *chose* jobs that were "traditional" when they joined FCDA programs. Thus the question that May does not ask is: Why did women conceive themselves as best qualified for the "traditional" civil defense jobs? This is an important question on how individuals construct their own identities—and the state can be viewed as an agent in the construction of identity. But May does not frame her puzzle in these terms, nor does she investigate this question. Instead, she asserts, incorrectly I believe, that the FCDA, as an agent of the state, was preconfigured to automatically conceive women and women's roles in civil defense in a paternalistic fashion. See also how author Philip Wylie, as a paid consultant to the FCDA, depicted women in his FCDA-sponsored novel *Tomorrow!* (New York: Rinehart, 1954). The tightness of the relationship between the FCDA and Wylie is fully documented in the Philip Wylie Collection, Firestone Library, Princeton University. See, for example, "Civil Defense Suggestion," Box Folder 4; "Civil Defense and Third War," Box 121, Folder 2.

102. See Guy Oakes and Andrew Grossman, "Managing Nuclear Terror: The Genesis of American Civil Defense Strategy, International Journal of Politics, Culture, and Society 5 (Spring 1992): 390–397; Oakes, *Imaginary War*, pp. 105–144.

103. On the Eisenhower administration, civil defense, and suburban America, see Oakes, *The Imaginary War.*

Chapter 5: Emergency Planning and American Political Development

1. See Michael J. Hogan, *A Cross of Iron: Harry S. Truman and the Origins of the National Security State* (New York: Cambridge University Press, 1998).

2. See, for example, John P. McCormick, *Carl Schmitt's Critique of Liberalism* (New York: Cambridge University Press, 1997), pp. 121–156.

3. Thanks to Allan Silver for graciously sharing a number of his ideas concerning the normalization of emergency and its effects on democracy, citizenship, and military strategy in the postwar era. See Allan Silver, "Democratic Citizenship and High Military Strategy: The Inheritance, Decay, and Reshaping of Political Culture," *Research on Democracy and Society* 2 (1994):317–349.

4. Thanks to Yagil Levy for suggesting this framework.

5. Harold D. Lasswell, "The Garrison State," *American Journal of Sociology* 56 (1941):455–468; idem, *National Security and Individual Freedom* (New York: MacGraw-Hill, 1950), pp. 23–49. Also see idem, *World Politics and Personal Insecurity* (New York: Free Press, 1965); and idem, *The Political Writings of Harold D. Lasswell* (Glencoe, IL: Free Press, 1951).

6. Lasswell, "The Garrison State," p. 448. A more sophisticated and comprehensive argument is made by Max Weber. It seems Lasswell essentially draws this notion directly from Weber's analysis of the same kinds of relationships between power, coercion, and legitimacy. See Max Weber, *Economy and Society*, vol. 2, ed. Gunther Roth and Claus Wittich (Berkeley: University of California Press, 1978).

7. Harold D. Lasswell, "Does the Garrison State Threaten Civil Rights?" *The Annals of Political and Social Science* 275 (May 1951):111–116; and "The Garrison State Hypothesis Today," in *Changing Patterns of Military Politics*, ed. Samuel Huntington (Glencoe, IL: The Free Press, 1962), pp. 51–70. See also Arthur E. Naftalalin, "Political Freedom and Military Necessity," in *The Garrison State: Its Human Problems* (Minneapolis: University of Minnesota Press, 1953), pp. 28–42; and Denis W. Brogan, *Democratic Government in an Atomic World: A Lecture Delivered under the Auspices of the Walter J. Shepard Foundation, April 24, 1956* (Columbus: Ohio State University, 1956).

8. Lasswell, *National Security and Individual Freedom*, p. 23.

9. See Clinton Rossiter, *Constitutional Dictatorship: Crisis Government in the Modern Democracies* (New York: Harcourt, Brace & World, 1948), pp. 3, 314.

10. Rossiter made the same theoretical move that Carl Schmitt made in his *Crisis of Parliamentary Democracy*, namely, that *extraconstitutional* means should be taken to save the constitution. See Rossiter, "Constitutional Dictatorship in the Atomic Age," *Review of Politics* 11 (October 1949):395–418; quotation p. 406. See also idem, "What of Congress in Atomic War?" *Western Political Quarterly* 3 (December 1950):602–605. The elite view of democratic politics in the United States is a characteristic trait of postwar liberalism, which I argue becomes the more confining and at times repressive Cold War liberalism. An excellent example of "guardianship" democracy can be found in David B. Truman's *The Governmental Process: Political Interests and Public Opinion* (New York: Alfred A. Knopf, 1951). On the responsibility of atomic-age citizenship, see especially Brogan, *Democratic Government in an Atomic World*, p. 31.

11. See Rossiter, *Constitutional Dictatorship*.

12. See George Schwab, *The Challenge of the Exception: An Introduction to the Political Ideas of Carl Schmitt between 1921 and 1936*, 2nd ed. (Westport, CT: Greenwood Press, 1989), pp. 44–61; quotation, p. 44. Neither Lasswell nor Rossiter ever developed any systematic definition of "emergency" or exactly who defines it. On Carl Schmitt's critique of liberal democracy, which Rossiter explicitly refers to in his work and which informs Lasswell's thinking even if by way of Rossiter (Lasswell refers to Schmitt only in a footnote in his early piece *World Politics and Insecurity*, 1935), see Joseph W. Bendersky, *Carl Schmitt: Theorist for the Reich* (Princeton, NJ: Princeton University Press, 1983); Carl Schmitt, *Political Romanticism*, trans. Guy Oakes (Cambridge, MA: MIT Press, 1986), esp. pp. ix–xxxv; and idem, *The Crisis of Parliamentary Democracy*, trans. Ellen Kennedy (Cambridge, MA: MIT Press, 1985). For a recent critical analysis of Schmitt's view of parliamentary democracy and his interpretation of the *Ausnahmezustand*, see Bill Scheuerman, "Is Parliamentarism in Crisis? A Response to Carl Schmitt," *Theory and Society* 24 (February 1995):135–158; idem, *Between the Exception and the Norm: The Frankfurt School and the Rule of Law* (Cambridge, MA: MIT Press, 1994), pp. 1–38; 121–188.

13. On this point, see especially Paul Hirst, "Carl Schmitt's Decisionism," in *The Challenge of Carl Schmitt*, ed. Chantal Mouffe (New York: Verso, 1999), pp. 7–17.

14. The "McCarren Rider" of July 1946 (to Public Law 490, 79th Congress) was the first step to Presidential Executive Order 9835, which set in motion the Truman administration's

Federal Employee Loyalty Program. For an interesting contemporary (1949) critical analysis of the loyalty program and its history, see Marvin H. Bernstein, "The Loyalty of Federal Employees," *Western Political Quarterly* 2 (June 1949):254–264.

15. See PHST, PSB, Box 337, "Staff Meetings 1952–January 1953"; PHST, PSB, Box 34, "Project East River" Folder.

16. See Theodore J. Lowi, *The End of Liberalism: The Second Republic of the United States*, 2nd ed. (New York: W.W. Norton, 1979), pp. 92–124, 295–310. See also idem, "The Public Philosophy: Interest Group Liberalism," *American Political Science Review* 61 (March 1967):5–24.

17. For two different treatments of the Berlin crises in 1948, see Frank Kofsky, *Harry S. Truman and the War Scare of 1948: A Successful Campaign to Deceive the Nation* (New York: St. Martin's Press, 1993); Samuel R. Williamson and Steven L. Rearden, *The Origins of U.S. Nuclear Strategy, 1945–1953* (New York: St. Martin's Press, 1993), pp. 77–100.

18. There is a large and growing historical literature on loyalty and political repression in the pre-McCarthy period. See, for example, the work of Athan Theoharis on the FBI, including *Seeds of Repression: Harry S. Truman and the Origins of McCarthyism* (Chicago: Quadrangle Books, 1971); and *Spying on Americans: Political Surveillance from Hoover to the Houston Plan* (Philadelphia: Temple University Press, 1978). Also see Sigmund Diamond, *Compromised Campus: The Collaboration of Universities with the Intelligence Community, 1945–1955* (New York: Oxford University Press, 1992); Robin W. Winks, *Cloak & Gown: Scholars in the Secret War, 1939–1961* (New York: William Morrow, 1987); Carl Bernstein, *Loyalties: A Son's Memoir* (New York: Simon and Schuster, 1989); Edward Pessen, *Losing Our Souls: The American Experience in the Cold War* (Chicago: I.R. Dee, 1993); and Christopher John Gerard, "'A Program of Cooperation': The FBI, the Internal Security Subcommittee, and the Communist Issue, 1950–1956" (Ph.D. diss., Marquette University, 1993).

19. See memorandum, May 29, 1946, from FBI director J. Edgar Hoover to RFC Chairman George E. Allan, PHST, PSF, Box 167, Subject File A-Bomb. The public also believed the Cold War was a real war. In a Gallup Poll conducted in August, 1950, 57 percent of those surveyed felt World War III was underway. In an earlier Gallup Poll conducted in January 1950, 70 percent believed the Soviet Union was "out to take over the world." By November 1950 (five months after the start of the Korean War), 81 percent of those polled thought the Soviets were seeking world conquest. See *Gallup Poll of Public Opinion 1935–1971*, vol. 2 (New York: Random House, 1972), pp. 949, 993.

20. On this specific point, see especially FBI Director J. Edgar Hoover's address to Dinner of Grand Lodge of New York, May 2, 1950, in PHST, Papers of Stephen J. Spingarn, Box 36, Internal Security, Loyalty Commission and Civil Rights folder, pp. 3–4. See also Bradley R. Usher, "Identity, Security, and Policy: Federal Employment and State Constructions of Homosexual Identity" (unpublished manuscript, 1996).

21. An interesting example of this can be illustrated by one of the many "personal and confidential" memoranda that J. Edgar Hoover regularly sent to the president and his aides regarding subversive activities. In December 1947, Hoover a sent a memo to Secretary of Defense James Forrestal about a set of books and maps purchased at a bookstore in New York City. The bookstore owner had been in touch with the local office of the Coast and Geodetic Survey Office in hope of getting some maps on "Hawaii, the Pacific, the Philippine Islands and Alaska." A person at the Geodetic Survey Ofice took it upon himself to consider this suspicious and reported it to the local FBI office. See Hoover to Forrestal, December 19, 1947, PHST, Papers of John H. Ohly, Box 73, Secretary of Defense Folder 3 of 3.

22. See, for example, National Security Council Directive 17, "The Internal Security of the United States," A Report to the National Security Council, June 28, 1948, PHST, PSF, Box 204, National Security Council Meetings Folder.

23. Ibid. For a careful study of the legal, organizational, and institutional changes that facilitated and rationalized the federal government's search for Cold War "subversives" and the

way in which the term itself was used by the government to collapse the private and public spheres, see Bradley Usher, "Federal Civil Service Discrimination against Gays and Lesbians, 1950–1975: A Policy and Movement History" (Ph.D. diss., New School for Social Research, 1998).

24. See Brogan, *Democratic Government in an Atomic World.*

25. Aaron Friedberg, "Why Didn't the U.S. Become a Garrison State?" *International Security* 16 (Spring 1992):109–142.

26. In Weberian terms the "power position" of the national security apparatus increased as agencies within the EOP and the DOD became more efficient in carrying out their objectives. This was quite apparent during the Eisenhower administration, which further streamlined the national security bureaucracy by using the NSC to its fullest extent, something President Truman resisted. On rationalization of bureaucratic power and its consequences, see Weber, *Economy and Society,* vol. 2, pp. 990–994.

27. On this point, see Michel Foucault, *Ethics, Subjectivity and Truth,* vol. 1, ed. Paul Rabinow (New York: The New Press, 1997), pp. 67–79.

28. On Cold War jurisprudence, see David Caute, *The Great Fear: The Anti-Communist Purge under Truman and Eisenhower* (New York: Simon and Schuster, 1978).

29. "Report by Ferdinand Eberstadt to Arthur M. Hill (Chairman, National Security Resources Board)," June 4, 1948. Papers of Harry S. Truman, White House Central Files, Confidential Files, Box 27 National Security Resources Board, Folder 1 of 10, p. 8. Hereafter, "Eberstadt Report."

30. Ibid. For a detailed analysis on the concern about war mobilization and its long-term effects on American democracy from the perspective of both Ferdinand Eberstadt and James Forrestal, see Jeffrey M. Dorwart, *Eberstadt and Forrestal: A National Security Partnership, 1909–1949* (College Station: Texas A&M University Press, 1991).

31. See Silver, "Democratic Citizenship and High Military Strategy."

32. Theodore J. Lowi, "Crossroads 1992: All Lights Stuck on Red," The Spencer T. and Ann W. Olin Address, Cornell University, June 5, 1992.

33. Millard Caldwell, Administrator of the Federal Civil Defense Administration, in U.S. FCDA, *Annual Report for 1951* (Washington, DC: GPO, 1951), p. vi.

34. State of New Jersey Department of Defense, Division of Civil Defense, *Proceedings of the Institute on Mental Hygiene Aspects of Civil Defense,* June 21, 1951, pp. 12–13.

35. On vulnerability and perception, see Andrew Grossman, "Atomic Fantasies and Make-Believe War: The American State, Social Control and Civil Defense Planning, 1946–1952," *Political Power and Social Theory* 9 (1995); Robert H. Johnson, *Improbable Dangers: U.S. Conceptions of Threat in the Cold War and After* (New York: St. Martin's Press, 1994), pp. 11–111; Ansley J. Coale, *The Problem of Reducing Vulnerability to Atomic Attack* (Princeton, NJ: Princeton University Press, 1947); John A. Thompson, "The Exaggeration of American Vulnerability: The Anatomy of a Tradition," *Diplomatic History* 16 (Winter 1992):23–43. On the concern about an atomic Pearl Harbor, see "Defense Lack Seen as Pearl Harbor," *New York Times,* October 10, 1949, p. 9; Thomas J. Kerr, *Civil Defense in the U.S.: Bandaid for a Holocaust?* (Boulder, CO: Westview Press, 1983), p. 24; U.S. Congress, Joint Committee on Atomic Energy, *Hearings, Civil Defense against Atomic Attack,* 81st Congress, 2nd Sess. (Washington, DC: GPO, 1950), pp. 140–150.

36. James V. Forrestal and Robert Patterson to President Harry S. Truman, PHST, PSF, Box 117, General File–Civil Defense Folder, "Determination of the Agencies Responsible for Civil Defense and Anti-Sabotage Activities," December 2, 1946.

37. NSC-17, June 28, 1948, "The Internal Security of the United States" PHST, PSF, Box 204, NSC Meetings File, p. 6.

38. Ibid., p. 6. This section is drawn in part from Kim Geiger and Andrew Grossman, "Preparing for Cold War: The Politics of Home-Front Mobilization, 1946–1952," Center for Studies of Social Change Working Paper No. 184 (April 1994).

39. For an interesting contemporary examination of how the concept of treason changed throughout the early Cold War period, see Rebecca West, *The New Meaning of Treason* (New York: Viking Press, 1964).

40. This quotation appeared in an FCDA poster that appeared in public spaces around the country in 1952. See advertising mats relating to Alert America campaign in PHST, Papers of Spencer Quick, Box 5, Civil Defense Campaign General–Folder 1.

41. The process of internalizing the early Cold War civic garrison modified behavior in the same mode that Foucault describes when he examines panopticism in another kind of "garrison": the jail house. See Michel Foucault, *Discipline and Punish: The Birth of the Prison* (New York: Vintage Books, 1995), pp. 195–228.

42. Superterrorism is defined as an attack using biological, chemical, or nuclear weapons with the intent to cause a serious disruption to the social order of the United States, including mass destruction, death, and panic.

43. See "Clinton Describes Terrorism Threat for 21st Century," *New York Times*, January 22, 1999, p. 1; "Pentagon Plans Antiterrorism Team," *Washington Post*, February 1, 1999, p. A-2; Richard Preston, "The Bioweaponeers," *The New Yorker*, March 9, 1998, pp. 66–75.

44. See, for example, Ashton Carter, John Deutch, and Philip Zelikow, "Combating Catastrophic Terrorism," *Foreign Affairs* 77 (November/December 1998):80–94; Charles L. Mercier, Jr., "Terrorists, WMD, and the U.S. Army Reserve," *Parameters* 17 (August 1997):98–118; and Chris Seiple, "Consequence Management: Domestic Response to Weapons of Mass Destruction," ibid., 119–127.

45. Public Law 104-132, Sec. 101-106 April 24, 1996.

46. See, for example, "The President's Words: Assessing the Risks of Germ Warfare to the U.S.," *New York Times*, January 22, 1999, p. A-9.

47. The main difference in how these two questions were framed and handled turns on the fact that in 1952 the Soviet Union was viewed by FCDA planners as the threat and thus civilian defense planning focused on strategic nuclear war and its consequences. Today, the United States government is concerned with non-nation-state actors using WMD. Current planning for FEMA and other national security agencies is thus a more complicated policy problem.

48. See, for example, "Pentagon Plans Domestic Anti-Terrorist Team," *Washington Post*, February 1, 1999, p. A2.

49. See, for example, B. W. Menke, *Martial Law—Its Use in Case of Atomic Attack* (Washington, DC: Industrial College of the Armed Forces, 1956). See also section 301 of the Civil Defense Act of 1950.

50. See Lowi, *End of Liberalism*, pp. 92–126.

51. Depression-era legislation is a classic example of this kind of lawmaking. On New Deal/economic crisis legislation, see especially ibid.; and Christopher L. Tomlins, *The State and the Unions: Labor Relations, Law, and the Organized Labor Movement in America, 1880–1960* (New York: Cambridge University Press, 1985), pp. 99–197. For an example of legal interpretation during a war emergency, see *Korematsu v. United States*, 323 U.S. 214 (1944), the decision that sanctioned the internment of Japanese Americans during World War II.

52. For a restatement of his classic bureaucratic politics model, see Graham Allison and Philip Zelikow, *Essence of Decision: Explaining the Cuban Missile Crisis*, 2nd ed. (New York: Longman, 1999).

53. On the issue of domesticating nuclear weapons, see Spencer Weart, *Nuclear Fear: A History of Images* (Cambridge, MA: Harvard University Press, 1989), pp. 128–154; and Paul Boyer, *By the Bomb's Early Light: American Thought and Culture at the Dawn of the Atomic Age* (New York: Pantheon Books, 1985), pp. 107–130, 289–367.

INDEX